SOUTHERN
SPLENDOR

SOUTHERN SPLENDOR

Saving Architectural Treasures of the Old South

MARC R. MATRANA,
ROBIN S. LATTIMORE,
AND MICHAEL W. KITCHENS

University Press of Mississippi / Jackson

www.upress.state.ms.us

The University Press of Mississippi is a member
of the Association of American University Presses.

Designed by Todd Lape

First printing 2018
∞

Library of Congress Cataloging-in-Publication Data

Names: Matrana, Marc R., author. | Lattimore, Robin Spencer,
author. | Kitchens, Michael W., author.
Title: Southern splendor : saving architectural treasures of
the Old South / Marc R. Matrana, Robin S. Lattimore, and
Michael W. Kitchens.
Description: Jackson : University Press of Mississippi, 2018. |
Includes bibliographical references and index. |
Identifiers: LCCN 2017039513 (print) | LCCN 2017041001
(ebook) | ISBN 9781496817648 (epub single) | ISBN
9781496817655 (epub institutional) | ISBN 9781496817662
(pdf single) | ISBN 9781496817679 (pdf institutional) | ISBN
9781496811004 (cloth : alk. paper)
Subjects: LCSH: Architecture, Domestic—Southern States. |
Historic buildings—Conservation and restoration—Southern
States.
Classification: LCC NA7211 (ebook) | LCC NA7211 .M38 2018
(print) | DDC728/.90975—dc23
LC record available at https://lccn.loc.gov/2017039513

British Library Cataloging-in-Publication Data available

CONTENTS

ACKNOWLEDGMENTS

Quality books don't just happen. They require a host of individuals willing to contribute something special and necessary to the final product. This book was made possible because of the generosity and support of countless people across the South who have dedicated themselves to documenting and preserving the past for future generations.

Leading the list of individuals who should be recognized are the principal photographers whose work illustrates the words printed on these pages. They are Jacques Levet Jr., Lesley M. Bush, and Danny Bourque.

Other photographers and historical repositories contributing images to this book are Amanda Cantrell, Bruce Schwarz, John M. Hall, Derek Orr, Chad Medford, the Carol M. Highsmith Collection of the Library of Congress, the Historic American Buildings Survey (HABS), Preservation North Carolina, the Palmetto Trust for Historic Preservation, the Historical Center of York County, South Carolina, and Rory Doyle of Cleveland, Mississippi.

In addition, the authors have also contributed photos. For identification purposes, each photographer's last name, or the initials for archival collections, are listed following related captions. A key to the photo credits is below.

Bourque—Danny Bourque
Bush—Lesley M. Bush
CAHPT—Classic American Homes Preservation Trust
HABS—Historic American Buildings Survey (Library of Congress)
Highsmith—Carol Highsmith Collection (Library of Congress)
Kitchens—Michael W. Kitchens
Lattimore—Robin S. Lattimore
Levet—Jacques P. Levet
Matrana—Marc R. Matrana

In every southern state people have graciously opened the doors to their homes. Their generosity has been matched by the kind and dedicated people of numerous historical societies and organizations, house museums, libraries, and university and state archives. These individuals and groups are listed below, by state, for easy and proper identification.

ALABAMA Robert Gamble; Carole King and Mary Ann Neeley with the Landmarks Foundation of Montgomery; Ninon Parker with the Colbert County Historical Landmarks Foundation, which now operates *Belle Mont*; Collier Neeley with the Alabama Historical Commission in Montgomery; and Henry P. Howard with the *First White House of the Confederacy*.

GEORGIA William N. Banks of *Bankshaven*; J. L. Sibley Jennings; Mary Linneman, Chuck Barber, and Kat Stein at the University of Georgia's Hargrett Rare Book and Maps Library; Sam Thomas at the *T. R. R. Cobb House* in Athens; Jonathon Poston and David Shaver at the Hay House Museum in Macon; and Lynn Speno and David Gomez at the Georgia Department of Natural Resources.

KENTUCKY David Stuart with the Ward Hall Preservation Foundation.

LOUISIANA Sand and Norman Marmillion of *Laura*; Jacques P. Levet Jr. for his help with *San Francisco*; Jim Blanchard and Kevin Kelly from *Houmas House;* John Cummings III owner of *Whitney*; Dr. Florent Hardy Jr., archivist of Louisiana and director of the Louisiana State Archives.

MISSISSIPPI Richard Forte Sr., Randy McCafferty, Richard Flowers, and the Combined Boards of Beauvoir for assistance with my research on *Beauvoir*; and Eustace Winn of *Hollywood Plantation* in Bolivar County.

NORTH CAROLINA Myrick Howard, Robert Parrot, and Ted Alexander with Preservation North Carolina; Kirk and Louisa Emmons, and Mary Alexander of *Creekside Plantation*; Amanda S. Cantrell of *Green River Plantation*; Delphine Jones of *Fox Haven Plantation*; Turner Sutton, Bobby Williams, and Gregory Tyler of the Historic *Hope Plantation*; Linda Wall of the *Joshua Hall Plantation*; the Town of Spindale (*Sidney Villa Plantation*); the Rutherford County Historical Society; the State Library of North Carolina.

SOUTH CAROLINA Michael Bedenbaugh with the Palmetto Trust for Historic Preservation; Richard Hampton Jenrette and Margize Howell of the Classic American Homes Preservation Trust (*Millford Plantation*); Michael Scoggins of the Historical Center of York County (Historic Brattonsville); Wade B. Fairey—Roots & Recall; Jackie Reynolds, Tim Drake, and Rebecca Pokorny of the Pendleton Historical Foundation (*Woodburn* and *Ashtabula Plantations*); Brian L. Robeson and Elizabeth Moss with *Rose Hill Plantation* State Historic Site; staff of Drayton Hall; Tommy O'Dell with the Historic Cokesbury Foundation (*Connor-Hodges Mansion*); the Anderson County Library; Kim

Worth, International Paper Corporation (*Kensington Plantation*); and Ola Jean Kelly, executive director of the Union County Museum.

TENNESSEE Dr. Michael and Bobbi Kaslow of *Rattle and Snap*; Jerry Trescott at curator at *Belmont*; Joanna Stephens, curator with the Battle of Franklin Trust at *Carnton*; Kelly Harwood at Gallery 202 at *Clouston Hall* in Franklin; Rick Warwick at the Heritage Foundation of Franklin; and Marsha Mullin with the Andrew Jackson Foundation at Andrew Jackson's *Hermitage*.

VIRGINIA Derek and Deborah Orr, owners of the Historic *Octagon House* (*Mountain View Plantation*); Leland Luck, official historian of *Berry Hill Plantation*; the staff of *Monticello*, the staff of *Arlington House* (Custis-Lee Mansion), the staff of the *White House of the Confederacy*, and the staff of the State Archives of Virginia.

Individually, the authors would also like to thank other people and organizations for their kind understanding and support during the countless hours required to research and to write this book.

MARC R. MATRANA Massive thanks to my wonderful wife, Heather J. Green Matrana; our amazing son, Bennett Dalton Matrana; my parents, Daniel and Jonnie Matrana; my father-in-law, David E. Green (who helped copyedit my work in this volume); and my mother-in-law, Jean Green. Also, thanks to my godmother Ann Sartin; Allen and Erin Green; many aunts, uncles, and cousins too numerous to name; friends Daniel and Bebe Alario, Dr. Sarath Krishnan, Shane Mabry, Dukes Richardson, and many, many more. My wonderful co-workers at Ochsner Medical Center, especially Lorrie Erario, Erin Pierce, and Andrea Brown. And, finally, Craig Gill, Steve Yates, Shane Gong Stewart, and the entire University Press of Mississippi team.

ROBIN S. LATTIMORE Shirley and Charlotte Lattimore, my extended family—Larry, Debbie, Rodney, Sarah Jo, Klint, Karsen, Brandon, Rebekah, Timothy, Mandy, Rye, Sadie, and Audrey; friends—Lesley M. Bush, Robert E. Carpenter III, Melvin LeCompte, C. Philip Byers, Charles Drawdy, Linda Lee Reynolds, and Maudie Katz; co-workers at Thomas Jefferson Classical Academy (CFA); fellow historians—Dr. James E. Kibler, Louisa Emmons, Alice Bradley, Todd Lavender, Michael Hardy, and Elizabeth Sherrill, president of the North Carolina Society of Historians; Justin Jones for photographic expertise and technical support; and the members of my history book club: Martha Schatz, Mary-Sandra Costner, Pam Childers, Londa Von Weter, Nancy Stroud, Lib Godfrey, Jeanne Goin Hagen, and Susan Todd.

MICHAEL W. KITCHENS Thanks and praise to my Lord and Savior, Jesus Christ, in whom all things are possible; Judith E. Kitchens, my mother, and Kimberly E. Berry and William H. Kitchens Jr., my siblings for their love and support; J. L. Sibley ("Sibbo") Jennings (recently deceased), David Sherman, and David Seibert, who unfailingly support my old house passion; my friend, Edward Balling; Douglas and Rachel Frey for being a reliable sounding board for my historic house manuscript ideas; Todd, Sharen, Trevor, Savannah, and Pearce Phinney; Sean, Lelee, Duff, and Shane Phinney; Miss Lyn Gordon and Theresa and Greg Gordon—the Phinneys and Gordons constantly encourage me in this and all endeavors and have welcomed me as family into their clan; Duff Phinney for being a constant encouraging support in my writing efforts and whose significant, God-given writing talents inspire me to work harder to improve my own writing projects; the entire Fiji Island Tailgate Crew; and Robert Gamble in Montgomery, Alabama, who is a reliable and constant support for my old house research endeavors.

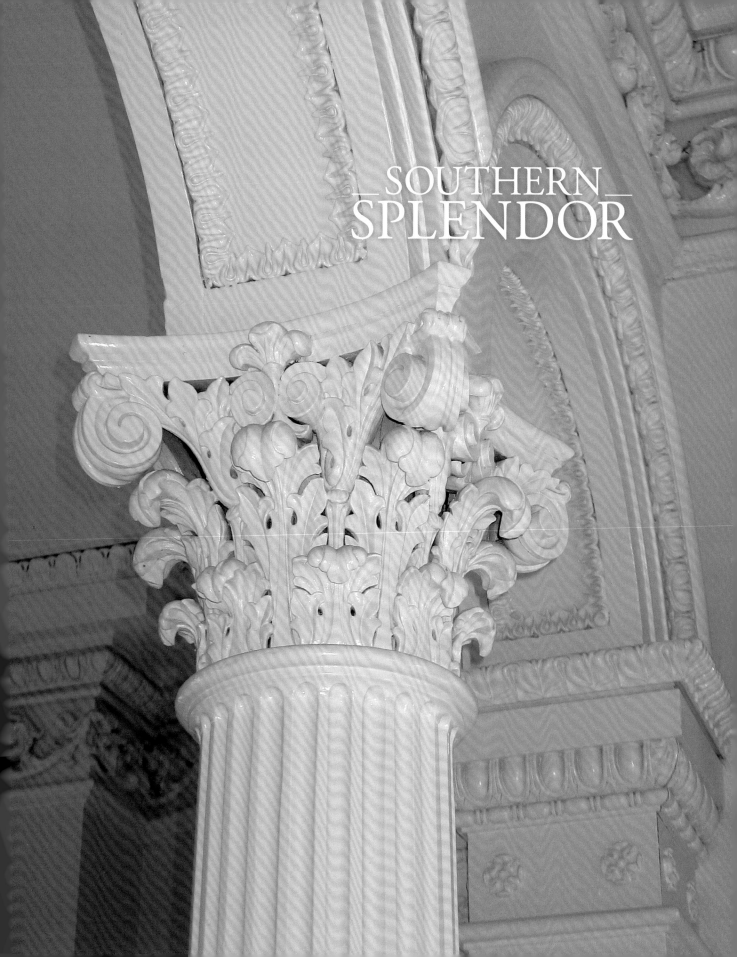

SOUTHERN
SPLENDOR

INTRODUCTION

No greater symbol exists of the American South than a grand plantation house set amid a fertile landscape of cultivated fields, pastures, and forests. Claiming near equal status with those dwellings are the town houses of planter families built in the region's trading centers and port cities. Such homes have long stood as icons of the South's storied past, particularly of the era before the Civil War (1861–1865) when cotton, sugarcane, rice, indigo, and tobacco ruled the region's agricultural-based economy and slaves worked the fields. More than a century and a half have now passed since these iconic dwellings were constructed, but the South's colonial and antebellum houses continue to have a powerful hold on the imagination and mindset of millions of people.

They are simultaneously beloved and despised, romanticized and demonized; contradictions that arise because each home rests at the heart of a complex web of human relationships that have shaped the social and cultural heritage of the region for generations. While they were made possible by an economic system that required the forced labor of enslaved people, the houses themselves, and the cluster of surviving outbuildings that often surround them, are no less landmarks of history. They are valuable links to the past that reveal much about the aspirations of long ago. Each one opens a window into a time that is very different from the present and provides a glimpse of an era that is only vaguely comprehendible today.

There is much to learn from studying the craftsmanship and architecture of each house and becoming familiar with the lives of the original owners. The history of the American South, however, was not shaped solely by such dwellings or the powerful and wealthy people who owned them. A deeper understanding of the work and hardships that occurred within the shadow of their walls is crucial in forging a true appreciation of each dwelling's significance as a symbol of a bygone era and an emblem of America's architectural heritage. It is equally valuable to consider how the South's plantation homes and their in-town counterparts have changed over time, and to recognize that far more houses of the planter class have been lost than have been preserved. Scores of those that remain stand in peril of complete loss if efforts are not made soon to protect them.

Like nearly all historic structures, despite their often commanding appearance, the South's plantation houses and companion in-town residences have proven to be fragile relics of history that have been vulnerable to dramatic change and ruin since they were first inhabited. Time, tragedy, neglect, and decay have taken a significant toll on them. Few planter homes that were constructed in the eighteenth and nineteenth centuries are still standing. Many of those that do survive exist in surroundings that are dramatically different from their original settings.

For every pre–Civil War residence that has survived in the South, there are dozens that have been lost. In 1861, when slavery had reached its zenith in the United States, approximately 46,275 plantations existed across the South.[1] While not all of those estates were anchored by a grand or substantial home, the majority did boast a residence that conveyed the position and wealth of the owner. Current estimates suggest that fewer than 6,000 antebellum plantation houses still survive in the entire South. A much smaller number of authentic pre–Civil War town houses built and used by planter families remain standing today.

An early culprit responsible for the loss of many southern colonial and antebellum dwellings was the Civil War itself; a conflict deeply rooted in opposing views of slavery and growing territorial animosities that brought an end to the plantation society of the Old South. Numerous stories survive that tell of marauding soldiers laying waste to plantation houses with fire and sword, while carrying away as many material treasures and food as their saddlebags could hold. It is unlikely that those perpetrators, swept up in the heat of battle or the powerful emotions that spawned individual acts of revenge, considered the long-lasting effect of the destruction; never realizing that their actions were robbing future generations of important pieces of history that had been meticulously crafted of wood, brick, and stone.

After the South's defeat new enemies emerged. With the loss of unpaid labor, fortunes fell and widespread poverty reigned in the South well into the twentieth century, making it difficult for plantation owners to keep or maintain their aging homes. Even when some owners were determined to survive and hold onto their estates they often found themselves overwhelmed with economic realities that undermined their intentions. Then when cotton prices plummeted during economic recessions and the boll weevil swept over the land in the early twentieth century, a significant number of families who had weathered the Civil War, Reconstruction, and its aftermath found themselves finally beaten by events beyond their control.

As older generations died away, younger family members often found the responsibility of maintaining ancestral plantations and town houses too daunting a task to undertake. Many simply moved away allowing their family homes to fall into ruins. Fields that once produced bountiful crops were left untended, and many rural estates were soon reclaimed by the forests and swamps that surrounded them. Thousands of plantation homes eventually succumbed to the elements and were lost to the rot, decay, and termites that resulted from neglect and abandonment. Others fell victim to fires ignited by lightning, accidents, or arson, as well as floods, storms, and other acts of nature.

After the Civil War, as the South transitioned from a primarily agrarian society to a more diversified manufacturing economy, many plantation properties were dismantled to make way for industrial, commercial, or residential development. In the twentieth century scores of antebellum homes were razed or burned in the name of progress when the land upon which they had stood for many years was claimed for a new purpose. Today, the only evidence that remains of many former plantation estates are their names on street signs and historical markers. At the same time, lots that once held the magnificent town houses of planter families are too often the sites of parking lots, hotels, and office buildings.

Despite all the seismic changes that have rattled the South through the years some homes have survived. Several have been saved by owners with deep sentimental attachments or an abiding knowledge of the historical importance of their ancestral home. Other owners have held onto their houses out of necessity because they could not afford to leave their antiquated dwelling. On occasion, the houses that remain were saved in the eleventh hour by groups of dedicated individuals, preservation groups, and historical societies determined not to let significant pieces of history slip away without a fight. In a number of cases, historic homes have found a champion in corporations or charitable foundations that provided the necessary funds to rescue and preserve them for the future. The efforts to save and preserve many properties were often as dramatic and remarkable as the houses themselves.

Early preservation efforts in the South, and across the nation, primarily focused on saving the homes of significant historic figures, or the structures where important historic events occurred. Over time, however, numerous preservation initiatives evolved to save structures valued for their architectural or cultural significance, regardless of their association with important people. Homes from modest log cabins to the most magnificent mansions began to be preserved. Preservation success stories and the excitement each project generated began to inspire other efforts all over the country.

Because the South's plantation homes and related town houses, both great and small, represent such a significant contribution to the nation's architectural heritage, it is not surprising that they have been the focus of preservation efforts through the years. In fact, the South has often been the leader in historic preservation, and the properties that have been preserved across the region rank among the leading historical attractions in the nation.

One of the earliest and most significant restoration projects in the country was on an agrarian estate in Virginia. Recognized as the first national preservation organization in America, the Mount Vernon Ladies' Association was formed in the mid-nineteenth century to preserve and protect the beloved plantation home of George Washington, which had fallen into great disrepair in the decades following his death in 1799.

From the very beginning, the goal of the Mount Vernon Ladies' Association was more than solely restoring Washington's plantation mansion. It was to also make it a place of scholarship dedicated to preserving both the architectural legacy of *Mount Vernon* and the political and military legacy of George Washington, while also opening the home and surrounding agricultural support structures to the public. The organization's work at *Mount Vernon* was just the beginning of a long and illustrious preservation story that became the model for other efforts around the nation and the South.

Inspired by the continuing work at Mount Vernon, private property owners, historical societies, and heritage organizations around the South began researching the histories of antebellum and colonial homes in their areas, and in turn began promoting and funding restoration and preservation projects that saved hundreds of colonial and antebellum houses from ruin. Still, while success stories were being written, tragic tales of loss continued. Even with the growing awareness of the importance of preservation in the twentieth century, many rural plantation homes and the town houses of planters continued to disappear from the landscape.

All the houses represented in this book are survivors and have been selected by the authors because they represent a broad range of architectural styles, and because they each convey a significant restoration or preservation story. The houses showcased here are among the last vestiges of a period of history symbolized by their very existence. They belong not only to ancestral owners and new buyers of historic properties who actually live in their historic dwellings, but also corporate and nonprofit owners that manage their former private homes as museums.

Despite overwhelming obstacles, the owners featured here have been able to preserve their homes and often put them in better shape than they have been in for decades. Some of the featured dwellings have been opened to the public as a way to produce much-needed revenue for repairs and to pay property or inheritance taxes. Other homes seen here are currently involved in extensive restoration projects and the final outcome of those projects is yet to be seen.

Collectively, the individuals and organizations associated with each home featured in this book have identified a myriad of reasons why they have chosen to preserve their own special piece of the past. At the same time, they have also echoed a common theme and a shared belief. They recognize that their historic residences could not be authentically replicated today, and that it is worthy of preservation because it stands as a tangible reminder of this country's incredible architectural and cultural heritage.

Beyond the physical survival of each historic home the question remains, however, as to how these dwellings, their material possessions, and their history will be viewed in the future. In his book, *Look Away: Reality and Sentiment in Southern Art*, historian Estill Curtis Pennington discusses some of the forces that seem poised to erode many of the long-held traditions of the South. He identifies the plantation mansion as an important symbol of the colonial and antebellum periods, and relates how powerful that symbol continues to be in the modern age. He delves into the symbols, songs, and literature of the South to draw conclusions about what the future may hold for the region's history.

Deeply rooted in the South's own perception of itself, and "central to the lyrics of the old minstrel song 'Dixie' is the passionate longing for old times not forgotten," writes Pennington. "Without regard to what those days may have meant or what they still mean to each individual, those lyrics sound the central theme of all things Southern: the past continues to exert a strong influence upon the present, because Southerners do not forget. Indeed, they yearn to remember, to recall, and to reflect." In that longing is the key to survival, Pennington believes.[2]

Pennington further relates that the South's penchant for remembrance and nostalgia successfully weaves together the often paradoxical elements of reality and sentiment.

The truth of how things were in the past and how we now imagine them to have been are magnetically joined by a force that makes separating the two virtually impossible. He contends that even at this time in the history of the United States, when great social changes have placed so many new road signs on the cultural terrain, the South is still imagined as a place where there is a near religious love of the land and where the structures of the past stand as sentinels guarding the region's history.

"There is no question that the South is changing," says historian and educator Chumley Cope, of Spartanburg, South Carolina. "But, I think the respect and sheer fascination that many Southerners have for their homeland will ensure that the greatest symbols of our plantation heritage will survive well into the future. The venerable plantation houses and in-town planter homes that survive are valuable pieces of that heritage and should be preserved at all cost."[3]

Saving the South's architectural gems has, in many cases, resulted in more than the preservation of physical structures. It has also evolved into preserving and recording the stories of families living in those homes, as well as the legacy of those laboring for the owner. The combination of architectural preservation with genealogy and the documentation of human toil has often resulted in a much richer testament of the past and a more balanced view of the region's history.

Significantly, the efforts and investment made toward restoration have often resulted in an economic boost to local economies, as well as to increased tax revenue. Beyond those benefits, many people see the importance of preserving the architectural treasures of the Old South solely in relation to what it means to the history of each surrounding community and to the families related to each historic site.

"The history of each Southern plantation is a living heritage," says Ted Alexander, regional director of Preservation North Carolina, one of the South's leading nonprofit organizations dedicated to promoting the preservation and restoration of historic homes. "While common themes and stories are interwoven through the history of plantations from the middle Atlantic states through the deep South, each one has its own personality and its own unique character. No other region of the United States can claim such cultural diversity and architectural splendor as the South. For every plantation house or in-town planter residence that is restored a little more of our collective history is preserved for future generations. And that is something that we should all treasure."[4]

LOUISIANA

Destrehan Plantation mansion,
front façade. (Matrana)

DESTREHAN PLANTATION

A Louisiana Legacy Lives On

♀ Destrehan, Louisiana

*D*estrehan Plantation in St. Charles Parish is often identified by its iconic mansion. This house, like the plantation itself, has gone through transformation after transformation as years of history layer on. The plantation site was once home to Native Americans, but later was developed into agricultural farms by early European settlers. In 1782, Frenchman Robert Antoine Robin de Logny retired from his post as the Spanish commandant of the Upper German Coast in Louisiana. He purchased two adjacent plantation farms and moved into a large principal house that was already on site at one of them.[1]

Once settled, he commissioned the construction of a new master house a small distance away. Logny hired a free mulatto named Charles (probably Paquet) to build the house, and the contract, which is still on file at the St. Charles Parish Courthouse, specified that the building was to be sixty feet long by thirty-five feet deep, surrounded by a twelve-foot-deep gallery. The gallery was to be supported by heavy, masonry piers, ten feet in height, and the second and principal story would have twelve-foot-tall ceilings. A dining room with Spanish tile floors was to be built on the first floor (as was tradition in early French plantation homes in Louisiana). For his work, Charles received, "one Negro, one cow with calf, fifty quarts of rice, and equal amount of corn, and one hundred piastres."

In 1786, Logny's daughter Marie Céleste married Jean Noël Destrehan, with whom she had fourteen children. The family purchased the plantation after Logny's death, and in the early 1800s added symmetrical wings (each with two rooms upstairs and two rooms downstairs, for a total of eight new rooms for this large family). These new wings were used as *garçonnières* or quarters for the young men of the family and their bachelor guests.

Jean Noël Destrehan was active in politics and was appointed by Thomas Jefferson to the first Legislative Council for the Territory of Orleans. He also served on a famous tribunal held at his plantation in which slaves involved in the 1811 revolt in the area

Solid marble tub at Destrehan Plantation. (Matrana)

were tried. The tribunal resulted in forty-five slaves (including three from *Destrehan Plantation*) being executed by firing squad for insurrection.

In 1816, Jean Noël's daughter Elénore Zalia married Stephen Henderson, who later purchased the plantation from the succession of his late mother-in-law, Marie Céleste. In 1839, after Henderson's death the plantation was sold to Pierre Adolphe Rost, the husband of Elénore Zalia's sister Louise. Rost completely transformed the old French-Louisiana home, updating it in the trendy Greek Revival style. Among other updates, he moved the location of doors and windows, added Doric columns outside and marble mantels inside, and enclosed the old back gallery to create an impressive entrance hall featuring two matching winding staircases. The result was an unusual house with Creole proportions and layout and Greek Revival finishes.

Upper gallery, facing the
Mississippi River. (Bush)

During the Civil War, federal troops seized *Destrehan* and the house was used as
the Rost Home Colony, one of four "home colonies" in the state, which served as self-
sustaining agricultural collectives that provided schools, commercial stores, and health
care for freed slaves. The colony provided a safe haven for persecuted freedmen and
provided a site for training and educating them with the necessary skills for survival in
post–Civil War Louisiana.[2]

Eventually, the plantation was returned to Rost and later inherited by his son,
Judge Emile Rost, who sold the plantation to developers in 1910; by 1914 the entire
plantation had been transformed into a company town for the Mexican Petroleum
Company. Slave cabins were removed and replaced by rows of houses for workers.
The mansion was transformed into a clubhouse. Later, the Amoco Corporation took
over control of the site, but closed operations there in 1959, leaving the plantation
abandoned.

Destrehan declined rapidly during the following years, as vandals ripped marbled
mantels from the walls and caused great damage as they searched for lost treasure.
Much of the original millwork, including many of the Greek Revival details, such as
pilaster capitals and exterior cornices, were stolen. The house was dealt another blow in
1965, when Hurricane Betsy caused even more damage.

Bedroom at Destrehan with French *prie-dieu* or prayer kneeler and painting of the Madonna and Child above the fireplace, highlighting the French Catholic culture of the Destrehan family. (Bush)

In 1968, a group of concerned friends convinced Amoco to replace the plantation mansion's dilapidated roof and secure the property against intruders. Enlivened by their success in this matter, the group organized themselves into the River Road Historical Society, a nonprofit organization that was granted a charter from the State of Louisiana in 1969. The society began raising a quarter million dollars to repair *Destrehan*, and in December 1971, Amoco graciously donated the mansion at *Destrehan* and nearly four surrounding acres to the group.

Around this time, the River Road Historical Society hosted its first Fall Festival, an annual event that continues today and remains a major fundraiser for the organization. By 1978, the society had successfully stabilized the decaying mansion and opened three rooms for tours.

The River Road Historical Society was greatly aided in its efforts at *Destrehan* by the Azby Fund, a nonprofit founded by Destrehan descendant Herbert J. Harvey Jr. (great-great-great-grandson of Jean Noël Destrehan) and named after his ancestral uncle Nicholas Azby Destrehan, last of the male line. Harvey and his father had made great fortunes in business, and the younger man left no descendants, so upon his death from amyotrophic lateral sclerosis (Lou Gehrig's disease) at the age of forty-three in 1981, the Azby Fund was endowed and has greatly supported preservation efforts at *Destrehan* ever since.

With both the will and resources to restore *Destrehan* to its full former glory, the River Road Historical Society set out to complete the project in the best way possible. Early on, they involved Eugene Cizek from Tulane University, an internationally respected preservation expert. Cizek led efforts that made *Destrehan* a pioneer of heritage education in the South, involving students from elementary through graduate school in the preservation process.

In 1982, with a matching grant from the Division of Historic Preservation of the Louisiana Department of Culture, Recreation, and Tourism, Cizek prepared a Historic Structures Report and Master Plan for the restoration and interpretation of *Destrehan Plantation*. An architectural conservator was brought in to analyze finishes, and William de Marigny Hyland, a historian and Destrehan descendant, prepared a three-part archival database, including a chain of title for the property, a family genealogy, and original source materials from contracts and inventories to newspaper articles. Other preservationists were brought in to conduct measured drawings, collect early photographs of the mansion, and interview people who remembered the house prior to its abandonment.

It was decided that the house would be brought back to its 1840's appearance, while attempting to communicate to visitors the evolution the house had realized through the decades. The restoration of the Greek Revival cornice was one of the first improvements made, and Cizek and his team used all available resources and clues from photos and oral histories to markings on walls and floors to try and re-create the finishes and adornments that had been stripped away from the mansion.

It was noted that many of the remaining details strongly resembled designs from the 1835 book *The Beauties of Modern Architecture,* so this volume served as inspiration

Ceiling medallion from Destrehan Plantation. (HABS)

for remodeling details for which no photos or other evidence could be found, such as cornices, mantels, and medallions. Rosettes from the extant staircase were copied onto cornices and around decorative medallions. Spanish tiles were replaced where necessary, doors, floors, windows, and walls were all restored and renewed, keeping as much of the original materials as possible. In some small areas, sections were left intentionally unfinished in order to show the evolution of the house over time or give insight into the underlying construction techniques.

To complete the renovation, period furniture was obtained, including several pieces original to the house that were purchased from Destrehan descendants. The restoration went on for years, as the River Road Historical Society continued to enlarge landholdings around the house. Today, the society has expanded the property to nearly eighteen acres. Other buildings have been added to the grounds, including a large mule barn from Glendale Plantation, which now serves as a special events venue, hosting weddings, educational programs, meetings, concerts, receptions, and other gatherings.

Destrehan was damaged by Hurricane Katrina in 2005, but the Azby Fund came to the rescue providing generous funding for full restoration. Just minutes from New Orleans, the plantation serves today as an unparalleled cultural and historical resource for the region. It remains the oldest documented plantation home in the lower Mississippi Valley, and in 2010, the plantation received the distinction of being named Louisiana Attraction of the Year.

Upstairs hall and stair landing at Destrehan. (Kitchens)

HOUMAS HOUSE

A Sugar Palace Reborn on a Wish and a Dime

⚲ Darrow, Louisiana

Today, *Houmas House* stands along the banks of the Mississippi River, a crown jewel among the parade of plantations that line the levees in this region. Flamboyantly restored and meticulously maintained, the house and its jaw-dropping gardens welcome throngs of guests every day.

Situated between New Orleans and Baton Rouge, *Houmas* was once among the lands the Houmas Indians called home. In 1774, these Native Americans sold a portion of these lands, destined to become a plantation, to Alexander Latil and Maurice Conway for $150 worth of goods consisting of copper pots, five pistols, powder, balls, butcher knives, white shirts, sugar, mirrors, and salt.[1]

Latil and Conway constructed a house on the property, and in 1775, Latil sold his interest in the estate to Conway. The property ended up in the hands of Daniel Clark, the first delegate from the Territory of Orleans to the US House of Representatives. Clark greatly improved the plantation, began cultivating sugar, and built one of the area's first sugar mills at *Houmas*. Clark's will later fueled the longest running legal case in US history, in which his child Myra Clark Gaines fought for her inheritance up to the Supreme Court.

In 1811, *Houmas Plantation* was transferred to Revolutionary War hero Gen. Wade Hampton. Hampton's financial agent in Charleston wrote:

> Your funds here, I believe, are sufficient to meet your engagements with Clark. The purchase you have made from Mr. Clark must certainly be an advantageous one; and will be a princely estate in a few years; and it cannot be said to cost you much more than $100,000, for with good management, the revenue from the places will pay the other $200,000, with the interest of only three percent. Although I feel pleased at the great bargain you have got, yet there is a jealously on my mind that the country will attract you too much from us here.

Houmas House Plantation as it appears today. (Matrana)

Hampton poured himself into sugar production, asking his son Wade Hampton Jr. to bring thirty slaves. The general himself brought an additional fifty slaves the first year. By 1817, ships were docking at the Houmas river landing to load up with "white gold." A German trader noted in his journal that year that he observed a three-masted ship loading at the "Hampton Place." By 1829, Hampton was listed as the largest sugar producer in Louisiana, refining 1,640 hogsheads of sugar and 750 hogsheads of molasses.

During his tenure at *Houmas*, Hampton enlarged a small 1805 master house that had been constructed in front of the original Latil house, creating a modest master house, with the original Latil house as an unattached rear dependency. Later, between

1829 and 1830, Hampton and his son greatly enlarged the master house, into a Greek Revival mansion, adding a second story, a immense attic with crowning cupola, and a three-sided colonnade of massive Tuscan columns enclosing a wide gallery.

Hampton died in 1835, leaving a vast estate of plantations and landholdings from Louisiana to South Carolina. Wade Hampton Jr. inherited his father's estate, but shared much of it with his half-sisters and their mother. They eventually sold *Houmas* to John Burnside, who quickly expanded the plantation further. By 1860, he owned 940 slaves in Ascension and St. James Parishes, and grew to become the wealthiest planter in the state.

At one time, Burnside had four sugarhouses on his massive estate. The Civil War certainly brought great changes to the *Houmas Plantation*, the greatest of which was the emancipation of the slave labor force. After the war, Burnside, who by then spent most of his time at his Washington Avenue home in New Orleans, began hiring Chinese and Irish workers to supplement the work of freed slaves.

Upon Burnside's death in 1881, *Houmas* was inherited by Burnside's childhood friend, Oliver Beirne. Seven years later, Beirne died, leaving the plantation to his son-in-law William Porcher Miles, who served as president of the University of South Carolina. By the turn of the century, Miles had consolidated *Houmas* along with several nearby plantations into the Miles Planting and Manufacturing Company, which held the estate for over forty years. Under the company, sugar manufacturing was consolidated into a central sugar factory; tracks were laid across the plantation fields, and steam engines transported cut cane quickly to ensure the highest yields.

Under Miles's care, the *Houmas Plantation* mansion was joined with the earlier colonial Latil house that sat near the rear of the mansion. This created one very large house, to accommodate the large Miles family and their guests.

In 1940, the plantation was acquired by Dr. George Crozat, a prominent orthodontist. For over a quarter century, Crozat devoted himself to preserving the mansion at *Houmas*. His influence was enormous and included relatively extensive alterations of the house. He preferred an austere, Federal style for the mansion, which he achieved exteriorly by removing decorative balustrades from the roof, taking down the cupola's crowning finial, and removing other ornamentation. Inside, his modifications were even more extensive. The floor plan was altered, most notably on the first floor by moving the dining room into one of the double parlors and creating a large ovaloid stair hall near the back carriageway (a covered breezeway between the main portion of the house and Latil house that had been incorporated into the larger structure). These changes created space to move the butler's pantry and created more storage and service space. Upstairs additional changes to the floor plan were made. Under Miles's renovation, the second floor contained nine large bedrooms. Crozat modified the connection between the principle part of the mansion at the Latil house, which removed two bedrooms, but allowed for the creation of a glass roof for portions of the carriageway, a larger second-floor stair landing, an elevator, closets, and modern bathrooms. Dr. Crozat died in 1965, still with additional plans undone for the house. His heirs held on to the mansion for decades, during which time it declined.

In 2003, *Houmas House* along with its contents were put up for auction. The house and every movable item in it were separately cataloged. The auction was highly publicized and collectors and dealers came from far and wide. The contents, including

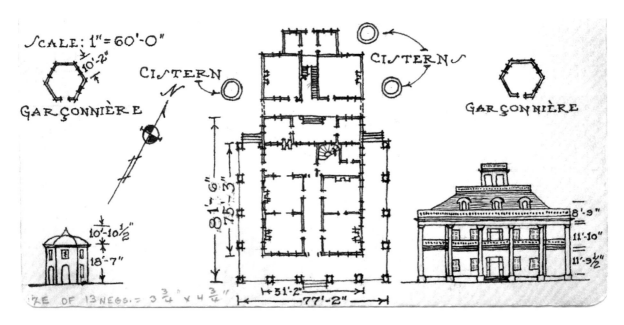

SCALE: 1" = 60'-0"

GARÇONNIÈRE

CISTERN

CISTERN

GARÇONNIÈRE

10'-2"

N

10'-10½"

18'-7"

81'-6"

75'-3"

8'-9"

11'-10"

11'-9½"

SIZE OF 13 NEGS. = 3¾" × 4¾"

51'-2"

77'-2"

The floor plan of Houmas House prior to the Crozat renovations. (HABS)

Houmas House Plantation prior to the Crozat restoration. Note the balustrades at the roof line and around the cupola; these would later be removed by Dr. Crozat, with upper balustrade being added back in the most recent renovation by Kevin Kelly. (HABS)

plantation records, family diaries, blueprints, the custom *Houmas* china, photographs, maps, and many other important historical pieces, were divided into over one thousand separate lots each going to the highest bidder. Stripped and empty, the mansion was sold separately.

The plantation estate was sold to real estate mogul and historic preservationist Kevin Kelly for $2.95 million. Kelly had long been a great fan of the estate, and had an

The spiral staircase at Houmas House. (Bush)

ironic visit to the plantation with a business colleague in 1987. Kelly had been touring the man around the River Road saving his favorite plantation—*Houmas House*—for last. When the two arrived, they were disappointed to find the old house in shabby shape: rundown, overgrown, and generally unkempt. They found a large sugar kettle there with a sign advising visitors to toss in a coin and make a wish. Kelly tossed in a quarter, his friend, a dime. Neither told the other what they had wished for, until news broke that an undisclosed buyer had purchased the plantation from the Crozat heirs and Kelly's friend called him. After learning that Kelly was indeed the new "mystery" owner of *Houmas*, both men revealed their wishes. Kelly wished that one day someone would restore *Houmas House* to its former glory; his friend had wished that one day Kelly would acquire *Houmas House* and restore it to its former glory. Both wishes were granted.

After acquiring the property, Kelly dove in to an extensive and costly renovation. Aided by his friend, artist Jim Blanchard, and others, Kelly rebelled against the white-walled ascetics of Dr. Crozat, making over the plantation in an exuberant and grand style. He poured millions of dollars into the restoration, updating the mansion's electrical, plumbing, and air-conditioning systems, and installing a sprinkler system. He renovated the large attic into his personal quarters complete with a large living room, kitchen, several bedrooms, and baths. After extensive research, the exterior walls of the

The entrance hall at Houmas House. (Matrana)

An ensemble of objects on a card table. (Matrana)

The carriageway that runs between the main house and earlier Latil house. (Levet)

main house were redone in an ochre-colored faux stone finish and the Latil portion of the house was painted brick red. The balustrade around the top of the roof was added back. Inside, the mansion underwent an equally flamboyant update. The walls now burst forth with color and the main entrance hall walls are covered with a mural depicting fields of sugarcane complete with local birds and even depictions of Kelly's beloved Dutch Labradors. The motif continues onto the ceiling, which shows a bright blue sky peeking through clouds. The colorful rooms are now chock-full with Kelly's extensive collections of period furniture, art, and seemingly endless antiques.

Beyond the main house, the restoration continued. The park-like grounds got a multimillion-dollar makeover and today are among the finest residential gardens in America, with meandering water features, classical marble statuary, and thousands of

Rear façade of Houmas House with the massive fountain installed by Kevin Kelly. (Levet)

varieties of indigenous flora. A few whimsical pieces—garden gnomes, pink flamingos, and some modern kinetic sculptures—remind visitors that these ornate formal gardens have a playful side as well. A massive fountain was constructed behind the Latil wing of the house, completely redefining the space. A large plantation store was constructed that incorporates salvaged materials from several historic buildings. It houses a massive gift shop, bookstore, theater, restrooms, and art gallery. The mansion's two iconic hexagonal *garçonnières* were transformed, one into a dark wood draped barroom called the "Turtle Bar" and the other into the well-appointed private residence for Jim Blanchard. Several classy restaurants were added throughout the estate, wedding and banquet facilities, an art gallery, overnight accommodations in the form of cabins, parking lots, and other structures were also added. Later, Kelly constructed an ornate Japanese tea pavilion on top of a large hill and waterfall, inspired by the famed pagoda once found in gardens of Valcour Aime's now-destroyed Petite Versailles Plantation. And, today, an outdoor amphitheater is being added for performances and other events.

The newly renovated mansion opened to the public in 2003, with the lavish wedding of Princess Grace and King Sam, Kelly's beloved dogs. The canine couple was dressed in full wedding regalia, and the entire wedding party was carried to site in horse-drawn carriages. Sam and Grace took their vows on the front steps and an unparalleled reception followed, with dancers in period costumes, a wedding cake in the shape of an exact replica of the newly renovated mansion, live music, and, of course, fireworks over the river.

Today, *Houmas House* is one of the most popular tourist attractions in Louisiana, and perhaps the entire South. Tour buses line up bringing hundreds and sometimes

An enormous oak tree on the grounds of Houmas House. (Matrana)

thousands of guests a day to the plantation. Tour guides lead spirited, unpretentious tours that often last an hour or more. Visitors are allowed to bang on the period piano, sit on the furniture, and enjoy the house and its priceless contents. Visitors are reminded the plantation is not a museum but rather still a private home; a fact further confirmed when guests see Kelly's pet dogs freely roaming the grounds. Most visitors don't even pay much mind to the bearded man in his t-shirt and shorts mulling about the gardens or riding around in a golf cart from building to building—little do they know that the man is the owner of the plantation and the person responsible for its rebirth.

The brightly colored exterior of
Laura, a Creole plantation. (Bush)

LAURA

Creole Traditions Rise from the Ashes

📍 Vacherie, Louisiana

The story of Louisiana's *Laura Plantation* is as complex and multilayered as any American estate can be. Over centuries, the mostly female-run Creole plantation has undergone several major transformations and has been brought from the brink of destruction more than once, most recently literally rising from the ashes after a devastating fire.[1]

The property originally served as a major ceremonial site for Native Americans long before Europeans set eyes on it. A large Acolapissa tribal ceremonial complex was built there by the early 1700s. It was known as "Tabiscanja" in the Mobilian tongue, meaning "long river view," due to the expansive view from the ceremonial mounds. It is said that an early Catholic missionary chopped down the central fourteen-foot-tall red-painted phallic totem or "baton rouge" in an effort to rid the site of "obscene" pagan symbols.

In 1785, four Acadian families—exiles from French Canada—received small plots of land from the Spanish government. They lived at the site with the Acolapissa. In 1804, Guillaume DuParc, the former commandant of Pointe Coupee, acquired the property and gave the Acadian families money to leave. DuParc allowed the Natives to remain on the property as he and a small number of slaves grew sugarcane and built a plantation house. It is said that Native American teepees surrounded the manor house in its earliest days, and the Acolapissa remained on the property as late as 1915.

DuParc began construction of his plantation mansion immediately after acquiring the property. It was completed eleven months later, having been built by highly skilled slave laborers. It was these Africans and their counterparts on the plantation who brought with them folktales from Senegal, which they passed down through generations of slaves. In 1870, the great Louisiana historian Alcée Fortier (grandson of St. James Parish sugar baron Valcour Aime) visited the former slaves in their cabins at *Laura* and transcribed their folktales, including *Compair Lapin* and *Compair Bouki,* known now to the English-speaking world as Br'er Rabbit and Br'er Fox. Today, these

The bright color palette at Laura continues into the interior. (Bush)

same tales are still being told in Senegal almost word for word as recorded by Fortier in Louisiana.

The West Indies–style mansion at *Laura* that the slaves built was a raised structure that rested on blue-gray glazed brick columns and walls. Underneath an eight-foot-deep pyramidal brick foundation provided much support. The wooden structure above was constructed from cypress inlaid with locally fired brick in the popular *briquette-entre-pôteau* (brick-between-posts) method, and then plastered inside and stuccoed outside. The exterior of the home conformed to Creole norms, being brightly painted in red, ochre, green, and pearl. The plan of the house was that of a traditional Creole home with no interior hallways or staircases. There was no front door, as inviting guests through a front door was considered rude. The men and women occupied different sides of the house, and male guests were welcomed into exterior bedroom doors on the men's side and then ushered into the men's parlor; female guests were likewise escorted through the women's bedroom. The Creoles believed that only Americans, whom they called *Les Animaux* (the animals), would bring guests through a front door. The

The view from the raised front gallery at Laura on a rainy afternoon. (Bush)

main house totaled approximately 24,000 square feet and there was a 2,500-square-feet detached kitchen behind the main house. A front door was eventually installed, but remained tightly locked until 1924 when eight family members were killed by a tornado at nearby St. Philip's Church; the archbishop of New Orleans visited to offer his condolences and he was allowed to enter through the front door.[2]

DuParc died in 1808, and at that time the plantation complex consisted of ten sizable buildings, including quarters for seventeen slaves, a barn, warehouses, and a small, rudimentary sugar mill. DuParc's wife, Nannette Prudhomme, took over operations of the plantation and built the *Maison de Reprise,* a house on the property where she could retreat from her family when necessary. The *Maison* was used as a hospital during the Civil War. Nannette was followed by three generations of DuParc's female descendants who ran the growing sugarcane plantation. The last of the female planters was Laura Locoul Gore, who in 1936 penned an amazing memoir of the plantation that now bears her name. The story has it that Laura's daughters were reading *Gone with the Wind,* and their mother immediately stopped them, "Don't read another word. I'll write it down," she told them. *Memories of the Old Plantation Home* was essentially lost for decades, a single handwritten copy of the manuscript being held in St. Louis by an old family friend, until 1993 when it was discovered and later published.[3]

Laura's memoirs tell of how the plantation flourished under the management of the Lacoul ladies. In 1830, Laura's grandmother, who then owned the plantation, bought thirty teenage female slaves from New Orleans and brought them to the plantation to have them impregnated. Within a few years, her breeding program resulted in what she called her "crop of children." As the slave population at *Laura* expanded, sixty-five cabins were built, four of which still stand today. By the time of the Civil War, 186 slaves resided at *Laura*, most of whom remained on the plantation after emancipation. After the war, Victorian-style millwork was added to the main house's porch and dormer windows, and a double-stair portico was built.

Laura Lacoul Gore eventually rejected her Creole culture and moved to St. Louis. She sold her plantation in 1891 to the Waguespacks, a family of French-speaking Creoles of Alsatian and Germanic descent. Laura specified in the sale that the plantation would retain her name. The Waguespacks squabbled among themselves, and arguments escalated to such a point that in 1905, one heir actually chopped off a portion of the main plantation mansion and moved it to a different location to serve as his residence.

The Waguespacks continued to grow sugarcane until 1981 when they sold their plantation to a group of politically connected investors, who planned to destroy the historic buildings and sell the cleared property to the state for the development of a new bridge across the Mississippi River at the site. Fortunately, a still-active earthquake fault on the property made the plantation an inadequate location for a bridge. The investors forfeited as their venture collapsed and the plantation then went into receivership. The plantation was largely forgotten. Abandoned, it quickly declined. *Laura* was sold at auction in 1992 to the St. James Sugar Cooperative.

In June 1992, a group of preservationists, led by Norman and Sand Marmillion, dreamed of an economic and historical venture that aimed to restore *Laura*, while attempting to prove that preservation can be financially transformative for a local community. "We want *Laura* to demonstrate that heritage tourism is a profitable economic alternative to heavy industry along the River Road and that a successful preservation effort rooted in economic incentives can save our heritage," said Norman Marmillion.[4]

The Marmillions and their supporters recruited investors at historical societies, civic clubs, and other like-minded organizations, and raised money to purchase the plantation in 1993. They began restoring the house. "They had huge vines of poison ivy growing through the shutters and 14 inches of cow manure in the basement," Norman Marmillion said. "It was hard as concrete. We had to use a pick ax to get it out."[5] Immediately, the group set up to create a plantation tour like nothing else. Life-sized cutouts of the DuParc and Lacoul family and their slaves stand in and outside the mansion and tours focus on the lives of the family members and slaves rather than furniture or other furnishings.

Slave cabins, once long abandoned in the fields, were secured to trailers and moved closer to the main house so that visitors could easily visit them. The way in which the plantation tour directly dealt with the issue of slavery was refreshing and unique. Tourists—both black and white—streamed in to hear a balanced story of plantation residents both in and outside the big house. *Laura* became one of the most popular tourist attractions in an area filled with plantations. Before long, an estimated 100,000 visitors each year toured *Laura*.

Then, tragedy struck. Eleven years to the day that the Marmillions acquired the plantation, a fire nearly destroyed it. Early on the night of August 9, 2004, an alarm sounded at *Laura*'s main house, but when a worker went to check on the mansion, he found nothing unusual. Later, a second alarm sounded and the house was ablaze with fire shooting out the roof. Firefighters worked for two hours to get the fire under control, pulling furniture out onto the gallery in an effort to save it. The roof collapsed, but

A storage room under the main house with wine rack, large olive jars, and a life-sized cutout that is used during interpretive tours. (Bush)

much of the remaining structure, while badly damaged, survived. Norman Marmillion said, "Seven fire trucks came out here and fought this blaze and beat it. It has survived floods and hurricanes . . . Oh Lord, this place has something that just won't stop."[6]

Shortly after the fire, the Marmillions vowed to rebuild the mansion. The tours never stopped; even the day after the fire, visitors were guided around the smoldering remains of the colorful house. The fire was an important part of the plantation's history, and the tour dealt directly with the tragedy just as it had with other difficult issues of the plantation's history. "Our tour had never been about the house and furniture," said Joseph Dunn, director of communications at *Laura*. "It's about the people who lived here. It's about their lives and about Creole culture."[7]

Shortly after the fire, plantation workers spent days sifting through the ashes and debris to salvage doorknobs, nails, hinges, and other artifacts to be used in the reconstruction. Soon, dozens of specialty shops across the state were working to restore windows, carpentry, and masonry work. Workers and craftsmen were hired to restore the house using original nineteenth-century techniques, binding vertical beams with peg joints and carefully repairing original plaster and other elements of the structure.

Two years after the fire, as the restoration continued, Hurricane Katrina brought another big blow. The Marmillions' home in the Lakeview region of New Orleans was flooded and tourism to south Louisiana screeched to a halt. *Laura*'s thirty-seven employees all lost their jobs. The Marmillions persisted, continuing to restore *Laura* and struggling to rebuild their own home.

Slowly, the tourists returned, employees were rehired, and *Laura* rose again, a colorful Creole phoenix. Today, visitors stream in once again to hear about a distinct culture, learn what life as a slave must have been like, and visit an estate "that just won't stop."

Nottoway Plantation. (Bush)

NOTTOWAY

Louisiana's Gleaming White Castle

📍 White Castle, Louisiana

The largest standing plantation mansion in the South sits near Baton Rouge on the banks of the Mississippi River. *Nottoway* was once home to the Randolph family, and it is the patriarch of this clan who built the 53,000-square-foot behemoth of a house that has endured so much, yet still flourishes today.[1]

John Hampden Randolph was born in Nottoway County, Virginia, in 1813, but moved to Mississippi at the age of six when his father was appointed as a federal judge. He grew up on a plantation in Woodville and learned how to be a cotton planter. He took over operations of his family's plantation when his father died in 1831, and six years later at the age of twenty-four, he married Emily Jane Liddell. In 1841, John moved his growing family to Louisiana, as he sought greater profits in sugar planting. He was unable to find any land for a plantation along the Mississippi River, as it had all been purchased by other planters. Instead, he purchased a 1,650-acre cotton plantation in a densely wooded area southwest of Baton Rouge. He called this estate Forest Home, due to the overgrowth surrounding the plantation's principal structure. Always a headstrong speculator, Randolph put up Forest Home as collateral to secure a $15,000 loan from the Bank of Louisiana, which he used in addition to a $37,000 loan from his father-in-law, for the construction of a steam engine sugar mill, levee, and drainage system. This faith in potential profits from sugar was well founded, and his ventures paid off. He used his profits from sugar making to purchase more and more lands along the river when they became available. Eventually he increased his holdings to over 7,000 acres.

As his wealth ballooned, Randolph hired famed architect Henry Howard to build for him the grandest plantation house along the Mississippi River. Howard did not disappoint, creating an iconic Italianate mansion that boasted sixty-four rooms spread across three floors, six interior staircases, three modern bathrooms with flushing toilets (unheard of at that time), 165 doors, and two hundred windows (365 openings in all, one for each day of the year). It also featured gas lighting with fuel that was produced onsite at a gas plant, a technological marvel at the time.

Interior column capital at Nottoway Plantation. (Bush)

Outside, the mansion was unlike any other. Towering square pillars reached up to a heavy cornice, all accentuating the vertical aspects of Howard's masterpiece. On the upriver side of the house, a grand semicircular projection—not unlike the southern façade of the White House—triumphantly completed this tour de force of plantation architecture.

Inside, exquisite hand-carved, Italian marble mantels surrounded the fireplace openings, and intricate lacy cornices and capitals detailed and richly decorated every conceivable inch of the interior. There was a bowling alley in the basement, but the home's crown jewel was its famed white ballroom, an ornate and luxurious space that hosted balls, society debuts, Randolph family weddings, and many other parties and events.

Surrounding the mansion, the estate encompassed nineteen hundred acres cultivated, and over fifty-five hundred acres of swampland. Buildings included dozens of slave quarters, a large schoolhouse, a greenhouse, stables, a massive sugarhouse, and a variety of barns, carriage houses, and other outbuildings.

Entrance hall at Nottoway Plantation. (Bush)

The Randolphs lived a life of luxury in *Nottoway* until the Civil War broke out. Initially, John Randolph was opposed to the war as he did not feel the South could win against the more industrialized North. Ultimately, he supported the war financially and three of his sons fought in the southern cause, the eldest dying in the Battle of Vicksburg in 1863. During the war, Randolph moved with two hundred slaves to a leased cotton plantation in Texas, where he was able to operate an agricultural business without hindrance from shipping blockades that were present in Louisiana. Because an abandoned plantation was certain to be occupied or burned by Union troops, the Randolphs made the difficult decision of having Emily remain at the plantation with her youngest children, including an infant, and just a few house servants. Both Union and Confederate troops camped on the plantation grounds at various times, and the plantation was shelled periodically by northern gunboats. In fact, a cannonball from the war can still be seen in one of the mansion's tall pillars today. Emily's courage is illustrated in the fact that when one northern gunboat approached the house from

Stair hall at Nottoway Plantation. (Bush)

Nottoway Plantation's famed White Ballroom. (Bush)

the river, she took her only weapon, a small dagger, and went out on the second-floor balcony to make her presence known. The officers, with their massive cannons, surely found the site of this petite woman on the balcony ironic. They disembarked from the boat and approached her. Shockingly, she invited them into the mansion and proceeded to entertain them with all the style and grace stereotypically fitting a southern plantation mistress. Stunned by her hospitality, the officers forged a fast friendship with this courageous little woman. She confided in them that all of the guns on the plantation had been confiscated, and she had no way of defending herself or her children on this massive estate. The commanding officer then handed her his own silver-mounted pistol. She is said to have later fired it to scare away thieves who were ransacking her chicken coups.

Randolph's Texas operations proved to be successful during the war. After the fighting ended, he started buying up plantations from less fortunate neighbors who were unable to pay taxes or mortgages. During his later years, Randolph's holdings slowly diminished as he himself slowed down. John Randolph died in 1883. Emily continued living at *Nottoway* until 1889 when at the age of seventy-one she sold it for the sum of $50,000, which she divided equally among her nine surviving children and herself. She spent the rest of her days between Forest Home Plantation, Baton Rouge, and New Orleans, where she stayed with her children and grandchildren.

Nottoway was purchased by Jean Baptiste Dugas and his former son-in-law Desiré Pierre Landry, who were sugar-planting partners. Landry's wife, Cordelia, had died at the age of thirty-four, and he remarried Marie Eugenie Folse. The couple moved into *Nottoway* in 1889 with their four-year-old daughter Beatrice. After both Desiré and Beatrice died, in 1897 and 1907, respectively, Marie sold *Nottoway* to Alfonse Hanlon in 1909. Hanlon was an experienced sugar planter who owned several plantations, but after losing his crop two years in a row to a hard freeze in 1911 and massive flooding in 1912, *Nottoway* was foreclosed and passed to Dr. Whyte G. Owen.

Dr. Owen, who served as surgeon general of Louisiana and president of the Louisiana Medical Society, attempted to operate *Nottoway* as a sugar plantation, but eventually sold most of the cultivated property, retaining for himself and his family the massive plantation mansion and immediate surrounding acreage. Dr. Owen died in 1949 at the age of ninety-one, and the plantation house passed to his son, Stanford Owen, who was raised in the house. Stanford served as the principal of White Castle High School and lived in the home with his wife, Odessa Rushing Owen, until his death. Odessa, a former professor at LSU, lived alone in the house and was extremely passionate about preserving the mansion. However, for all of her determination and fervor, she woefully lacked the massive resources required to maintain the home. The mansion fell into grave disrepair, with clutter piling up and wallpaper peeling down. The once gleaming white pillars were now shabby and dark gray. Broken light fixtures hung from walls and ceilings, while water flooded through holes in the roof when it rained. During storms, Odessa would run through the corridors with large buckets to try and catch the deluge pouring in.

In 1980, Odessa came to the conclusion that she could not continue to care for the plantation alone. She began searching for a proper buyer for the old house. She entertained many offers, but ultimately rejected all of them, feeling that everyone she spoke

with either was disingenuous or did not have the passion or means to restore the house
in the way she felt was appropriate. Finally, she read an article about Arlin K. Dease, a
young Baton Rouge contractor who had meticulously restored three other antebellum
houses. She contacted Dease, who was thrilled with the opportunity presented to him.
He purchased *Nottoway* in 1980 for $570,000 with the agreement that Odessa would
be allowed to live in the house for the remainder of her days.

After purchasing the mansion, Dease immediately hit the ground running, bringing in crews of up to sixty men at a time who worked twelve hours a day restoring the
house. The mansion was opened to the public just three months after Dease acquired
it. Dease was aided in his efforts by Stephen Saunders, who did comprehensive research
on the plantation, leading to its inclusion on the National Register of Historic Places.

In 1985, the plantation was purchased by Australian multibillionaire Paul Ramsey,
who owned over 150 hospitals in Australia, the United Kingdom, France, Indonesia,
and Malaysia, as well as numerous television and radio stations. Ramsey fell in love
with the house after staying there during a business trip, and he was determined to play
a part in the estate's preservation. While the rest of southeast Louisiana faced economic
downturns related to the desertion of the oil industry to Houston, Hurricane Katrina,

Nottoway Plantation, front
façade. (Bush)

Garden statue at Nottoway Plantation. (Bush)

and other tragedies, Ramsey steadily poured tens of millions of dollars into *Nottoway*. He greatly expanded the grounds, restoring formal gardens and building dozens of historically blended outbuildings from event and meeting facilities to bed and breakfast accommodations and more.

All the while, Odessa Owen remained in her quarters at the plantation, operating a quaint shop under the main house where she sold dolls, crafts, and other handmade items to tourists. She continued to live on the property until her death in 2003 at the age of ninety-five.

Paul Ramsey died in 2014, leaving his $3.5 billion fortune to a charitable foundation. Because of his generosity and the passion and vision of other owners of the property, *Nottoway* continues to thrive and serve as an economic powerhouse for the area. Today, the area immediately beneath the white ballroom has been glassed in and serves as a charming restaurant; hundreds of brides clamor to book weddings at *Nottoway*; and visitors enjoy expansive resort facilities including a swimming pool, tennis courts, state-of-the-art meeting facilities, several large event venues, a fitness center, a salon and spa, shops, and more—all perfectly blended into the historic landscape.

Nottoway remains a symbol of Louisiana's past but is also a gleaming example of how investment in historic preservation can spur successful economic growth.

SAN FRANCISCO

Quintessential Steamboat Gothic Sails
into the Twenty-First Century

♀ Garyville, Louisiana

The exuberant mansion at *San Francisco Plantation* explodes onto the River Road frontage in a splash of color and elaborate ornamentation. It defines the Steamboat Gothic style, and one rule holds true throughout: there is nothing "usual" about this mansion.

The plantation's history can be traced back to the 1820s when Elisée Rillieux, a free man of color, began buying tracts of land, small plantations, and slaves to establish a large sugar plantation in St. John the Baptist Parish. Elisée never intended to be a planter himself; he and his brother, Francois, were speculators. Francois created an estate that later became Godchaux Plantation. Elisée followed his brother's example, and only three years after assembling his plantation, he sold it to Edmond Bozonier Marmillion and his partner Eugène Lartigue for the enormous sum of $100,000. Elisée made a very handsome $50,000 profit from the deal.

Marmillion and his family owned other estates in the area. But, it was on this tract that Marmillion sought to build a showplace mansion. The house was built between 1853 and 1856 and is thought to be a replacement for an earlier house that was probably badly damaged or destroyed during flooding caused from the crevasse of 1852. The bumper crop of sugarcane the following year likely provided the surplus funds necessary for the elegant mansion's construction.

San Francisco is indisputably one of the most unusual plantation mansions along River Road and arguably has one of the most beautiful interiors. The exterior of the house is the pinnacle of Steamboat Gothic style—the house looks in many ways as if it should be floating down the Mississippi rather than sitting alongside it. The house has been called a "layer cake." Simple square pillars support the upper and principle floor; dainty Corinthian columns support an unusual deck that is surrounded by a fully louvered attic. An immense cornice with Italianate brackets visually anchors the top portion of the mansion. Gothic-style windows adorn the dormers, and a copula crowns the top like a wheelhouse. The house is a mishmash of ornate styles beautifully

San Francisco Plantation. (Levet)

Steamboat Gothic detailing on the San Francisco Plantation house. (Levet)

blended together with color. Pale blues, creams, yellows, and whites highlight the complex designs and detailing throughout. Two large cisterns frame the mansion, crowned with Moorish-style, bell-shaped toppers.

The plan of the mansion is as unusual as its famed exterior. The principal floor is arranged in three rows. The front row is three rooms across, with a central reception room and two flanking drawing rooms. A broad gallery wraps around the front and sides of this row of rooms. The reception room opens into a secondary reception room,

Upriver drawing room. (Levet)

which is the central room of the middle row. This middle row is five rooms wide, with the gray sitting room and the green sitting room flanking the central reception area, and a boudoir and a children's room on the ends of the rows. The back row of rooms contains a large loggia (three rooms wide) with double staircases. This long room is flanked by bedrooms. Below, the ground floor features a larger central dining room, which is oriented under the space occupied by the front and middle reception rooms upstairs. A U-shaped billiards room and back entrance room wraps around much of the dining room. Storage rooms for china, wine, and food flank the billiards room.

Downstairs, the interior of the house is quite simple; upstairs, *San Francisco* boasts some of the most ornate, colorful, and beautiful painted rooms in the South. The upriver drawing room was painted in a pale violet with the cornices and ceiling being adorned with richly detailed hand-painted floral motifs and medallions. The downriver drawing room was decorated in a masculine style, with dark geometric designs on the ceiling, doors, and cornices. Images of deer, Roman-style faces, and antique vases and vessels were framed in perfectly painted rectangles, circles, and diamonds. In the nearby pale-blue boudoir, faux gold latticework framed pudgy cherubim who adorn the ceiling.

Edmond Marmillion passed away in 1856, less than one year after the home was completed. The day after Edmond's death, his oldest son, Valsin, returned from Europe and was forced to take over the plantation. Following the Civil War, *San Francisco* was acquired by Achille Bougère in 1879. During this period, a few alterations were made

San Francisco   43

Detail of the ceiling fresco in the boudoir. (Levet)

Downriver drawing room with richly painted doors and ceiling. (Levet)

Ground floor patio, San Francisco Plantation. (Levet)

to the house including the addition of two rooms on the first floor. It was the Bougères who gave the home its current moniker. Originally, Valsin Marmillion had said he was "sans fruscins," meaning without a penny in his pocket, a comment about the extraordinary debt he incurred in running the plantation and maintaining the mansion. So, the plantation was called San Fruscins for a while, but evolved into "St. Frusquin" and, in 1879, changed to "San Francisco" by the Bougères.

When the Bougères moved to a house in La Place in 1905, they took the original furniture from the plantation mansion, and unfortunately, this furniture was subsequently destroyed by fire. The Ory family purchased the house, and beginning in 1954, they leased it to the Clarks, who opened the house to the public. The plantation property, including the house, was purchased by the Energy Corporation of Louisiana in 1973, in order to construct an oil refinery. Fortunately, the chairman of the company, Fredrick Ingram, was an admirable man with great appreciation for history. He wished to see the mansion at *San Francisco* restored and arranged for the house and a few acres of surrounding property to be donated to the newly created nonprofit San Francisco Plantation Foundation. After extensive research, restoration of the house began in 1975, with borrowed funds. The following year the Energy Corporation of Louisiana was purchased by Marathon Oil, which had long been active in the Louisiana oil and gas industry. Marathon agreed to underwrite the cost of restoration (some $2.5 million at the time), and continues its support today. Marathon's support of the 1970s restoration of the house was sincerely appreciated, but at the same time anger was mounting over their neglect of Welham Plantation in St. James Parish. While the restoration of *San Francisco* was complete in 1977 thanks to the generosity of Marathon executives, those same executives sent a bulldozer through the historic halls of Welham, destroying it completely just two years after the restoration of *San Francisco*. There was no logical explanation for their contradictory handling of these two historic properties.

The 1970s restoration of *San Francisco* was done with the utmost professionalism. The house was restored to the period of 1860, when it was at its height of elegance. Outside, the slate roof was repaired, much of the millwork was revamped or replaced, and exterior stairs were refurbished. The real challenge came on the inside of the house, where overpainting and neglect had badly damaged the unique and stunning wall and ceiling paintings. Archeologists, historians, artists, contractors, and others conducted thorough analysis of paint samples and flakes. They used special high-powered lighting to see under layers of paint at the designs hidden underneath. Ultimately, these painstaking efforts were not in vain, allowing restorers to uncover and restore and in other areas replicate the famed paintings down to the most minute detail. By the 1970s one of the beautiful double staircases in the back loggia had been removed and had to be replaced—its twin was used as a model to make sure the staircase was an exact replica of its original predecessor. Painted floor cloths were replicated and period furniture and other furnishings were brought in to complete the project.

San Francisco has inspired films, books, and many works of art. Frances Parker Keyes set her novel *Steamboat Gothic* there. In 1978, the house was declared a National Historic Landmark, and became a favorite destination among tourists and locals alike. In 1992, *San Francisco* welcomed its millionth visitor, and it is now visited by over 100,000 guests annually. Major repairs took place in 2014 and 2015. Additional restoration work continues today.

Today, the biggest threat to the plantation is the river that inspired its eclectic exterior. Over the years, the Mississippi has inched closer and closer toward the mansion, with the levee and River Road sitting almost at the plantation mansion's front steps today. Other Louisiana plantation houses such as Avondale and Uncle Sam have ultimately been victims of the river's harsh encroachment, but hopefully creative solutions over the coming decades will allow *San Francisco* to continue to thrive and to inspire visitors for many, many years to come.

WHITNEY PLANTATION

A New Day Dawns

◉ Wallace, Louisiana

*W*hitney Plantation, once home to a German immigrant family that found great success in the antebellum sugar trade, has recently been opened to the public as a monument to the memory of slavery. Just a few years before, the plantation house was surrounded by a foreboding fence and dense foliage. At that time, a handmade sign at the gate near the old plantation store warned of "armed personnel." From the River Road in St. John the Baptist Parish, the estate looked overgrown and decrepit. But, beyond this misleading façade, just a few hundred feet from what the average passerby saw, preservation was percolating.

The historic property was purchased by prominent New Orleans attorney John Cummings III more than a decade ago. He quietly worked for years to make his longtime dream a reality. Cummings, an unassuming gentleman with a white beard and rosy cheeks, stated his goals clearly, "We want to remember the forgotten ones," referring to slaves whose forced labor fueled production on antebellum plantations throughout the South. Their individual stories have largely faded into the past.

To this end, Cummings diligently worked to restore and preserve *Whitney Plantation* and expand it into a living history museum with a particular focus on slavery. Cummings's grand plans are now a reality. For example, Cummings acquired Antioch Baptist Church—a large building built in 1861—and moved it from the town of Paulina to *Whitney*. He had the building chopped into three pieces, shipped across the Mississippi River, and reassembled. He placed curious statues of black children dressed in the typical clothing of slaves around the plantation's buildings, a reminder of the children who grew up in slavery across the South. Authentic down to every detail, except the eyes, which were left eerily hollow; these statues are the creation of Ohio artist Woodrow Nash, who was commissioned to produce forty-two of the realistic depictions of youths in sculpted stoneware and bronze patina.

Outside the church, workers dug a large lake that serves as the terminus of the estate's new water system, a series of creeks and water features, that meanders through

The Antioch Baptist Church, which was moved to Whitney Plantation in recent years. (Matrana)

Two of the forty statues of slave children by Ohio-based artist Woodrow Nash that can be found at Whitney Plantation. (Levet)

Kitchen at Whitney, the oldest kitchen in Louisiana. (Matrana)

tall cattails and water lilies. On the opposite side of Antioch sits *Whitney*'s "virtual cemetery," where Cummings plans to place dozens of old iron crosses, and build other monuments to slavery.

The Field of Angels sits farther back—granite plaques engraved with photos of slave children commemorate the area that memorializes slave children who died before their second birthday. Here, a striking statue of a bare-breasted African angel, wings outstretched, kneels down as she gazes into the face of a small child in her arms.

A few of *Whitney*'s original slave cabins remain on site, but many more have been brought in from neighboring estates to re-create the slave village. A few original buildings remain at *Whitney*—including the oldest kitchen in Louisiana and the sole surviving French barn in America—and Cummings has amassed several dozen others. An unusual antebellum greenhouse is slotted to serve as a cafeteria and meeting space. Several buildings from Tezcuco Plantation, whose noted Greek Revival master house was destroyed by fire in 2002, will serve as offices and dormitories.

Cummings envisions a portion of the plantation serving as a high-tech research complex and domicile for students and scholars who come to Louisiana to study southern plantation culture and slavery. He has already hired noted historians to begin

Detail of the front façade of the master house at Whitney Plantation. Note the faux marble detailing. (Levet)

extensive research into the area's antebellum history. In addition to academic support, Cummings plans to elicit support from celebrities to spread the word of his plantation preservation project.

The large Creole-style master house with its unusual faux marble and unique exterior murals sits at the center of the sprawling plantation complex. The one-of-a-kind exterior murals—found on no other plantation mansion anywhere in the South—were the work of Dominique Canova for the Haydel family, who owned the estate in the nineteenth century. Canova, thought to be a nephew of Napoleon's famed artist Antonio Canova, came from Italy and painted frescos in many of New Orleans's notable buildings. The masterpieces at *Whitney* have recently been restored by artisans from Rome.

The mansion was constructed around 1790 by the Haydels, about a quarter century after they originally acquired the property, and it was expanded in 1803.[1] The house

Master house at Whitney Plantation, front façade. (Matrana)

Master house at Whitney Plantation, rear façade. (Matrana)

was nearly identical to the mansion built by Haydel relatives at nearby Evergreen Plantation, although today, the two houses look nothing alike because the mansion at Evergreen was later remodeled in the Greek Revival style. *Whitney*'s master house was pure Creole in character and form, melding French, Spanish, and Creolized West African/West Indian architectural traditions. Unlike Anglo-inspired plantation houses, the stairs at *Whitney* were all exterior, there were no hallways in the house, and the central dining room occupied a large part of the raised basement. The mansion is large, with a seventy-foot-long gallery running the length of the front of the house and a smaller

Whitney Plantation pigeonaire.
(Levet)

"cabinet gallery" enclosed on three sides in the rear. A French colonial Norman Truss–style roof sits atop it all.

The Haydels retained ownership of their Creole mansion and surrounding estate until 1867, when it was acquired by the Bradish Johnson Company. A survey conducted soon after noted that the plantation had a wooden sugarhouse with a steam-powered sugar mill and open kettles in the boiling house section. By 1869, the plantation annually produced 182 hogsheads of sugar and 3,500 barrels of corn. By this time emancipated slaves at *Whitney* were earning on average between 40–60 cents per day for their labor.[2]

A great fire destroyed the sugarhouse at *Whitney* around 1880, and the plantation passed through several owners before being bought by the Barnes family in 1946. They used the estate as a weekend getaway, where they rode horses and hosted picnics under a large pavilion they built.

In 1990, the Barnes sold *Whitney* for nearly $8 million to the Formosa Chemical Corporation, a Taiwanese industrial giant, who planned to build the world's largest rayon plant there. Because the plant was projected to pump 53 million gallons of wastewater into the Mississippi River each day and consume eight hundred tons of wood daily, many environmentalists cried foul.[3] For years the plantation sat vacant and decaying.[4] But, Formosa's plans ultimately fizzled, and John Cummings III purchased the plantation from the chemical company in 1998, beginning his massive and unique preservation effort.[5]

Along with the rest of the complex, Cummings restored the master house to its original splendor as well, spending a fortune to furnish it. He has acquired among many other pieces an inlaid cherry wood sideboard, circa 1800, made in Natchez, Mississippi;

an important cypress armoire; an early nineteenth-century Louisiana cypress blanket chest; and a colonial West Indian commode.

In addition to a museum's worth of antiques for the mansion, Cummings amassed over fifty large original cast-iron sugar kettles for display on the estate. These are scattered in little groups all around the plantation. He found dozens of authentic plantation bells, and has his own functioning blacksmith shop that produces everything from hardware for doors and windows to replicas of period tools. He's also brought in over seven tons of cypress each month to repair buildings and construct other various structures.

The historically minded attorney amassed a small, but dedicated group of full-time artisans for the estate, such as Russell Stagg, a man Cummings considers "a genius." Stagg successfully replicated one of the plantation's original pigeonaires. Using original materials, he re-created the tower-like structure, which appears in every way to be a decaying, forgotten piece of the past.

Beyond the pigeonaires and other plantation buildings, toward one corner of the estate, sits an enormous barn-like structure, which hides a modern workshop. One end of the space is taken up by stacks of historical books and artwork. This is where the attorney and his staff research everything from original French colonial tools to early abolition speeches. Above, an open loft is lined with dozens of statues, some by Woodrow Nash, and others by various artists. Several of the lifelike effigies sit with their legs dangling over the edge of the space. "Go on up there," Cumming instructed, "but be very careful." The loft is filled with hundreds of centuries-old antiques, relics of our southern past that Cummings hopes all tell a very important story in a unique way.

In contrast to the artifacts above, the center of the warehouse is dominated by a massive, ultramodern machine: a high-tech laser engraver commanded by a sophisticated computer system. Guided by the mind and hand of one of the plantation's permanent craftsmen, the device helped make one of Cummings's most ambitious visions for *Whitney* a reality.

With the help of renowned historian Gwendolyn Midlo Hall, the attorney amassed the names of over 107,000 Louisiana slaves—each engraved into granite. Dozens of thin table-sized gray slabs were produced, each covered with names, images, and original quotes from these "forgotten people." Cummings explained that like the Vietnam Memorial, the sheer number of names in stone is astonishing. But, unlike the harsh lines of the sharp, calculated monument in Washington, the granite plates were placed in a more chaotic assemblage—much like slavery itself. The plates are displayed along an allée named after Gwendolyn Midlo Hall, the noted historian who built the "Louisiana Slave Database" and served as a mentor to dozens of students of American slavery. This important monument serves as a permanent reminder of those whose toil and suffering made plantation life possible.

Cummings opened *Whitney* to the public in December 2014, as the nation's first major museum devoted to slavery. It has garnered much media attention, with articles in the *Smithsonian* magazine, *Los Angeles Times*, and many others. *Whitney* is like no other place in world, and its message is meaningful and in many ways startling. Diverse visitors now come from far and wide to visit the plantation and take a tour that focuses deeply on the horrific institution of slavery.

Front façade, St. Joseph
Plantation. Note cousins working
to finish restoration. (Kitchens)

ST. JOSEPH PLANTATION
A Family Affair

📍 Vacherie, Louisiana

In the shadow of Louisiana's famed *Oak Alley Plantation*, another very different but no less historic plantation has been restored by oodles of cousins from far and wide who all feel a wonderful and warm connection to their old family home.

St. Joseph Plantation was owned in antebellum times by the Scioneaux family, who built an impressive raised Creole-style mansion on their large sugar plantation around 1830. The house was simply laid out with two rows of five rooms, forming ten principal rooms.

The house differed starkly from many of its gilded neighbors on River Road. The house lacked opulent decorations and embellishments; its size and proportions were enough to impress. It has the distinction of being the 1838 birthplace of Henry Hobson Richardson, the famed architect for whom the Richardsonian Romanesque architectural style is named.

In 1840, the plantation was sold to Dr. Cazamine Mericq and then later to Alexis Ferry and his wife, Josephine, daughter of Valcour Aime, a famed Louisiana planter and personality known as "the Louis XIV of Louisiana." Aime's nearby *Petite Versailles* Plantation was a showplace with some of the finest gardens on the continent at that time. Ferry used Josephine's dowry money to purchase *St. Joseph* and to remodel the house. He added four smaller rooms and enclosed the ground floor to create a basement with service rooms that served a variety of functions.

After the Civil War, the house was sold at a sheriff's sale. Joseph Waguespack purchased it and it has remained in his family ever since. Waguespack also later purchased nearby *Felicity Plantation*, an estate that had been built with dowry money from Josephine's sister. He combined the two estates in 1901 into the St. Joseph Planting and Manufacturing Company.

Through the generations, the house served as the nexus of a working plantation, a family business that is still in operation today. Like many planter families in the area, the Waguespacks and descendants created a family corporation to maintain their

A small cabin and sugar kettle.
(Matrana)

Cabin in the fields at St. Joseph.
(Bush)

Doorways, showing the arrangements of the rooms at St. Joseph. (Matrana)

family sugar-planting business rather than subdivide the lands *ad infinitum* through the generations. Cousins all hold stock in the company and elect a board of directors from their ranks who oversee day-to-day operations and financials of the corporations.

These business partners not only share ownership in their family business, but also share fond memories of good times had in their family's plantation house. Christmas was an especially important time at the old plantation house. "There were no decorations, all the emphasis was on the food," Joy Rousell, a family member, recalled. "My grandmother and mother always made a giant pot of super gumbo, salads, baked fish, roasted turkeys, chicken pies with delicious, big chunks of chicken, angel food cakes and ambrosia made by the dishpan-full with a mixture of peaches, oranges, pineapples and cherries . . . The children all sat on long benches at the kitchen table eating and telling stories while the adults ate in the dining room. Then we'd play tag on the outside stairs, running up one side and down the other."[1]

In the 1970s, as the older generation faded, the old plantation home was shuttered and abandoned. The sugar-growing operations continued, stockholder cousins of the

corporation met annually for a business meeting the second Monday of every March, but in the early 2000s those same cousins, who as children enjoyed wonderful family dinners and holidays, decided they wanted more from their plantation than the profit from the annual sugar crop—they wanted their memories to be brick and mortar again, they wanted to save their old family home. Lead by family corporation president, Joan Boudreaux, cousins upon cousins came out of the woodwork to help. They came from near and far, from various backgrounds and professions, and various branches of the family tree—many had never met one another, but together they banded together with one great goal in mind.

Boudreaux organized a restoration committee to oversee the work, recruited volunteers for specific tasks, and published a monthly newsletter to announce updates and work agendas. The first task was accessing the damages: there were significant structural damages caused by water being trapped in the plaster-covered brick and by a half foot of mud on the ground floor. There was termite damage, rotten door frames, and cracked paint and sealant.

Starting in the sweltering summer of 2002, every Tuesday, Thursday, and two Saturdays a month, between twenty-five and thirty cousins gathered to work on the house. With the exception of plumbing and electrical work, which was done by professionals, the family members provided all of the labor for the project. This cut costs considerably and allowed the project to stay in budget. They sought guidance from the Louisiana Historic Preservation Society and others in order to maintain historical accuracy.

Maintaining the historical integrity of the house was paramount. Boudreaux explained, "We take a minimalist approach. We fix what we have to and anything that we can leave and not touch, we are. We aren't trying to achieve perfection, just trying to let the house tell its story."[2] Every step was done with as much historical accuracy as possible. Tongue-and-groove boards were found on the property from an old collapsed slave cabin that matched those of the house perfectly; so these were incorporated instead of using new materials. Caulking was made onsite by hand using a traditional method of mixing lime, flour, and boiling water.

The cousins worked hard. Even tough octogenarians helped provide heavy physical labor, and they all seldom took breaks, except for a hearty pot-luck lunch. Those cousins who couldn't be there in person often sent over roasted meats, casseroles, and classic Cajun dishes to show their solidarity and support.

Twenty-six sets of French doors had to be refurbished. "Each door was very time consuming because each had three actual parts: the shutters, screens and glass and wood doors," Boudreaux explained. "They had to be sanded, sometimes stripped down to the original cypress, primed, painted, and the screens changed."[3]

The project got an unexpected boost when over $30,000 worth of plants was donated for landscaping by Universal Studios. The film *The Skeleton Key* had been filmed at nearby Felicity Plantation, and set designers had created dense gardens and swamps; when they tore the set down, they gave hundreds of plants—including ferns, monkey grass, azaleas, roses, and lagustrums—to Joan Boudreaux and her cousins for use at *St. Joseph*.

Once the restoration was nearing completion, the family threw open the doors of *St. Joseph* and opened the plantation for tours. True to form, the tours were not stuffy, scripted walk-throughs, but instead warm, down-to-earth visits led by the cousins themselves, who peppered in their own memories of holiday dinners with relatives and firsthand accounts of the recent restorations. The tour guides did not back away from the history of slavery (although the family purchased the house after the Civil War) and instead sought records and historical accounts to better document slavery at *St. Joseph*.

Uniquely the cousins did continue a number of important Creole rituals and routines that have really set *St. Joseph* apart from other publicly opened plantations. For example, every October, the old house is draped in black for a traditional mourning tour. One of the only plantations in the South to showcase antebellum mourning customs in this way, the family hauls a casket into one of the front rooms and shows visitors what it would have been like to host and attend a traditional family funeral in the Old South, particularly in a French-speaking Creole household. Likewise, a traditional St. Joseph altar is erected in the house every March to honor the more than one hundred Italian immigrants who worked the fields of the plantation at the turn of the century. These unique and intensely authentic experiences have brought in curious tourists and further boosted foot traffic to the old house.

In 2005, the cousins' restoration efforts at *St. Joseph* were formally recognized when they were awarded the Bricks and Mortar Award by the Foundation for Historical Louisiana. Family members continue to give tours of the plantation house and grounds, while operating a profitable modern sugar corporation on the estate.

MISSISSIPPI

Beauvoir with flanking cottages
on each side. The house looks
out on the beach and the Gulf
of Mexico. (Levet)

JEFFERSON DAVIS'S BEAUVOIR

The Rebirth of a Presidential Estate following Hurricane Katrina

♦ Biloxi, Mississippi

The stately raised home, known as *Beauvoir* or beautiful view, due to its beachfront location in Biloxi, was never used as a plantation, but commands a prominent place in history, as it served as the retirement home of Confederate president Jefferson Davis.[1]

The property upon which *Beauvoir* was built was purchased by John Black in 1832. He paid the United States $100 and change for approximately eighty-five acres that fronted the Gulf of Mexico, holding the property for six years before selling it to John Henderson. Henderson expanded the landholdings, adding an adjoining eighty-one acres to the plot, but sold both parcels a year later. The new owner of one of the pieces, Hanson Alsbury, was forced to relinquish his interest in the site in 1843, when he was sued by a creditor. The land was sold at auction, being purchased by none other than former owner John Henderson, whose bid of only eight dollars proved to be the highest. Henderson later regained ownership of the remaining portion of the estate he had originally assembled after he filed suit against the owners for nonpayment under the vendor's lien. Henderson held the property for five more years, before selling it to James Brown for $2,000.[2]

From the very beginning of his ownership of the estate, Brown made his intentions of building a "family residence" quite clear. He immediately moved into a small double dogtrot house on the property, and soon began construction of the house that would later serve as the home of the Confederate president. Brown served as his own architect and construction superintendent, personally overseeing all aspects of the ambitious project.

He built a sawmill nearby the site, and moved slaves from his Madison County Plantation to his new estate. They provided the great majority of the labor to build the new house. Slaves cut cypress from the Back Bay swamp area of the plantation to build the frame of the house. Longleaf pine lumber was used for the floors. The slate for the roof was imported from England. It was delivered to nearby Ship Island and sent in barges to Brown's estate.

Brown's mansion was a highly raised cottage-style dwelling. The main portion of the mansion was of a traditional plan with a wide center hall running from the front door to the back door. Two rooms placed back-to-back flanked either side of the central hall. Two symmetrical wings, built as independent structures, with their corners connecting to the corners of the main portion of the house extended out of the back. A broad front porch, supported by heavy square pillars with recessed panels, wrapped around the front and sides of the main portion of the house and met the front of the two wings. A back veranda partially encircled the U-shaped area created by the back of the house and the central sides of the wings. Wide, centrally located stairs led up to the front and back doors.

The house was built with its semitropical, coastal environment in mind. Raising the main floor high above the ground provided protection from floods while also allowing for significant ventilation to keep the house cool in the sweltering Deep South summers. The area under the house was also used for cool storage—a dry well and food cellar were constructed there during the Brown periods. Above, the floor-to-ceiling triple sash windows were flanked and protected by heavy shutters, which added protection from storms. The roofline of the mansion was constructed with a high peak and steep slope with hurricanes and other tropical storms in mind.

Outside, a number of ancillary buildings and support structures were constructed. Brown built two identical one-room cottages flanking the front of the main house;

Front porch at Beauvoir. (Levet)

one was used to house the governess, and the other housed a Methodist minister who occasionally visited the area. It became known as the "Circuit Rider's House."

Beauvoir, then commonly known as "The Brown Place," was purchased by Sarah Ann Ellis Dorsey for $3,500 cash on July 7, 1873. Sarah, a noted writer from the famed Percy clan, was the daughter of prominent planter George Percy Eillis and his wife, Mary Magdalen Routh, and she spent much of her early life on her parents' plantations in Louisiana and Mississippi. She later attended Madame Deborah Grelaud's French School in Philadelphia, where she was a schoolmate of Varina Howell's, who later married Jefferson Davis. Sarah also knew Jefferson Davis and was a frequent visitor at *Hurricane*, the plantation home of Jefferson Davis's brother Joseph.[3] After completing her education in England, Sarah married Samuel W. Dorsey. Sarah lived with her husband at *Elkridge Plantation* in Louisiana, where she taught her slaves to read and write and built a chapel for them.

The *Elkridge Plantation* was burned during the Civil War and later rebuilt. After the war and following her husband's death in 1875, Sarah rented out her Louisiana plantations and moved permanently to *Beauvoir*. It was shortly thereafter that *Beauvoir* received its name. Kate Lee Ferguson, a cousin of Sarah's, recalled the exact moment:

Years have fled since we two drove from the old Barnes Hotel at Mississippi City that evening so we might inspect the place. It was in the sunset of a beautiful June day that my cousin Sarah Dorsey walked down the deserted pathway of the old estate once owned by the Browns, and as she reached the tall green gate opening to the sea, she threw its portals apart, exclaiming, "Oh how beautiful! Look Catherine, the beautiful view! I shall call it Beauvoir!" And so it remained.[4]

Initially Sarah Dorsey lived at *Beauvoir* with her cousin, Mrs. Cochran, and later with her half-brother Mortimer Dahlgreen, and her niece Mary Ellis. Dahlgreen provided a fine description of *Beauvoir* in a letter to his stepmother:

> Beauvoir, my present place of abode, is a tract of land comprising over one thousand acres, and faces on the Gulf of Mexico and backs on Back Bay. It is situated just halfway between Mississippi City and Biloxi (being five miles from either). This interesting house is built in a true old Southern style upon columns twelve feet high; it is one hundred feet wide by one hundred and twenty feet deep, with a large gallery running around the entire house. On either side of the main house is a beautiful little cottage, which are [*sic*] kept for visitors & c . . . On every hand the grand old live oaks rear their proud heads high towards heaven, draped in their picturesque garb of iron gray moss, the token that they have stood the fierce howling storms of winter, and the burning sun of summer for many a long year, while scattered throughout the yard among the other shade trees, are the cedars, acorn, hickory nut, and the beautiful sweet scented magnolias. On either side of the house extending far back in the rear is an immense orchard of orange trees, which are now in full bloom. The house faces the Gulf and is just 100 yards from the beach.[5]

Jefferson Davis first visited *Beauvoir* in 1875, a decade after the Civil War ended. He was in the area inspecting several lots of land his wife had purchased years before. Sarah Dorsey was away on a visit to her plantations, but Davis took this opportunity to look over *Beauvoir*. In a letter to his wife he described the estate as "a fine place, large and beautiful, and many orange trees yet full of fruit."

It was also during this time that Jefferson Davis began eyeing the Gulf Coast as a place to write his memoirs. He came to the area again in December 1876 to visit some relatives and search for a quiet place to write. He again visited his lots and had the underbrush cleared, but did not find these suitable for his needs. Soon thereafter Sarah Dorsey learned of Davis's efforts to find a place to work on his memoirs. She contacted him and invited him to use the East Pavilion at *Beauvoir* for this purpose. She further suggested remodeling the cottage by enclosing in the East Gallery, which could serve as a bedroom and dressing room. She suggested that the main room be converted from an office to a library. And she further offered her own assistance as secretary. Davis found the arrangement quite suitable, and insisted on paying $50 a month, to cover expenses including room and board for himself and his servant Robert Brown. By January Davis was at *Beauvoir* and soon had begun work on his book. Maj. W. T. Walthall joined Davis and Dorsey on the Gulf Coast, providing them with official documents and letters to aid in the writing of the manuscript.

Davis was enthralled with the environment that surrounded him at *Beauvoir* and on the Mississippi Gulf Coast. He loved the climate, the breezes, and the general atmosphere of coastal life. He noted that the "soft air is delicious." His wife, however, still in

England, was not as pleased with the idea of living on the Gulf Coast, and she had misgivings about her husband's living arrangements and relationship with Sarah Dorsey. He wrote to Varina on June 11, 1877:

> . . . permit me to correct an apprehension you have fallen into, about Mrs. Dorsey's invitation to you. She several times spoke of her desire to have you on the coast, but . . . you had such unfavorable recollections of it, that you had earnestly urged me neither to buy or build there, she thought if you would try it again, your opinion would change, and beginning with only a brief visit in view, you would end by a more permanent stay. The salt air, and salt baths have been of service to me generally.

Reluctantly, Varina finally traveled to *Beauvoir* and surprisingly, she quickly grew fond of the estate and endeared herself to Sarah Dorsey. The Davises purchased *Beauvoir* from Dorsey, paying their first installment in 1879. Dorsey later willed the remaining portion of the property to Davis, but he insisted on paying the outstanding installments to her estate. Davis moved into the main house and completed work on his memoirs, *The Rise and Fall of the Confederate Government*.

The Davis family lived happily at *Beauvoir* in 1889, when Davis died in New Orleans, while on a trip. He was buried there in an elaborate funeral, but four years later, his body was moved to Richmond, Virginia. *Beauvoir* was inherited by his youngest daughter Winnie, but upon her death in 1898, its ownership reverted back to her mother, Varina. Varina sold the estate to the Mississippi Division of the Sons of Confederate Veterans (SCV), who have owned the house ever since. She stipulated that the property should serve as a Confederate soldier's home, and that the house itself should become a shrine to her husband's memory. Mary Hunter Southworth Kimbrough, a close friend of the Davises, thereafter devoted the rest of her life to championing the cause of the veterans home and Jefferson Davis shrine and in aiding the Mississippi Division of the Sons of Confederate Veterans in making Varina's dream a reality.

The Confederate Veterans home at *Beauvoir* admitted its first resident in 1903. The State of Mississippi took over operations at the home and over the ensuing years, twelve large dormitory buildings would be constructed on the site, as well as a large hospital, chapel, dining hall, and other buildings. At its height, the soldier's home housed over 250 Confederate veterans, their wives, and widows. Life for the veterans was described as idyllic, as many locals volunteered there and supported the veterans and ensured their comfort and enjoyment.

The last Confederate veteran to live at *Beauvoir* left in 1951, at the age of one hundred, and the homes' last two remaining residents, both Confederate widows, were transferred from *Beauvoir* to Greenwood in 1957. Complete control of the property reverted back to the Mississippi Division of the Sons of Confederate Veterans, and the site's sole purpose was now to serve as a shrine to Jefferson Davis.

Preparations had already begun to open the property as a historic site. In the early 1950s restoration work had begun on the main house and cottages and a lagoon and water features were installed, which separated the principal buildings from the estate's cemetery, which housed many of the deceased veterans.

The old dormitory buildings were demolished and the old hospital was converted into a visitor's center, housing a gift shop, exhibits, restrooms, and ticket sales. The site flourished as tourists steadily visited, but in 1969, the estate was ravaged by Hurricane Camille. The hurricane caused much damage across the property, nearly destroying the library cottage, where Jefferson Davis wrote much of his memoirs and ripped the whole roof off the hospital building. Exhibits under the main house were tossed far and wide, but volunteers from nearby Keesler Airforce Base recovered 97 percent of them. One worker who stayed on site during the storm died of a heart attack as the hurricane passed, and others barely survived. *Beauvoir* was closed for an extended period of time, but after meticulous restoration efforts, the home once again flourished.

In 1998, the Jefferson Davis Presidential Library and Museum was opened on the property. It was a $4 million state-of-the-art facility with a ticket area, auditorium, and museum on the first floor and a large research library, archives, and administrative offices on the second. In 2002, the most ambitious and detailed master plan for the estate was unveiled, which focused on the extensive development of $35 million botanical gardens at *Beauvoir*.

Beauvoir continued to thrive until tragedy again struck in 2005. Hurricane Katrina, the most devastating natural event in United States history, took more than eighteen hundred lives and caused more than $80 billion in economic damages. It severely damaged thousands of historic architectural treasures in Louisiana, Mississippi, Alabama, and to a lesser extent other areas. It completely destroyed many historic homes across the Gulf South, and *Beauvoir* was almost one of them.

The hurricane struck land early in the morning on August 29, 2005, heralded along the Mississippi Gulf Coast by massively strong winds and flooding of biblical proportions. Buildings along the beachfront, including massive casino complexes, were tossed about, often floating miles from their original location. In New Orleans, failure of the federally built levee system led to even more massive flooding, which devastated great portions of the metropolitan area.

In the aftermath of the storm, Rick Forte, director of *Beauvoir*, stayed near his radio at his home in Hattiesburg, Mississippi, listening for news of the events that surrounded him. He soon heard on a radio broadcast that *Beauvoir* had been completely destroyed by the storm.

Forte decided to check the damage for himself. When he arrived on the grounds, what he saw before him was a "foreign object," as he described it. The mansion at *Beauvoir* had not been completely destroyed as reported in the earlier broadcast, but it had been so badly damaged as to make it unrecognizable. The front and side porches that surrounded the mansion had been completely ripped away, and a large portion of the roof had collapsed. According to Randy McCafferty, the architect who later led restoration efforts of the house, the only thing that kept the back of the mansion standing was the support of a few old shutters, which surrounded the back porch—the entire structural integrity of the back portion of house had fallen, wedging the shutters between the supporting beams above and the porch and underlying supports below. "If it wasn't for those shutters," Randy said, "the entire back portion of the house would've collapsed."

The house survived even in this damaged state, largely due to thoughtful design. It had been constructed to weather just such an assault. It was built on slightly elevated

Margaret Davis Hayes Memorial Room. The Victorian burled walnut bedroom set was given by Jefferson and Varina Davis to their daughter Margaret as a wedding present in 1876. She returned the furniture to her parents after they moved to Beauvoir. (Levet)

ground, with the main structure elevated on twelve-foot-tall piers, which largely allowed the floodwaters to surge past. Its broad low-hipped roof with slopes on each side was also less vulnerable to wind damage than traditional vertical roofs. The chief architectural historian for the Mississippi Department of Archives and History, Richard Cawthon, explained that "the house was designed to accommodate weather conditions that occurred on the Gulf Coast. It was constructed to maximize its survivability."[6]

Unfortunately, although the mansion itself at *Beauvoir* survived major damage, many of the other important structures on the estate were completely destroyed. The library cottage where Jefferson Davis had written *The Rise and Fall of the Confederate Government* was completely destroyed as was its twin, the Hayes cottage, along with several other buildings including the director's home, a replica of the soldiers' home

Dining room at Beauvoir, with period mirror over the fireplace mantel. (Levet)

barracks, as well as a museum dedicated to Confederate soldiers. The large Jefferson Davis Presidential Library lost its first floor, which housed a number of important artifacts, but the second-floor reference library survived, and most of its important documents and books were preserved.

After an extensive inventory was completed, *Beauvoir* officials realized that they lost a third of the historical artifacts housed on the estate including many Confederate uniforms and weapons, the saddle upon which Jefferson Davis road into the Mexican-American War, and the wooden caisson that carried his body to the grave. A few weeks after the storm about seventy-five national guardsmen and personnel from the Departments of Homeland Security and Natural Resources joined *Beauvoir* officials and volunteers from the Mississippi Sons of Confederate Veterans in fanning out across the property looking for lost artifacts. *Beauvoir*'s director, Rick Forte, noted that the amount of debris was unimaginable. He was amazed to see mounds of crushed and mutilated artifacts juxtaposed with a dainty piece of fine crystal, which was left untouched. Important artifacts recovered during the search included the original death mask of Jefferson Davis, a silver christening cup given to Jefferson Davis Hayes, as well as a number of important Confederate items. The jacket of a Confederate soldier was found hanging from a bush.

After Hurricane Katrina, the 2002 master plan for the estate was abandoned. Director Rick Forte and his team realized that past planning and development efforts were no longer applicable or appropriate as much of the previous efforts and progress of past planning had simply been washed away or otherwise destroyed. It quickly became clear that a new master plan was needed.

In May 2006, at the request of the Mississippi Department of Archives and History, a team of experts from Colonial Williamsburg visited *Beauvoir* and drafted a plan report. The team consisted of two senior architectural conservators, the Colonial Williamsburg Foundation's vice president for research and historic preservation, a senior historical architect from the National Park Service (Boston office), and four additional architectural conservators who were trained and employed at Colonial Williamsburg. Along with input from the Beauvoir Combined Boards, the efforts of the Williamsburg experts led to the creation of a new and updated master plan.

Obviously, the plan called for the repair of the hurricane-damaged main house, and restoration of its surroundings to the Jefferson Davis period, but it also set forth a wider plan that will guide the development of the estate for several years to come. The plan began by broadly dividing the fifty-two-acre site into four areas: two devoted to historic period areas, including the mansion and surrounding structures; a third devoted to an environmental and nature area; and the fourth, a modern interpretation area, which included a new and improved presidential library and museum.

The updated plan sought to consolidate modern visitor areas around the presidential library, while best utilizing the estate's property to preserve its historic past. Earlier concepts of developing a new main entrance on Beauvoir Road, were abandoned in favor of keeping the main entrance on Highway 90 at the south end of the property. Plans for a new visitor's center on Beauvoir Road were scrapped, placing this function as well as ticketing areas within the new presidential library building to consolidate multiple functions and allow for the streamlining of staffing.

The creation of a new Jefferson Davis Presidential Library and Museum to replace that destroyed by the hurricane was among the most ambitious parts of the new plan. The new building is now open to the public and it is larger than the previous library and combines soft areas (theater, offices, and gift shop) located on the first floor and the critical areas (museum, collections, archives, and library) located on the more flood-resistant second floor. A third floor houses electrical mechanisms, heating, air conditioning, emergency generators, and other mechanical facilities, high above any potential floodwaters. And, the always at-risk first floor was wired independently of the other two floors, so that in the event of another catastrophic storm the lower floor can be easily disconnected, making power and utilities available immediately to the other floors.

In addition to the presidential library, the new master plan sets forth an ambitious vision for the entire estate, aiming at restoring the two historic period areas as closely as possible to their original states when Jefferson Davis resided there. The earlier 2002 plan, for example, called for developing the entire grounds into botanical gardens, while an updated plan concentrates botanical development by focusing on historical restoration of Varina Davis's rose garden, kitchen gardens, and surrounding orchards, as described by Varina in original letters.

The 2002 master plan also called for the rebuilding of the Confederate Veterans Hospital Building. Although the new plans repeal this concept, it calls for the remaining original slab of the hospital building to be used as a multipurpose area to host picnics, receptions, and more. Historic cannons and a large flag will further mark the area.

The plan also calls for the reconstruction of the several of the outbuildings original to the Davis era, including a dual dogtrot kitchen (four-room structure), which would house a reconstructed kitchen and storeroom as well as modern public restrooms. The Foreman's House will serve as a guest cottage, as well as a maid's quarters. The original carpenter's shop and carpenter's residence are also to be rebuilt, with a modern security office scheduled to be built in the carpenter's residence. Other structures to be rebuilt include barns, a carriage and harness shop, and stables. Additional outbuildings, including a sheep pen and a chicken house, are also being considered. The director's home would be rebuilt, possibly on high ground east of the museum and with a view of both the museum and the mansion.

The cemetery area of the estate is also undergoing updates. The large United Daughters of the Confederacy arch that was torn to pieces by Hurricane Katrina was restored and moved from the front of the master house to the front of the Tomb of the Unknown Confederate, allowing for a more historically accurate entrance at the front of the mansion, and an even grander memorial at the celebrated tomb. An ancestor's walk is planned to lead up to and through the arch into a brick patio area within a semicircular colonnade that will surround the tomb.

The fourth quarter of the plan calls for the restoration of an environmental area, with the replanting of a primitive forest complete with a nature trail. Oyster Bayou and the bay-head swamp, which runs through the area, would be returned to a natural and historic drainage area similar to the way it was when Davis lived here.

As *Beauvoir* evolves over time and planning strategies adapt to meet the advancing times and unique situations of each generation, one thing holds true, the wishes of Mrs. Davis still guide the primary objectives and vision for this historic presidential estate. Hurricane Katrina was inarguably the worst disaster to befall *Beauvoir*. It may also have been one of the most serendipitous. The monster storm ravaged the estate, but also plotted a path for its rebirth. The necessary restoration of the house has uncovered new and extraordinary knowledge about the history and construction of the mansion, while meticulously and artfully revitalizing the home's grandeur as it existed during Jefferson Davis's days there. The tempest also ultimately led to the designation of federal funding for the erection of a new, larger presidential library complex and broader improvements as well. While *Beauvoir*'s course through history was certainly rerouted by Hurricane Katrina, these detours have led to new plans for the future. South Mississippi historian Charles Sullivan noted that *Beauvoir* "is a tangible connection to a past that wasn't so long ago. In the 7,000 years of human history, the Civil War was just an eyeblink ago. It just happened. Because of *Beauvoir*, Jefferson Davis is still with us. In the words of William Faulkner, 'The past is not dead. It is not even past.'"

THE HOUSE ON ELLICOTT HILL

A Natchez Treasure

📍 Natchez, Mississippi

The house on *Ellicott Hill* stands as a monument to the site where Natchez became American. It was on this lofty locale, in 1797, that US major Andrew Ellicott raised the American flag and took possession of Natchez and all the Spanish lands east of the Mississippi River above the 31st parallel. This transfer had been previously agreed to by a treaty between Spain and the United States in 1795, but the Spanish remained at the site until 1798, as the exact location of the 31st parallel was disputed.

The famous Hill took Ellicott's name and after the American flag was planted, the hill passed from the ownership of the Spanish governor's mother-in-law to James Moore, a prominent Natchez merchant. It was he who built the house there between 1797 and 1801. The house on the hill originally fronted Canal Street, which was at the time the front street of the town on a large public green space or Spanish promenade.

Moore constructed a house whose exterior would have fit in perfectly in the West Indies, with a high-pitched central roof surrounded by a much-lower-pitched roof, which covered the galleries and peripheral rooms of the structure. The house was raised and supported by thin pillars. The floor plan was also reminiscent of a West Indies style, with no interior hallways, an exterior staircase, and a large central grand room flanked by smaller peripheral rooms on the upper principal floor. The ground floor was accessible by three exterior bridges.

The interior of the home, in contrast to the Caribbean style outside, was done in high Federal style, with elegant moldings, detailed fanlights, and vaulted ceilings. The central grand room on the principal floor boasted an interesting dome, from which the chandelier hung. This metal dome was said to have come from a ship, and it was painted over to look like plaster.

James Moore married in 1799, and as his family expanded, his wife preferred to reside at the family's plantation on Liberty Road, a property now known as *Oakland*. Moore chose to rent the house on *Ellicott Hill*, and one of his first tenants was Samuel Brooks, a cousin of President John Adams. Brooks lived in the house during the

The House at Ellicott Hill prior to restoration. (HABS)

time when he served as the first mayor of Natchez, and he later became the first state treasurer of Mississippi. Later, Moore rented the house to Dr. Frederic Seip, a graduate of the Medical College of Philadelphia who used the residence as both a home and a location for his medical practice.

The house was purchased by Orlando Lane in 1825. Lane also rented the house, and a variety of tenants called it home. It was during this time that the house was used as a coffeehouse for patrons of a nearby hotel. In 1850, the house was sold to five promi- nent Presbyterians who established the Natchez High School for Boys, an elite private boarding school, on the premises. The school remained open until 1878, when the house served as a barracks for workers at the nearby cotton mills.

The cotton mills shut down in the 1920s, and the house on *Ellicott Hill* was aban- doned and quickly began to deteriorate. Within a few short years, it was in a truly deplorable, dilapidated state. On August 13, 1934, the house was purchased by the Natchez Garden Club for $2,000. The club members engaged famous New Orleans architect Richard Koch of the architectural firm Armstrong and Koch (later Koch and Wilson) to oversee restoration of the house. They paid the architect $150 plus expenses related to his travel. Work began the next year and was completed by 1937.

Roane Fleming Byrne, chairman of the restoration committee, wrote on January 27, 1937: "Dear Mr. Koch: Ellicott's Hill has passed through troubles and excitements too

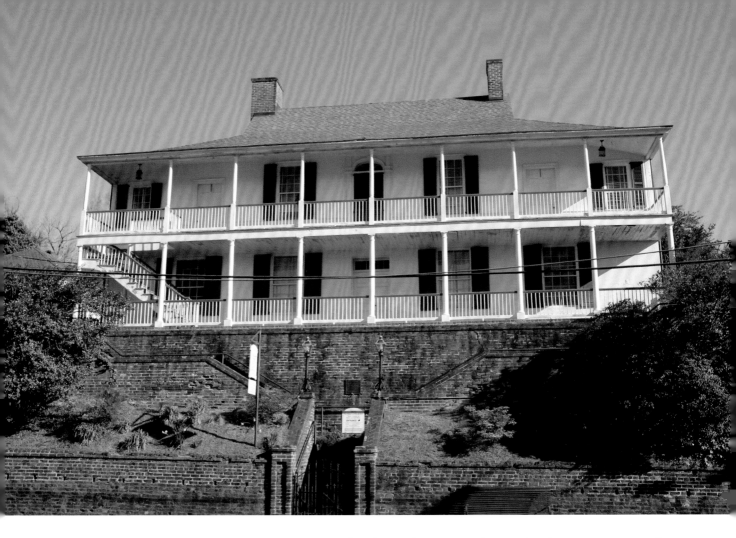

The House at Ellicott Hill after restoration. (Matrana)

numerous to enumerate here but we have managed to weather the various storms and expect to open the place with ceremonies and celebrations during the garden club's pilgrimage of March 28–April 4, 1937. The house and the hill are attracting a great deal of interest wherever they are advertised, especially among artists, writers, etc. Stark Young seems really crazy about the place and has given us some very interesting relics."

The Natchez Garden Club's charter was revised in 1976, and as a result the house on *Ellicott Hill* was transferred from the garden club to the Preservation Society of Ellicott Hill. The society completed a three-year restoration project from 2003 to 2006, which significantly rehabilitated both the exterior and interior of the home. Interestingly, the firm of Koch and Wilson again oversaw the project.

Today, research into the architecture and history of Ellicott Hill's famous house continues to reveal important information about the past. For example, the house was once identified as Connelly's Tavern, but it is now known that this historic business was actually located one block further east.

The house on the hill is the last remaining eighteenth-century merchant's house in the area, and has the distinction of being the first historic property restored by a civic organization in the state of Mississippi. The Preservation Society of Ellicott Hill has opened the house for tours, and in remembrance of Maj. Andrew Ellicott's flag raising, a 1797 fifteen-star American flag still flies over the site today.

Twin winding staircases in the
Rotunda at Waverly Plantation.
(Kitchens)

WAVERLY

A Palladian Treasure of the Deep South

◉ Near West Point, Mississippi

The unique and imposing mansion at *Waverly Plantation* has stood near the banks of the Tombigbee River for more than 150 years. Once the proud home of George Hampden Young and his family, the mansion later fell into decline and was abandoned for a half century. Fortunately, before it was too late and lost forever, the Snow family found the decaying behemoth hidden in the woods, and devoted their lives to returning it to its former glory.[1]

The plantation site, which now lies in Clay County, Mississippi, was originally occupied by Chickasaw Indians, who later ceded their tribal lands to the US Government in the Treaty of Pontotoc. The lands that were to become *Waverly Plantation* were acquired by Col. George Hampden Young of Ogelthorpe County, Georgia. Colonel Young and his large family moved to the area around 1836. He began planting cotton, an operation that thrived, and he was quickly able to expand. Young called his plantation *Waverly* for his favorite collection of stories, *The Waverley Novels*, by Sir Walter Scott.

Young was noted to be particularly interested in the lives of his many slaves, as evidenced in a series of letters from the mid-1840s in which he attempted to reunite his slave Moses with the slave's wife, who was living on a different plantation.

As his cotton empire grew, Young began designing a proper plantation mansion for his estate. The house was built in the 1850s. The floor plan was a modified Palladian design with a grand central rotunda flanked by four chambers and recessed loggias on the front and back forming a standard "H" room arrangement favored by the famed sixteenth-century Italian architect Andrea Palladio. Atop the main house set an enormous octagonal cupola that dominates the façade of the mansion. The impressive rotunda featured twin curving staircases and three octagonal balconies, one on top of the other.

The basic design of the house is said to be that of Colonel Young's with some collaboration from the Italian architect Charles Pond of St. Louis. The exterior of the house was an amalgamation of various styles, with Greek Revival predominating. The home's recessed galleries were supported by fluted cypress columns topped by Ionic capitals

Waverly Plantation rotunda, note the red Venetian glass surrounding the front door. (Kitchens)

further ornamented with dogwood blossom rosettes. The steps leading up to the front and rear gallery were of marble. Square pilasters ornamented much of the exterior of the house. Small octagonal columns with Egyptian capitals supported an entablature crowning the front entrance. The recessed front door was flanked by sidelights and topped by a transom of red Venetian glass. Iron banisters were brought in from Mobile, and the exterior of the home was painted in several shades of gray and slate blue.

Inside, the second floor had a similar plan to the first, with four bedrooms flanking the rotunda, two on each side. Each bedroom had access to either the front or rear balconies. The Egyptian bedroom was the most elaborate with the color scheme of lavender and peach and elaborate decoration including window and door facings that

Entrance, Waverly Plantation. (Kitchens)

Column capital, Waverly Plantation. (Kitchens)

were topped by stylized lotus motifs. The third floor, which was used for storage, supported the enormous cupola above. Colonel Young kept a desk in the cupola, a room he probably used as a private study.

The home was a masterpiece of modern conveniences, complete with gas lights. Outside the mansion behind the kitchen stood the cook's house and smokehouse. A brick office building was constructed near the mansion. There was a bathhouse in the garden, as well as a privy that boasted marble seats of various sizes and a marble shelf for chamber pots—all unique luxuries at the time. The family also had a small in-ground pool, approximately eight feet in diameter with steps leading down into it. This was fed by an artesian well. There were benches surrounding the pool and a dressing room on each end, one for men and the other for women. The property also featured a large icehouse, three guest houses, and a gas plant in which pine knots and stems were burned, with the resulting gas pumped into the main house to supply the gas lights.

The colonel and his family lived an idyllic life at *Waverly* until the Civil War broke out, and six of the Young sons went off to battle. One of them never returned. After the war, Reconstruction brought with it a number of major changes; the greatest of course was the loss of the slaves. But rather than languish as many plantations did, *Waverly* actively thrived after the Civil War, and the Young family successfully expanded their holdings during this time.

After Colonel Young's death, the plantation was eventually held by his last two remaining sons, George and William. George died on Christmas Day 1906 at the age of seventy-nine, leaving William alone at *Waverly*. William hired a young African American boy to aid him during his later years. The boy, Luke Richardson, later recalled that his employer held lively gambling parties at the plantation. While assisting during the parties, Luke often got tipped with poker chips. He said that the next morning when he cashed in his chips, he'd be "rich." Luke helped William plan his annual Emancipation Day celebration, in which he hosted a large party, complete with a big barbecue, for all of the African Americans who worked in and around the area, in order to celebrate the freeing of slaves.

Over the years, William grew very fond of his companion and when Luke reached the age of sixteen, William offered to send him to college. Luke was more interested in marriage and declined the offer. So William instead traveled to Columbus, where he bought Luke a ring to give to his girlfriend. After the wedding, William allowed the couple to live in the brick office building next to the plantation mansion; they remained on the estate for the rest of their lives and raised their children there. Upon William's death, the plantation passed to his surviving sisters, Lucy and Sue.

The mansion was eventually closed and abandoned. It became a playground for curious young people from around the area, and was a popular site for wild fraternity parties. It is said that the names of every young couple in the area were scrawled around the rotunda walls. During this time, many of the outbuildings were torn down by tenant farmers who sought wood and bricks for other structures. Heaps and heaps of original plantation papers, letters, and historic records were lost forever when they were burned by one of the tenant farmer's wives and her daughter-in-law. They explained that when children played in and around the mansion they would scatter these papers everywhere and the farmers were tired of dealing with it.

After fifty years of vacancy and decay, a remarkable thing happened in October 1961. A man traveling to his home in Jackson stopped into a small antique store owned by Robert and Madonna Snow of Philadelphia, Mississippi. The man was coming from West Point and casually mentioned the abandoned plantation house he had seen languishing in the dense woods of Clay County. Robert Snow was intrigued, and took his wife to go and visit the place himself. He noted that the house seemed to rise up out of a jungle of dense growth. He noted that vines clung to the exterior walls of the house, that the porch floor had collapsed, and that the marble steps were scattered throughout the yard. The red Venetian glass that surrounded the front door was broken, but inside

Waverly Plantation today.
(Kitchens)

the most impressive site of the rotunda, with its many balconies and stairs, still was an awe-inspiring sight. Despite that birds were nesting in the chandeliers and squirrels ran across the halls, the original French mirrors remained over the fireplaces, and other details were also relatively untouched.

After some digging, Robert was able to locate one of the heirs to which the abandoned monstrosity belonged. He offered to buy the house. The co-executioners of the estate decided they would contact the other heirs and come to a decision. Robert later recalled that he spent the night at home scared to death that the heirs would not sell; his wife spent the night scared to death that they would sell. Her fears were realized. The Young family heirs sold *Waverley* and a small amount of surrounding acreage to Robert and Madonna Snow in the early months of 1962.

Soon, the Snows were faced with the gargantuan job of restoring *Waverley*. They noted that it took years to fully oust a colony of bats from the attic. Enormous beehives had to be removed from the galleries, one of which weighed over two hundred pounds. It took the couple more than eight months to restore the rotunda, as they had to refinish each of the 718 hand-turned mahogany spindles around the staircases and balconies while still in place. The couple completed virtually all of the restoration themselves along with the help of their children. They cleaned, repaired, repainted, and replaced from top to bottom.

They decided to keep the house in a condition that was as historically accurate as possible. They maintained only a small kitchen and sitting room for their private

Parlor at Waverly Plantation. The parlor's alcove has been the site of countless family weddings, christenings, and other special ceremonies from the home's earliest days through the present. (Kitchens)

family space. Over the years, hundreds of artifacts original to the estate made their way back to the home. An entire set of *The Waverley Novels* once belonging to Colonel Young were returned by a former Mississippi State student who took them for safekeeping during the years of the plantation's abandonment. During the restoration, the Snows received quite a great deal of publicity; even the *New York Times* picked up the story of their restoration efforts. Visitors started to come in droves, sometimes walking into the house without even knocking, strolling through the grounds, and generally interrupting many of the restoration efforts. Robert Snow became more and more frustrated, and one day made a cardboard sign that read "Visitors $1 Each." He placed this in the driveway and posted an assistant in the yard, who quickly came back a short time later bearing fistfuls of one-dollar bills. It was clear at that time that visitors could help fund the restoration efforts. A year later, Madonna quit her job and became the full-time tour guide of *Waverley* plantation.

The Snows ran *Waverley* as a business, but continued to use the house as their private home where they raised their four young children. All of the children helped in the restoration effort. Daughter Melanie recalled, "When Momma and Daddy told us about Waverley she said that Cindy and I would be like little princesses in a big castle in the woods. Then we got here and it was dirty and full of spiders and we didn't want to be princesses anymore!" The Snows' youngest son, Gage, was involved in some particularly memorable incidents. Once, when his mother was leading a tour group of garden club ladies dressed in white gloves and hats through the rotunda, three-year-old Gage, standing on one of the balconies above, took the opportunity to pull down his pants and "christen" the ladies below as only a young boy could. He giggled wildly as the women squealed and tried to dodge the spray from above.

Over the years, the family has celebrated countless holidays, birthdays, and marriages within the plantation home. The Snows have welcomed thousands of guests, including celebrities, nobility, politicians, and other notable visitors. Their remarkable work in bringing *Waverley* back to life was recognized with a National Restoration Award, and the naming of the property as a National Historic Landmark. Madonna Snow died suddenly in 1991, and her daughters Cindy and Melanie took over day-to-day operations at the plantation until the mid-1990s, when they hired additional staff to help.

The house is still owned by the Snow family and tours are still provided by them. The house is again showing some signs of its age, but new generations of Snows continue to breathe life into the old home their grandparents and great-grandparents saved many years ago.

John Burrus's imposing Hollywood
plantation sits upon a low ridge
overlooking cotton fields and forests.
(Image courtesy of Rory Doyle)

HOLLYWOOD PLANTATION

From *Hollywood* to Hollywood

♀ Bolivar County, Mississippi

J ohn Crawford Burrus built the imposing mansion at his *Hollywood* plantation in the 1850s. It was named for the profusion of holly trees growing wild on the property. He could not have foreseen that almost a century later, another more famous Hollywood would visit the property to make a film about rival cotton gin owners in Mississippi. Burrus's *Hollywood* was new and represented the best of what could be experienced during his generation. However, Hollywood, California's version of Burrus's *Hollywood* was that of a dilapidated structure representing only a sad reflection of what once was. Today, the mansion has been restored to approximate its 1850s condition.

John Burrus was born in Alabama in 1814, but just seven years later, both of his parents died within just a few months of each other. John's brother-in-law, George Fearn, was appointed as John's guardian. He sent Burrus to live with relatives in Virginia so that he could get a good education. John attended the University of Virginia, then returned to Alabama to study law under his uncle, Judge Daniel Coleman. Meanwhile, George Fearn was investing John's funds in fertile virgin lands in northwest Mississippi. Fearn moved Burrus's slaves to the property he purchased there and had them clear land for planting. John used these Mississippi lands occasionally to hunt and fish. With no permanent residence on the property, Burrus and his friends would pitch tents or stay in the overseer's cabin when on their hunting jaunts.[1]

Around 1845, Burrus bought a large tract of land about five miles from the Mississippi River and not far from his other property. On the new property, he built a large log home with six huge rooms and a long gallery. Then in 1858 he built a more permanent and larger home on a spot specially chosen for the purpose. The home he called *Hollywood* was completed in 1861 and the Burrus family moved into it at about the same time as the War between the States erupted.[2] The large Greek Revival country residence was built from hand-hewn timbers of cypress cut from the property. Family tradition holds that an architect from New Orleans was retained to design and build

After years of occupancy by tenants and long periods of vacancy, Hollywood plantation suffered almost to the point of being lost. (Image courtesy of Eustace Winn)

A tornado in 2001 caused the collapse of the front gable and columns, architecture unique to Hollywood. (Image courtesy of Eustace Winn)

the home. As originally built, *Hollywood* had a grand circular staircase near the entry, fine double parlors for lavish entertaining, and four spacious bedrooms upstairs. The house was documented in 1936 for the Historic American Building Survey.

John Burrus was unable to join his friends and neighbors in the war due to a physical disability. However, he aided the cause by becoming a large financial contributor and by donating nearly all of his stock of prized horses to provide mounts for the Mississippi cavalry. When the war came to his doorstep, his family fed and housed soldiers and tended to the needs of the sick and wounded. In fact, family tradition relates that John and his family impoverished themselves in their zeal to aid the southern war cause.[3]

Hollywood plantation, now known as Baby Doll House, is Bolivar County's only remaining grand residence from the antebellum period. (Image courtesy of Rory Doyle)

Confederate general William Starke camped on the Burrus plantation for several months during the war. During that time, the Burrus's fine mansion was used as a hospital. Months later, when the war was all but over, *Hollywood* plantation hosted famed Confederate general Jubal Early, who was hidden there for several weeks after Union officials put an arrest bounty on Early's head.[4] However, Charles Burrus, one of John's sons, was able to evade federal forces and bounty hunters when he smuggled the general across the Mississippi River one night. General Early then was able to escape to Texas where some Confederate troops were still engaged in the conflict. He ultimately made his way into Mexico, then to Cuba and Canada until he was pardoned by President Andrew Johnson in 1868.

After the war, the Burrus family was financially ruined, but citizens of Bolivar County, both black and white, were desolate. Union forces had destroyed some of the levees that held back the flooding fury of the Mississippi River. This action caused the flatlands of the county to flood with only ridgelines remaining above water. Man and beast were relegated to seeking what little higher ground could be found. Many of these ridges were situated on Burrus's property and the Burrus family did all they could to feed and care for the stranded. Burrus and his sons used canoes to deliver food and necessary items to whoever needed it.[5]

After John Burrus Sr. died, the home and surrounding plantation tracts were inherited by John Burrus Jr. The younger Burrus had distinguished himself in service to the Confederate army during the war. After the war, Burrus served in various municipal positions and in the Mississippi state house of representatives and state senate.[6] John Jr. and his family resided at *Hollywood* until they moved out in 1916.

Once the Burrus family vacated the property, it suffered from decades of use by tenants. By the 1950s the house was only a shadow of its former beauty. However, in 1955 movie producers from Hollywood, California, chose the old Burrus place as the setting for a new and somewhat controversial screenplay written in part by Tennessee Williams. The film was later called *Baby Doll*. The movie starred Carroll Baker and Karl Malden, and actor Rip Torn appeared in the picture in his first role on screen. When the movie was released in 1956, it was controversial for what was considered then as overt sexual content. Nonetheless, the movie secured several Academy Award nominations, including those for Best Actress and Best Adapted Screenplay.[7]

In the years after the spotlights and cameras had moved on, the Burrus house suffered from neglect and vandalism. But in 1974, the Burrus heirs donated the house to the Bolivar County Historical Society. Apparently unable to keep up such a large house, the society mothballed the house, but kept it in a reasonable state of preservation. Then, in 1987 the historical society returned the house to the Burrus heirs.

Again, the house went through a period of neglect and vandalism. Still more damage was inflicted on the historic structure in 2001 when a tornado nearly destroyed the house, causing columns on the front to collapse and the front gable to crumble. Fortunately, Dr. Eustace H. Winn Jr. of Greenville, Mississippi, came to the rescue. He installed a tin roof on the house to protect the structure from damaging rain and leaks. The house was mothballed once again until four years later when Dr. Winn established the Burrus Foundation to help fund the restoration of the structure. After years of hard work and great expense, the Burrus house, now referred to as the Baby Doll House, is fully restored. To make the home more usable to modern guests, it was modified slightly to add electricity, plumbing, and air conditioning. This remarkable structure is now opened to visitors for tours and rental for weddings, family gatherings, and other special events.

ALABAMA

Belle Mont today stands amid
cedars planted as an alley over
150 years ago. (Kitchens)

BELLE MONT PLANTATION
Jeffersonian Classicism in the Deep South

📍 Colbert County, Alabama

Thomas Jefferson will forever be remembered in this country for the many contributions he made to forming and governing America. But, this Founding Father also provided America with its own classically inspired architectural style. Jefferson is well known for designing his home, *Monticello,* near Charlottesville, his plantation home at *Poplar Forest*, and campus buildings at the University of Virginia. He also designed the homes of at least a dozen of his friends and neighbors in Virginia. While Jefferson's architectural creations lean heavily on the design ideals of Italian architect Andrea Palladio (1508–1580), the structures Jefferson planned were uniquely his own. He developed a new architectural style, heavily influenced by classical forms, which were embraced by the nation he helped to establish.

While all of the elements used by Jefferson in his residential building designs had been used in the past, his adherence to a specific set of features was unique and identifiable. Jeffersonian architecture employs a Palladian-inspired form with a central core flanked by symmetrical wings, portico-and-pediment entry, red brick construction, classically ordered trims and moldings (particularly in the Tuscan style), white-painted trim, sand-painted columns, and suppressed stairways. Virtually all of these stylistic elements are found on other Virginia homes on which Jefferson is known to have been consulted for their designs, including *Lower Brandon* plantation, *Bremo* plantation, and *Belle Grove* plantation. However, this architectural style was not confined to Virginia. *Belle Mont*, sometimes referred to as "*Belmont*," in Colbert County, Alabama, is also a fine example of Jeffersonian classicism.

Indeed, because Alabama's *Belle Mont* is so squarely in keeping with the Jeffersonian building ideal, many speculate as to how directly its association with Jefferson might be. *Belle Mont*'s builder was Dr. Alexander Mitchell, who moved to Alabama from Louisa, Virginia, in 1818. Some who have researched *Belle Mont* and its history suggest that one or more of the craftsmen who worked under Jefferson at *Monticello* or at the University of Virginia came to Alabama before 1828 and either designed or heavily

HABS photograph of the rear courtyard with a fruit tree growing in its center and displaying courtyard walls scored to resemble blocks of stone. (HABS)

influenced the design of Dr. Mitchell's home.[1] Others have speculated that because Dr. Mitchell's father lived very close to *Monticello,* Thomas Jefferson may have personally drawn the plans for the Mitchell residence to be built in Alabama.[2] Jefferson's papers, now housed at Harvard University, contain a home Jefferson designed that is very similar to *Belle Mont,* with a U-shaped floor plan forming a courtyard. However, regardless of precise origin of its design or how the home took its form, *Belle Mont* is undeniably built in the Jeffersonian style and bears nearly all of the characteristic elements of Jeffersonian Classicism.

Belle Mont was constructed between 1828 and 1832. While the home was being built, Dr. Mitchell moved his family into a log house, which once stood next to the brick mansion. Apparently, the east wing of the house was completed first, and Dr. Mitchell moved his family into that portion of the house while construction on the rest of the home continued. Once the mansion was finally completed in 1832, the Mitchells had erected an imposing brick residence that crowned a steep knoll overlooking the Tennessee River valley, including the 1,680 acres of cotton- and corn-producing land encompassed by their plantation. The finished structure has a two-story central pavilion measuring twenty-four feet by twenty-four feet with a two-tiered, pedimented portico shading the front entrance. Its brick walls are a sturdy fourteen inches thick. On either side of the residence's central block are one-story wings extending about twenty-five feet on either side of the façade, and sixty-five feet to the back. The U-shaped floor plan creates a pleasant courtyard behind the central block. The courtyard is laid with square bricks and the floor rises nearly five feet above ground level. Its colonnaded loggia provides shade to all but the center of the courtyard. The home's occupants used the courtyard as an outdoor living room to entertain guests and as a pleasant space to shell peas or carry out other daily chores. However, Mitchell sold *Belle Mont* just a year after it was completed and moved to Philadelphia—the home of his second wife.

1930s photograph of Belle Mont taken for the Historic American Building Survey showing some of the deterioration already occurring there. (HABS)

In 1833 Isaac and Catherine Baker Winston purchased *Belle Mont* and its acreage. They and their heirs made it their family's home for the next century. The Winstons were also of Virginia stock. In fact, Isaac's family tree's closest branches include such notable Americans as Dolly Madison, Patrick Henry, and Isaac Cole, who was a close personal friend and secretary to Thomas Jefferson.[3] Isaac and Catherine furnished *Belle Mont* to suit their tastes and their concept of their position in society. So during their occupancy it was an exceptionally fine residence for a house in a relatively remote location.

For exterior trims, particularly the exterior columns on the loggia, white paint was mixed with course sand and the mixture was applied to wooden columns and other trim to give it the look and feel of stone. Walls of the loggia were painted to resemble gray blocks of stone. Interior walls were either covered in French wallpaper or painted in bright colors, while the baseboards were marbleized to simulate expensive, imported marble. Door and window trims were grained to resemble rosewood. Some of these faux finishes remain at *Belle Mont* today; either as remnants of the original finish or as modern attempts to return the home to its original splendor.

Isaac Winston Sr. apparently managed his plantation efficiently. By 1850 Winston's *Belle Mont* was valued at $54,000. Just after Alabama seceded from the Union in 1861, Winston, who by then was in his early to mid-sixties, volunteered for service in the Confederate army. Although he served briefly in Virginia, in 1862 he became so severely ill that he was sent home to recuperate.

Winston was home at *Belle Mont* in May 1862 when Union soldiers invaded northwest Alabama after the carnage at the Battle of Shiloh. As the Union army passed through Colbert County (then Franklin County), they stole and destroyed a great deal of property at Winston's plantation. Writing of the depredations visited upon *Belle Mont* by Union soldiers, Isaac Winston Jr. describes the event to the *Montgomery*

Belle Mont's dining room as it appears today with faux-grained doors and baseboards, and original flooring. (Kitchens)

Bedroom in the east wing of Belle Mont with original paint treatment and huge paneled door opening onto the courtyard. (Kitchens)

Daily Advertiser in a letter dated December 1862, recounting how the invading soldiers took all of his slaves, twenty-eight horses and mules, four wagons, three hundred bales of cotton, destroyed his crops, tools, and farm animals, and left his family and their remaining servants without food to survive. He describes how nineteen of his servants did not want to leave *Belle Mont* and secured a pass from the Union officer to return to their homes there.[4] However, theft and destruction by Union forces was only part of the horror visited upon the Winstons. In outrage over how enemy soldiers treated his family, Isaac Winston Jr. wrote to their commander, Maj. Gen. Don Carlos Buell, to lodge a complaint and to seek redress. He writes:

Photograph taken in the early 1980s capturing the extent of the home's dilapidation just prior to the Alabama Historical Commission's efforts to restore it. (Image courtesy of Robert Gamble)

Because I dared to avow my principles and remonstrate with the men who intruded upon my family at all hours, robbed my garden, and [because I] refused to sell them articles I could not spare, I was threatened with arrest and forced to fly from my home leaving my wife and children unprotected. Col. Straight has had hauled from my cribs nineteen wagon loads of corn under protest from me that he was depriving my family of bread[,] and knowing I will never accept one cent by way of compensation. What is money worth when we should want bread? I had no corn to spare, will now be compelled to buy. . . . When Gen. Mitchel's Division were here they took from me forty hams of bacon besides constantly intruding upon my family threatening me with violence, forcing locks and robbing constantly. . . . On no other plantation was such a large amount of quantity of corn taken, leaving so little, thus proving it was done through malice and spite.[5]

Isaac Winston Sr. died in 1862. *Belle Mont* remained in the Winston family, but family members moved away and used the plantation house more as a country retreat than as a residence. Family gatherings at *Belle Mont* eventually died out altogether and the mansion was left abandoned. In 1941 the home was sold by Isaac Winston's descendants to J. C. Fennel and Gordon Preuit. By 1969, the house was once again left abandoned and had become heavily vandalized. Over the next dozen or so years, kudzu swallowed *Belle Mont*, covering it like a green blanket. Finally, in 1983 the house and thirty-five surrounding acres were donated to the Alabama Historical Commission (AHC) in an effort to save the house on its original setting.

Since coming under the ownership of the Alabama Historical Commission, *Belle Mont*'s decline has been stayed. The AHC has spent over $500,000 to stabilize the structure and to begin to return it to its antebellum grandeur. During its years of abandonment, some of the home's finest features were destroyed or stolen, such as the fanlight above the front door, some of its fine black marble mantels, and some of its early paneled doors. However, thanks to the AHC's efforts, the house was slowly returned to its original condition and was opened to the public for tours. In early 2016 the AHC turned over management and operation of the property to the Colbert County Historical Landmarks Foundation, which continues to open the home for tours in an effort to tell the story of *Belle Mont*. In hopes of raising funds to continue the restoration of the mansion, Colbert County Historical Landmarks is also opening the house for special events such as weddings and family gatherings.

CHEROKEE
Palace for a Plantation Industrialist

♀ Tuscaloosa, Alabama

I n the decades leading up to the War between the States, cotton is the crop to which today's history novices default as the probable source for the wealth of any particular southerner. While the cultivation, harvesting, and shipping of cotton was certainly a very large contributor to the fortunes of many southerners, it was not their only source of income. Indeed, some of the southern elite derived only a fraction of their fortunes from those snowy bolls. Robert Jemison Jr. of Tuscaloosa, Alabama, is a good example.

Robert Jemison Jr. was one of Alabama's richest citizens in the years leading up to the War between the States. Although he operated several plantations in western Alabama totaling nearly ten thousand acres, Jemison's business and income-generating interests were widely diversified. His primary source of income seems to have come from export trading. However, his other commercial interests included stagecoach lines, road building, coal mining, sawmill operations, iron smelting, and leasing some of his slaves to others as contractors trained in trades such as carpentry, blacksmithing, and masonry.[1] For years Jemison oversaw these varied interests from his plantation, *Crab Orchard,* later renamed *Cherokee Place*, near Northport in Tuscaloosa County. But by the mid-1850s, he was ready to build a town house in Tuscaloosa that would provide more convenient quarters from which to conduct his business while at the same time enabling his family to entertain their many business and social guests in town.

Jemison is believed to have retained the services of Philadelphia architect John Stewart, the partner of the widely renowned architect Samuel Sloan, to build his new home. Stewart was already in Tuscaloosa to oversee the erection of the huge Italianate structure that would be Bryce Insane Hospital, originally known as the Alabama State Hospital for the Insane, which had been designed by Sloan & Stewart. Jemison played a key role in getting the hospital built in Tuscaloosa so that the state's mentally ill could be humanely housed and treated.[2]

While John Stewart supervised the building of Jemison's new town house, he was aided in its construction by an army of skilled craftsmen and laborers Jemison already had on hand in the many slaves who were highly trained in carpentry, blacksmithing, and masonry. In fact, nearly everything Jemison needed to build the house was available from one of his business interests. Lumber for the home was felled at his plantation *Cherokee Place* and then sawn at his sawmill. Nails and iron for construction were acquired by or made at his blacksmith shop. His new mansion's state-of-the-art interior gas-lighting system and gas stoves were powered by coal mined by one of his companies. Construction on Jemison's home began in 1859 at approximately the same time as construction on Bryce Hospital had been substantially completed, which enabled John Stewart to devote sufficient time to engage in overseeing its progress. Even with all of these advantages, the large edifice Jemison erected in Tuscaloosa took nearly three years to complete.

Stewart's plan called for an enormous and rambling brick mansion with two and a half stories over a full English basement. A broad veranda stretches around three sides of the structure providing ample space to entertain guests or to lounge in a rocker while watching the many travelers plying the oft-traveled road in front of the house leading from Tuscaloosa to Greensboro. The interior is treated with wood trims milled on his plantation and carved by artisan slaves. Two of six stairways in the home are "public" stairways in which Jemison's carpenters carved deep paneling trimmed in native walnut, oak, and chinaberry wood. Interior doors are fourteen feet tall with first-floor

Today, Cherokee dominates Greensboro Avenue in Tuscaloosa and provides a beautiful setting for events such as weddings and family gatherings. (Kitchens)

When Cherokee was photographed for the Historic American Building Survey in 1934, the home was covered in wisteria vines. (HABS)

Massive, sliding pocket doors open from Cherokee's library onto the wide central hall and display some of the skillful craftsmanship that went into the woodwork and trims of Jemison's mansion. (Kitchens)

ceilings rising eighteen feet. Stewart's intent for the residence was to awe those entering its halls.

Jemison's finished home, which he called *Cherokee*, was one of the largest homes—containing twenty-six spacious rooms—built in Alabama just before the War between the States and contained many conveniences unknown to but a fortunate few. *Cherokee* was the first residence in Tuscaloosa to have fully plumbed bathrooms, and it was one of only a few houses to have its own gas plant that provided fuel to gas-powered lamps, chandeliers, and a gas stove in the home. An antebellum version of an intercom system was installed that connected the basement kitchen to Mrs. Jemison's room upstairs by

Jemison imported Carrara marble mantels from Italy that had been intricately carved. (Kitchens)

means of a tube. This speaking tube enabled Mrs. Jemison to have frequent and detailed conversations with the kitchen staff without having to traverse several levels of stairs.

The large cupola crowning the structure served as more than an aesthetic feature. On hot summer days, the cupola's large windows would be opened, creating a powerful updraft that lifted hot, stale air from the rooms below, and pulled it through the center of the home and out of the cupola. The resulting effect is akin to that of an early air-conditioning system, which was surprisingly effective. The home's basement level contains a large ballroom, a billiard's room, dressing rooms, a two-story conservatory, and a dry well used to store and cool large quantities of ice. All of these features were designed to ensure the complete comfort of Jemison, his family, and their many important guests.

Lavish entertaining was a frequent occurrence at *Cherokee* during the Jemisons' occupancy. Then as now, entertaining friends and clients can be a significant benefit to one's business interests, but lavish entertaining enabled Jemison to hone his political talents as well. He served in both the Alabama state senate and the house of representatives. In 1861 he represented the anti-secession party in Alabama's debate on whether to leave the Union. Though he was opposed to secession, he still joined the Confederate cause when Alabama seceded. A few years later, after William Lowndes Yancey died while serving Alabama in the Confederate Senate, Jemison was appointed to fill his seat.

Jemison's service in the Confederate Senate almost resulted in his newly minted mansion being destroyed. A detachment of the Union army set out for Tuscaloosa on March 29, 1865, to destroy the town's manufacturing facilities and to free Union soldiers being held in Confederate prisons there. Union forces arrived in Northport on April 3 and took Tuscaloosa on April 4. Unfortunately, Senator Jemison happened to be home from Richmond, Virginia, at that time. When Union commanders discovered his presence at home, a squad of soldiers was dispatched to *Cherokee* to take him into custody. However, by that time, Jemison was hiding in a nearby swamp. In frustration,

The entire exterior of Cherokee is covered with a gray-green stucco, which is scored to simulate large marble blocks. (Kitchens)

one of the officers ordered the burning of *Cherokee*, but permitted Mrs. Jemison just fifteen minutes to remove her valuables from the home. While Mrs. Jemison hastily gathered that which was most precious to her, two boys, apparently engaging a dangerous game of pranking the Union soldiers, approached *Cherokee* and yelled, "Forrest is coming." Gen. Nathan Bedford Forrest had been the pariah of the Union army and was known to ruthlessly destroy enemy assets. The soldiers preparing to burn the Jemison house immediately dropped their torches and fled to safer quarters. The boys' prank saved the house from certain destruction.[3]

The Jemison family continuously occupied *Cherokee* for the next eighty years. In the 1940s J. P. and Nell Burchfield purchased the house, which by that time had become dilapidated. The Burchfields undertook a major restoration of *Cherokee* without substantially changing its original design. But the Burchfields only occupied the house for about twelve years. The house was then put to use as the Friedman Public Library in 1955, and it remained useful in that capacity until 1979. But *Cherokee* once again fell into decay for several years. The City of Tuscaloosa acquired the mansion in 1991 and deeded it to the Jemison-Van de Graaf Mansion Foundation to restore and preserve the house. For years the foundation has worked hard to preserve the antebellum mansion and return it to its former splendor.

Today, the Jemison-Van de Graaf Mansion Foundation operates the house as a tour house and events facility while they continue to raise money to return the architectural gem to its 1860 condition and appearance.

The First White House as
it appeared in 1934 when
photographers from the Historic
American Buildings Survey visited
Montgomery. (HABS)

FIRST WHITE HOUSE OF THE CONFEDERACY
Witness to History

♥ Montgomery, Alabama

When William Sayre built his home in the fledgling town of Montgomery in the early 1830s, who could have predicted that the home would be the virtual heart of a new nation just three decades later? Sayre retained the services of contractor A. M. Bradley to build a commodious townhome at the corner of modern-day Lee and Bibb Streets. In 1855 Col. Joseph S. Winter took ownership of the home and undertook a renovation to make the Federal-style house more fashionable. He added a number of Italianate details, including brackets under the eaves and a front portico with rusticated detailing underneath. He also enclosed the rear porch to make a large room which served essentially as a cross hall. After the extensive renovation, Winter's home was aided by a full complement of service buildings on the property and a large residence with reception halls, spacious dining room, double parlors, and large bedrooms.[1] One curiosity about this residence is the fact that although the house was a frame structure, many of the outbuildings were constructed of brick, some of them being two stories. It was far more common in that era to find the main house built of brick with frame outbuildings complimenting the main structure.

Just a few years after Winter completed renovations on the old Sayre house, it was sold to Col. Edmund S. Harrison, who purchased it for a town house. Montgomery had become Alabama's capital in 1846, and many wealthy and influential Alabamians sought accommodations in the capital city to entertain important guests and remain near to those making the state's laws. As tensions between North and South crescendoed and southern states began to secede, the entire South's focus turned to Montgomery as a suitable city in which to hold a convention of states to discuss forming a new nation.

In early 1861 a rapid, almost dizzying, succession of events brought Montgomery into national prominence. On January 11, Alabama adopted its Ordinance of Secession. On February 4, the Confederate States of America were organized as a new nation. Four days later a Provisional Constitutional Congress convened at the Alabama State Capitol Building to elect a new president. Jefferson Finis Davis was elected the very

The presidential dining room played host to many of the mid-nineteenth century's political and social leaders. (Photographs in the Carol M. Highsmith Archive, Library of Congress, Prints and Photographs Division)

next day by unanimous vote as the new nation's president. On February 18, Jefferson Davis arrived in Montgomery by midnight train and at 1:00 in the afternoon he was inaugurated as the Provisional President of the Confederate States of America. Montgomery seemed an unlikely city for such activity. It was still a small town with just eight thousand residents and half of those residents were slaves or free persons of color. Then, all at once the town became a national capital and the center of furious activity to organize and govern a new country.

The new nation's president would need a suitable home in which his family could live. The home had to be sufficiently large for the president to entertain guests and conduct private meetings. Recognizing these needs, Col. Edmund S. Harrison offered to lease his new townhome in Montgomery, fully furnished and fully staffed with servants, for the enormous sum of $5,000 per year. Although many questioned the exorbitant cost of the lease as being unpatriotic and an effort to price-gouge the new government, an agreement was reached to pay Harrison's price to lease the mansion. President Davis's family moved into the new White House on March 4, 1861.

President Davis's wife, Varina Howell Davis, seems to have been pleased with the Confederate White House. In her memoirs, she writes, "The house chosen for us was a gentleman's house, roomy enough for our purposes. It was on the corner of the street looking towards the capitol. We lived there three months, and the most brilliant levees were held, and the handsomest dinners given while Mr. Davis was President of the

The First White House of the Confederacy in Montgomery is a fine example of a nineteenth-century Italianate mansion. (Kitchens)

Confederacy."[2] Mrs. Davis was accustomed to lavish entertaining as she had experienced the excesses of galas and soirees in Washington, DC, when her husband was United States senator from Mississippi. Historian Thomas M. Owen writes of those early, heady days in Montgomery in 1861: "The town had filled with literally hundreds of the political, military and business leaders of the South, many accompanied by their wives and daughters. These made a brilliant company. The young gallants and maidens took long rides on horseback, or in handsome turnouts, or spent the mornings in attendance upon the sessions of Congress. The native grace and charm of Mrs. Davis, and her long residence in Washington, and other social centers, gave her acknowledged leadership."[3]

However, not all activity in Montgomery was so festive. President Davis utilized one of the outbuildings on the White House grounds for his office. Late one evening as he worked in his study, he glimpsed a would-be assassin making his way to the office's open window. Davis acted quickly by pulling a pistol from his desk drawer and fired at the attacker, who hastily made an escape. Thereafter, Mrs. Davis moved the president's office into the library in the main house for more security.

First White House parlor with chairs used by President Davis's family. The chair with the white placard is the chair sent to President Davis for his use and comfort while he was imprisoned at Fortress Monroe in Maryland after the war. (Kitchens)

Montgomery's position at the center of the universe was short lived. Just three months after the Davis family moved to the Executive Mansion in Montgomery, the Provisional Confederate Congress decided to move the Confederate capital to Richmond, Virginia, and ordered that the Confederate Congress reconvene in Richmond on July 20, 1861. On May 26, 1861, President Davis left Montgomery to relocate in Richmond. Varina Davis stayed in Montgomery a while longer to oversee the packing of family personal items and furniture that the Davises had moved to the First White House just months before.[4]

After the First White House was no longer the executive mansion, a succession of Montgomery's finest families took ownership of it, including Col. William Knox, George Matthews, Fleming Freeman, William Crawford Bibb, Mrs. James Ellsberry, and Mrs. Libby Agnew Kenny. It was later purchased by Archibald Tyson of Lowndesboro, Alabama, and finally by Mrs. Robert Ridley and Lewis Render of Georgia. For decades the house, known at that time as the "Jeff Davis House," was leased to tenants.

In 1897 a newly organized United Daughters of the Confederacy (UDC) in Alabama held their first state convention. After it was proposed as a UDC state project to

The First White House welcomes visitors for tours and is opened daily for much of the year. (Kitchens)

preserve the First White House of the Confederacy, a committee was formed, headed by Mrs. Jessie Drew Beale. Mrs. Beale had had a long friendship with Varina Davis and as a result of that friendship, Varina Davis agreed to donate the bedroom furniture President Davis used at *Beauvoir* on the Mississippi coast during his retirement there. After several years of failed attempts to achieve their goal, the UDC seemed to abandon their project. Fortunately, a group of twenty-seven ladies were unwilling to allow the effort to preserve the First White House to die. In 1900 these ladies formed the White House Association of Alabama, which was patterned after the Mount Vernon Ladies' Association of the Union that had rescued Washington's Mount Vernon in Virginia. All of the Davis family furniture that had been donated by Mrs. Davis was signed over to the White House Association in 1902. The Render family who owned the First White House was unwilling to sell the lot on which the house was located because the value of the property had become so great. However, they were willing to sell the house so that it could be moved. The White House Association, however, was unable to raise sufficient funds to have the home moved to another property.

By 1919 the house seemed doomed. It had become a boardinghouse for trainmen and was allowed to deteriorate into a deplorable condition. Demolition was imminent and efforts to save the house continued to be stalled. It was at that moment that Gov.

Thomas E. Kilby signed into law a bill that dedicated $25,000 in state funds for the purchase of the house and secured its relocation to state-owned property across from the state capitol building. The historic house was purchased for the meager sum of $800. After carefully documenting the house in photographs, the home was dismantled and cut into thirds for the move. On its new lot, the edifice was reassembled, restored, and returned to its 1861 appearance.[5]

On June 3, 1921, the restored First White House of the Confederacy was opened with great fanfare and ceremony. After a parade, which ended on the lawn of the capitol, the White House Association gave the house to the people of the State of Alabama. Legislation a few years later retained the house as a property of the State of Alabama, but handed over management of the historic property to the White House Association. As a consequence, the state owns and maintains the house and the grounds, but the White House Association owns and maintains the furniture, paintings, and other items in the house.

The First White House of the Confederacy has long been a popular tourist attraction. Around 100,000 tourists per year visited the house in the 1970s. Wear and tear from the heavy traffic through the house necessitated another renovation in 1976 in which floors were reinforced to accommodate the weight and wear of visitors.

Today, thousands of visitors continue to frequent the home. They are treated to dozens of historic artifacts that once belonged to or were used by President Davis and his family. Included in the inventory of items now seen in the home is the table on which Jefferson Davis wrote *Rise and Fall of the Confederate Government*; a mahogany sofa owned and used by President Davis in the Montgomery White House; a canopied bed made especially for Jefferson Davis; the Davis family Bible; a mahogany chair Jefferson Davis used while in prison at Fortress Monroe; and myriad other items of furniture, clothing, and personal effects of the Davis family. These and many other artifacts can be seen at the First White House of the Confederacy, which is opened to the public for self-guided tours on nearly a daily basis.

GAINESWOOD

Rambling Exterior, Resplendent Interior

♀ Demopolis, Alabama

By 1860, Alabamians were accustomed to seeing imposing Greek Revival mansions. The state had hundreds, if not thousands, of them, especially in the Black Belt region. But no one, either then or now, would expect to see a Greek Revival residence from that period so entirely unique as *Gaineswood*.

Gaineswood rose from rather modest beginnings. The first dwelling on the site now known as *Gaineswood* was a utilitarian log house built by Gen. George S. Gaines, an Indian agent who developed a very close relationship with Choctaw chief Pushmataha in 1815. In 1819, General Gaines was appointed as the spokesman for the White Bluff Association to purchase a site on White Bluff along the Tombigbee River for the development of a town. This town later became the city of Demopolis. Gaines purchased for himself acreage close to the Tombigbee River, but just outside of the town limits. On that site he built a comfortable log home. Once the Choctaws were removed from western Alabama to the West in the 1830s, a flood of settlers came to Alabama's western Black Belt to buy fertile land to farm. One such settler was Nathan Bryan Whitfield.

Whitfield came from a prominent North Carolina family. His father attained the rank of general in the Colonial army and his uncles all served in the American Revolution as patriots. Nathan Bryan Whitfield also accepted the mantle of leadership by serving first in the North Carolina house of commons and later in the North Carolina senate. He made his first trip to Alabama's Marengo County in 1833 to visit his uncle, Col. J. R. Bryan. Whitfield was smitten by the lush countryside and inexpensive land, so he purchased a plantation consisting of several thousand acres about fifteen miles south of Demopolis. He named the plantation *Chatham*. However, after losing three of his children to yellow fever within just a few weeks, he moved his family to a healthier location near Demopolis.[1]

Whitfield had become friends with George S. Gaines and was well acquainted with Gaines's home near Demopolis. In 1842 he purchased Gaines's fifteen-hundred-acre property just south of Demopolis. However, the log house that Gaines had used for

his homestead would not suffice for Whitfield's residence. Whitfield set out to build a home that would suit his family's needs and reflect his own ideals of design and comfort. However, because Whitfield planned on building a large and unique home, he first had to build his own village where the work of fashioning raw materials into a home could be done. Buildings to accommodate carpenters and plasterers were erected along with structures to house machinery required to fashion wooden columns and cornices. He also built separate structures to serve as brick kilns and batter houses.[2] Whitfield used predominantly the labor of skilled slaves, free men of color, and itinerate craftsmen to execute his plans for the home.

The house Whitfield had in mind took nearly seventeen years to complete. Its design and redesign was entirely the creation of Whitfield himself. He was aided with some of the finer architectural details by his extensive collection of architectural books, including Minard LaFever's well-known works *The Modern Builder's Guide* and *The Beauties of Modern Architecture*, James Stuart's *The Antiquities of Athens*, and others. When he began construction in 1843, he initially called the estate *Marlmont*, but by the time the home neared completion, he renamed it *Gaineswood* to honor his friend, George S. Gaines.[3]

Whitfield apparently tore down the log house in which Gaines had once resided. The house he built at Gaineswood possessed a layout and design that was entirely unique for its day and time. Upon completion in 1861, Whitfield's residence was a rambling, unconventional structure uncannily similar to ancient Roman villas uncovered at Pompeii or Herculaneum. The front door is still centered in the front of the two-story structure, but rather than entering through a front porch, the entrance is reached

Gaineswood has been restored to reflect its 1850s appearance. Its exterior stucco has been scored to resemble large stone blocks, in keeping with its intended classical theme. (Kitchens)

by walking through a Doric porte-cochère with round, fluted columns. He hired an itinerate artist from Poland to paint a fresco of a flower wreath on the porte-cochère's ceiling. His intention was to have his guests ride up to the front door in their carriages and disembark the conveyance while under the sheltering cover of the porte-cochère. In poor weather, this covered entrance would be preferred to the more typical homes of the time that had no shelter between the carriage lane and the front portico.

The entire home is built of brick, which is stuccoed over, and then scored and colored to resemble ashlar blocks. On either side of the main block of the structure are one-and-a-half-story wings fronted by squared columns. Centered on the north side of the house, Whitfield built a Doric portico matching the design of the porte-cochère entrance portico, but leaving visitors confused as to whether the front of the home was its north side or its west entrance underneath the porte-cochère. Everywhere one looks on the mansion's exterior are unique and visually appealing architectural details. However, it was Whitfield's interior design elements that make *Gaineswood* one of the nation's irreplaceable architectural treasures from the antebellum period.

One enters *Gaineswood* through a narrow hallway with the customary rooms on either side. While this entry hall is attractive enough, it does not hint to the grandeur that lies beyond. The parlor on the right is a large square room capped by a huge dome. The pinnacle of the dome is a cupola three feet in diameter with windows that flood the room with light all around.

Gaineswood's parlor sits just to the right of the central hall and is remarkable for its huge plastered dome and fine classical decoration. (Kitchens)

The interior of the dome is practically dripping with intricate layers of plaster anthemion. Even the flat portion of the ceiling is plastered with panels, rosettes, and Greek-inspired decorative designs. The plasterwork continues in dentil molding and decorative friezes on the walls just underneath the ceiling, and in a repeating pattern of plaster anthemion continuing along the upper portion of each door frame. Just beyond the domed parlor is a small cross hall followed by a domed dining room. The dome and decorative features of the parlor are replicated in the dining room.

If the heavily ornamented domes were not enough to impress Whitfield's visitors, then the drawing room across the central hall would definitely do the trick. It has been referred to as the most elaborate and spectacular room in any private residence

Gaineswood's large dining room is flooded with light from the dome, much as the room would have appeared in 1860. (Kitchens)

in America. The drawing room is the largest room in the house, measuring twenty feet by thirty feet. At each end of the room is a large fireplace with a gray Italian marble mantelpiece. The two long sides of the room are lined with spectacular fluted, Corinthian columns and pilasters, while the short sides of the room continue the theme with Corinthian capitals over fluted pilasters. But covering this resplendence is the coffered ceiling containing more plaster decoration than perhaps any other room in Alabama. Each panel formed by the coffers contains its own ceiling medallion. Anthemion in a continuous repeating train cover all sides of the coffers beams along with other intricate plaster elements spreading over the bottom edge of the coffers. The room was recognized then as now for its beauty. Family descendants recall tales of fine balls held in the drawing room during which friendly Indians still living in the area peered in through the windows to watch the festivities and admire the resplendence of it all.[4]

In many of the finer mansion houses of the period, it was fairly common to include decorative wood and trim in the public rooms where guests could appreciate the time and expense that went into installing it, but this sort of decorative ornamentation was nearly always left out of nonpublic rooms such as bedrooms. However, Whitfield incorporated high-style, intricate plaster trim and architectural details even to the bedrooms and utilitarian rooms in the house.

Among many unusual features at *Gaineswood* was "The Ring." The roof over the home's second floor contained a round observatory on which an open cupola was built. Family tradition holds that the family often gathered in the small cupola to

The drawing room at Gaineswood may be the most elaborately decorated room in the antebellum South, with plastered coffered ceiling, Corinthian columns, and gray marble mantels. (Kitchens)

Close-up view of the intricate plaster moldings and column details found in Gaineswood's master bedchamber. (Kitchens)

Painting of Gaineswood just after its completion in 1860 providing a glimpse of the lake that once was beside the mansion. (HABS)

hold musicales. Music was a common form of entertainment at Whitfield's home for he was known to be a multitalented musician competent at playing the pianoforte, violin, bagpipe, and harp. Whitfield even invented an instrument, which he called the "flutina." A flutina is a blend of a pianoforte and an organ that sounds similar to a flute. One of Whitfield's flutinas still resides at *Gaineswood*.[5]

Whitfield's design and planning genius was not confined to the musical and architectural realms. He also designed the grounds surrounding the house. He built a lake just off of the north side of the house. Centered in the lake were two small islands on which poplars, cedars, and crepe myrtle trees were planted. A huge artesian well nearby supplied both the lake and the house with water. Water pressure from the well was sufficient to push water into the house for use by its occupants. Not far from the lake, Whitfield built a Greek-styled gazebo to provide shade to those strolling the gardens and enjoying Alabama's salubrious southern air.

The War between the States touched, but did not destroy, *Gaineswood*. In 1864 when Confederate general Leonidas Polk, known as the Fighting Bishop, visited Demopolis, he used *Gaineswood*'s grounds to encamp his troops. General Polk's decision to bivouac at *Gaineswood* was not merely chance, for Polk and Whitfield had been classmates in North Carolina.[6]

The war, nonetheless, devastated Whitfield's finances. Although he kept *Gaineswood*, he could barely maintain it. The home began to decay. In the decades following the war, its dilapidation was so severe that Mulberry trees grew through the home's floor and into the skylights of the dining room, while goats slept in the magnificent drawing room.

Fortunately, in 1896 the home was purchased by Whitfield's daughter, Mrs. Charles Dunstan, who began a complete restoration of the house. But *Gaineswood* soon was sold again and for the next five decades the home passed through an array of owners until it was purchased by Dr. and Mrs. J. D. McLeod. Dr. McLeod was an Alabama native who had decided to retire to his home state after living much of his adult life in Ohio. When the McLeods bought *Gaineswood*, it had once again fallen into disrepair. After two years of arduous work, they were able to return the home to its original grandeur.

Finally, in 1967 *Gaineswood* was purchased by the State of Alabama, which undertook another restoration and opened the historic home to the public in 1975. *Gaineswood* was added to the National Register of Historic Places in 1972 and designated a National Historic Landmark in 1973. Over the intervening years, the Alabama Historic Commission, which now operates the home as a museum, has acquired many of the original Whitfield family pieces that once were housed there. The home remains open today as one of the nation's most fascinating house museums, offering tours that take visitors into the heart of Old South resplendence.

HARRIS-TATE-THOMPSON HOUSE
Alabama's Repatriated Beauty

📍 Tuskegee (moved to Montgomery), Alabama

The jewel of Alabama's eastern Black Belt is the town of Tuskegee. This small city boasts of dozens of imposing antebellum homes that still stand as evidence of the wealth and sophistication that it displayed during decades prior to the War between the States. The town has gained national acclaim for the school that Booker T. Washington established there in 1881—the Tuskegee Institute. The president of modern-day Tuskegee University lives in Tuskegee's grandest remaining antebellum residence, known as *Grey Columns*. Another of Tuskegee's most impressive prewar residences still stands, but not in Tuskegee. The Harris-Tate-Thompson house, long considered one of the most imposing homes in the region, was disassembled around 1980, moved in pieces to a warehouse in Georgia, and then reconstructed in Montgomery, Alabama's Old Towne District in 1988.

The beginnings of the Harris-Tate-Thompson house are somewhat uncertain. It was originally built by Peter Coffee Harris, a nephew of famed general John E. Coffee of the War of 1812. Peter Harris was one of the original settlers of Tuskegee, and he built the first house in town on a site just north of the town square. Then in 1850, Harris built a mansion on the same site with the intention of making it one of the most impressive homes in Tuskegee. Just three years later Harris sold his newly completed mansion to Judge Thomas Stribling Tate. Tate was a native of Edgefield County, South Carolina, but he moved to Russell County, Alabama, where he prospered as a probate judge, county clerk, and sheriff until he relocated to Macon County. As a Tuskegee resident Tate was elected to the state legislature.[1]

Tate's imposing residence is a Greek Revival mansion with Italianate details. The person responsible for the design and construction of the home is not known. However, it is one of the great vernacular structures in Alabama. Six fluted columns along the façade are capped by huge capitals evocative of those used by the Egyptians rather than those used by the Greeks or Romans. Each capital is more than three feet tall and carved from a single piece of solid cedar with cast-plaster floral designs attached to give

The Harris-Tate-Thompson house on its original site in Tuskegee. The veranda easily accommodates nineteen people for a celebration. The photograph appears to have been taken in the 1890s. (Image courtesy of Landmarks Foundation of Montgomery)

HABS image from 1934 of the cross hall showing the unique decorative elements above interior doorways and the domed ceiling where the hallways intersect. (HABS)

1970s image of the Harris-Tate-Thompson house in Tuskegee with obvious deterioration to the veranda. (Image courtesy of Landmarks Foundation of Montgomery)

the impression of modified Corinthian capitals. Windows of the first floor extended from the floor to ceiling. Other unique architectural features include the use of quoins on the corners and a one-of-a-kind, lyre-themed iron balcony extending nearly from one end of the façade to the other. Italianate features include a bracketed cornice and a low-hipped roof. At the back of the structure is a two-story portico with six octagonal columns. The interior floor plan has four large rooms divided by cross halls running north to south and east to west. The cross halls intersect at the center of the structure, and feature heavy plaster corbels that appear to support a vaulted ceiling. In the center of the dome created by the vaulted ceiling is an intricate plaster medallion. Apparently, the house was built with a running water system, as the attic appears to have had a tank or reservoir, which, with the aid of gravity, would deliver water to various faucets in the residence.

In 1880 William Phillip Thompson purchased the house and raised a family there. He was a highly successful Tuskegee merchant. William's son, Charles W. Thompson, inherited the house in 1891 after his father's death. Charles sold his father's mercantile business and focused his efforts on organizing the Bank of Tuskegee. In 1896 Charles was appointed to the staff of Alabama's governor Joseph E. Johnston. A year later he was elected to the Alabama state senate, and in 1901 he was elected to represent his district in the United States Congress. Thompson's rising political prominence was affirmed in 1898 when United States president William McKinley visited Tuskegee to speak at Tuskegee Institute. President McKinley stopped at Charles Thompson's house for a visit, and later spoke to town citizens from the balcony of Thompson's imposing home.[2]

Generations of the Thompson family continued to live in the house until it was sold out of the family in 1975 and acquired by a local bank. The bank used the structure to store old files, but did not maintain the house properly. Even so, the

Image of the shallow domed cross hall intersection while the Harris-Tate-Thompson home was being dismantled in the late 1970s. (Image courtesy of Landmarks Foundation of Montgomery)

Rear veranda of the Harris-Tate-Thompson home as it was being reconstructed in Montgomery at Old Town. (Image courtesy of Landmarks Foundation of Montgomery)

Harris-Tate-Thompson house in 1979 was in much the same condition as it had been in the 1850s with only rudimentary electricity having been added to modernize it.

It was at about this time that the house was sold to Hayes Gilliam. Gilliam had long admired the house and wanted it for himself. However, he wanted to live in the house on his property in Carroll County, Georgia. Caring for the house as he did, Gilliam carefully deconstructed the historic structure, recording each board and post by number so that it could be precisely reconstructed on his own property. Hundreds

The Harris-Tate-Thompson house as it stands today in Montgomery. The house is currently being leased as office space for businesses. (Kitchens)

of photographs were taken of the house as it was deconstructed to help ensure that neither time nor faulty memory would prevent a successful reconstruction. The unique plaster medallions and corbels were photographed and pieces were retained to make copies or replacements in its rebuilt iteration. Finally, the entire house, now in thousands of parts, was kept in a storage facility in Carroll County, Georgia. There the home, in its elemental form, remained for several years, while Gilliam waited for the time, money, and energy to reconstruct it in the location he had planned.

Landmarks Foundation of Montgomery learned of Gilliam's removal of the house from Tuskegee. The Landmarks Foundation for years had been developing a district in downtown Montgomery at which historic antebellum structures, mostly residential, were moved to create an entire neighborhood of period structures. The organization wanted to have an array of homes in the district (Old Alabama Towne) that represented the varied styles of architecture utilized in early Alabama. One house style they were missing, however, was the grand, two-story columned mansion so iconic in the South. Landmarks Foundation looked at a number of homes to move to Old Alabama Towne, but none fit the bill like the Harris-Tate-Thompson house.

In 1981 Landmarks Foundation contacted Mr. Gilliam to investigate whether he would be willing to sell the deconstructed house to them. At first he resisted the idea since he still planned to rebuild the house for his personal use in Georgia. However, he soon changed his mind and agreed to sell the house, in its elemental form, to the Landmarks Foundation. So that it would be reconstructed properly, he also agreed to provide the foundation with his personal assistance in rebuilding the house as it originally stood. He had taken hundreds of photographs of the details of the home as it was being deconstructed to make it easier to reconstruct the house fitting the parts together just as they were originally, and he agreed to provide Landmarks with those photographs. Once the purchase was arranged, Landmarks Foundation dispatched eight large trucks to transport the house parts from the warehouse in Georgia to a warehouse in Montgomery where it would be stored until a lot in downtown Montgomery could be secured as the new site for the Harris-Tate-Thompson house.

In September 1988, the effort to re-erect the home began. Some referred to the gargantuan effort as "the world's largest jigsaw puzzle." Although the home on its original location in Tuskegee did not sit upon a basement, the elevation of the new site made it possible to rebuild it atop a basement, which would be used for offices and event space. Finally, in May 1991 the Harris-Tate-Thompson house stood precisely as it did in Tuskegee. It was soon opened to house the Montgomery Chamber of Commerce's Visitor Center and the public was allowed to tour the mansion.[3]

Today the Landmarks Foundation leases the house as office space for law firms and other businesses. The Harris-Tate-Thompson house returns to Montgomery some of the antebellum architectural grandeur that once filled the city. However, perhaps more than any other city in Alabama, Montgomery has lost the vast majority of its antebellum mansions to "progress" and development. Sprinkled about the city are a handful of other grand mansions from the period, but the Landmarks Foundation of Montgomery has done more than any other organization to protect the city's early architectural heritage and provide citizens and visitors a glimpse of the stateliness of Montgomery when it served as the capital of the young Confederate nation in 1861.

STURDIVANT HALL

Belle of the Black Belt

♀ Selma, Alabama

W hile truly imposing mansions were built here and there across the South before the War between the States, no southern city of a similar size had as many large-scale, costly mansions as Natchez, Mississippi. Before the war Natchez was the second wealthiest city, per capita, in America—second only to New York City. Natchez's elite citizens built enormous mansions featuring the finest and costliest architectural elements available. Enormous sums were spent by homeowner after homeowner to construct a home that would be more impressive and more lavishly appointed than that of their neighbors. Perhaps no home in Alabama best compares with the imposingly sumptuous mansions of Natchez more completely than Selma's *Sturdivant Hall*.

Selma was and is a town filled with impressive antebellum homes. Selma has its fair share of beautiful historic structures reflecting the significant wealth it once sheltered for cotton barons in surrounding areas. But probably the most imposing, the most impressive, and the most elaborate mansion built in Selma or the Alabama Black Belt in antebellum times is the Watts-Parkman-Gillman house, known today as *Sturdivant Hall*.

Sturdivant Hall was built during the flush times of the early 1850s. The structure was started in 1853 by Col. Edward Watts. Watts was a wealthy planter who commissioned Thomas Helm Lee, a cousin of Robert E. Lee, to build the home. Educated in the ancient classics, Watts may have actually conceptualized the home himself and then engaged Lee to bring his vision into reality. Watts wanted his new mansion to be the finest mansion in the region. It appears that he achieved this goal. He certainly spared no expense, as it cost him the princely sum of $69,000 to construct.[1] By comparison some of the very fine homes built during the same time period cost $15,000 or less.

Watt's mansion home occupied most of a city block. Sprawling around the sizable structure were gardens and broad lawns. Rising from the center of the property is a Greek Revival masterpiece with towering "Tower of the Winds" capped columns supporting a heavy entablature. The home is built of brick on a slightly raised foundation.

Sturdivant Hall presents the most imposing presence of any house in Selma and is befitting of the enormous residences built in Natchez, Mississippi, during the 1850s. (Kitchens)

In the 1930s Sturdivant Hall was starting to suffer from neglect, but the beauty of the juxtaposition of huge columns and lacey iron balconies and verandas is still obvious. (HABS)

Sturdivant Hall's central hallway is tiled in black and white marble that leads to the rear door surrounded by unique door trims. (Kitchens)

The entire exterior is stuccoed in a pleasant gray-blue shade and its decorative wooden trim is painted in medium and dark shades of gray. In sharp contrast to the solidity of the brick walls and columns is a very delicate and highly intricate cast-iron balcony railing extending across most of the second-story façade. The lacy ironwork is echoed in a very small balcony on the right side of the house and a larger one-story cast-iron porch on its left. Crowning the roof's peak is a rather small cupola used to help draw warm air from the home's interior, functioning as a sort of air-conditioning system.

Sturdivant Hall's interior is distinguished by a T-shaped hall, which divides the home down the center from front to back and is intersected by a hall to the left leading to a side door opening to the side porch and gardens. The most elaborately appointed room in the mansion is the drawing room, which measures twenty feet by thirty feet

The interior of Sturdivant Hall is resplendent with architectural decoration such as fluted columns, pilasters flanking each window, and exceptional plaster cornices and moldings. (Photograph in the Carol M. Highsmith Archive, Library of Congress, Prints and Photographs Division)

and contains layers of plaster decorations on the cornices, friezes, and ceiling medallion. The parlor, dining room, and library are also found on the first floor, and they bear some of the same plasterwork found in the drawing room. Inside and out, *Sturdivant Hall* is one of the region's largest and most elaborately decorated residences.

Watts and his family enjoyed their Selma mansion until 1864 when they sold it and moved to Texas. A very youthful John McGee Parkman, then just twenty-six years old, purchased the home. Parkman was a dry goods clerk who found a way to grow his business during the difficult times imposed on Selma during the War between the States when the city was occupied by Union forces. He also found a way to make income as a bookkeeper, bank teller, and cashier. From these endeavors the ambitious Parkman seems to have been able to accumulate sufficient income to purchase *Sturdivant Hall* for $65,000, and then he moved his young wife and their two children into what was perhaps the finest residence in Selma.

Parkman was selected as the president of the First National Bank of Selma in 1866. He took the reins of the bank at just the wrong time. Because the bank had heavily speculated in cotton during the war, and because the price of cotton crashed just after the war, Parkman's bank was financially devastated. Union general Wager Swayne seized an opportunity to take control of the bank and arrested Parkman. The young executive was imprisoned at Cahaba, just south of Selma.

Parkman's arrest and imprisonment outraged the citizens of Selma, who devised a plan to attempt to free him from the oppressive military authorities then exerting

Centered on nearly an entire city block, Sturdivant Hall reigns supreme as Alabama's Black Belt queen. (Kitchens)

authority over the citizenry. A Mardi Gras parade was organized to process down the street in front of the Cahaba prison with the purpose of distracting prison guards so that Parkman would have an opening to escape. The staged Mardi Gras spectacle worked as planned. Guards were distracted, and Parkman was freed from his cell. He successfully escaped to the river. However, Parkman was never seen thereafter. Many have speculated that a prison guard glimpsed him escaping across the river and shot him. Since he never made it back to his family, he was believed to be dead. At the time of his death, he was just twenty-nine years old.[2]

Although Parkman's widow tried to find a way to keep her beautiful home, she soon found it impossible to maintain for very long. Three years after her husband's death, the home was sold at auction for the paltry sum of $12,500.[3] The winning bid belonged to another local banker and businessman, Emile Gillman. Gillman renamed the home *Gillman Hall*. He and his descendants would live there for nearly eighty-seven years.

Although the Gillman family carefully maintained the house for most of the time they owned it, the family seems to have been unable to keep up the house after 1947. When the Gillman descendants sold the home in 1957, it had deteriorated rapidly after a decade of sitting abandoned. During these years of abandonment, vandals had managed to rip out all but a few of the valuable chandeliers. Although vandals caused some damage to the interior of the home, they did not destroy most of its fine architectural features. Fortunately, a group of Selma's concerned citizens banded together to find a way to save this irreplaceable home. It was at this time that Robert Daniel and

Elizabeth Sturdivant donated their collection of antiques to the City of Selma along with a $50,000 endowment to find a proper setting in which to display the collection. Another $25,000 was raised by the City of Selma and Dallas County to purchase the Gillman's mansion in order to secure it to serve as a museum to display the Gillman's exceptional collection of antiques. Once the mansion was secured, it was renamed *Sturdivant Hall* to honor the chief donor who made its purchase possible.

For ten years Selma's citizens assisted in making repairs to the mansion. Once the home was sufficiently restored, it was opened to the public as a historic house museum. Today the mansion is operated by the Sturdivant Hall Museum Association, who raises money through tours, events, and donations to continue the slow process of restoring the mansion.

GEORGIA

The Gordon-Blount house was
moved from Jones County,
Georgia, to its current site south
of Newnan around 1970 and
now sits on a commanding hill
overlooking broad lawns and a
serene lake. It is now known as
Bankshaven. (Kitchens)

BANKSHAVEN
New Setting for a Georgia Architectural Gem

◍ Jones County, moved to Coweta County, Georgia

*B*ankshaven, historically known as the Gordon-Bowen-Blount-Banks house in Haddock, Georgia, is one of the state's most outstanding examples of late-Federal plantation architecture. Its designer and builder was the renowned carpenter-architect Daniel Pratt (1799–1873). Pratt was raised in Temple, New Hampshire, where he apprenticed as a teenager with master carpenter Kimball Putnam. When only twenty-one years old, Pratt borrowed $25.00 from a relative to purchase fare on a ship headed to Savannah, Georgia, from Boston, Massachusetts. The ambitious young Pratt decided to move to the balmy climes of the southern states where Eli Whitney's cotton gin had made it possible for planters to become wealthy on cotton crops and where Pratt hoped to find an anxious clientele needing his considerable carpentry skills to construct the many mansions in which planters clamored to live.[1]

Pratt spent just a year in Savannah before he moved in 1821 to Milledgeville, which was then Georgia's tiny capital city.[2] He understood that families of wealth and importance would be moving to the area even though Milledgeville was just a short distance from territory still owned and occupied by Indians. While in Milledgeville, Pratt was engaged to build at least eight substantial homes for wealthy citizens. Because of Pratt's innate sense of scale, proportion, and craftsmanship, the homes he built became some of the most beautiful and unique residences in the entire state. Included in his resume of Milledgeville-area residences are *Westover*, *Boykin Hall*, *Jackson Hall*, and the Orme-Crawford house in Baldwin County, and *Lowther Hall*, the Pratt-Moughon house, and the Gordon-Bowen-Blount house in Jones County. Only two of these homes remain standing today, but all of them were known to have exhibited a similarly outstanding use of plaster cornices, medallions, and arches, finely carved wood mantels and trim on the interior, and exquisite arched transom lights over the front doors—a feature for which Pratt was well known and greatly admired. These homes are now renowned for these unique characteristics, resulting in what architectural historians

The Gordon-Blount house is seen here as it originally stood on its Jones County, Georgia, site for nearly 150 years. (HABS)

refer to as the "Milledgeville-Federal" style. Many historians believe that Pratt personally executed much of the fine woodwork in the homes he built.

Pratt stayed in the Milledgeville area for only ten years. During this time, the ever industrious Pratt also worked with Samuel Griswold in Jones County, Georgia, in manufacturing cotton gins. Seeing the promise of developing his own manufacturing business to serve planters farther west, Pratt moved to Alabama with enough mechanical parts sufficient to build and sell dozens of new cotton gins. On a site just north of Montgomery, Alabama, Pratt began manufacturing and selling his cotton gins, and by 1860 he became the state's first industrial millionaire. The village that grew up around Pratt's manufacturing facility became known as Prattville. It was there that Pratt built one final house—a home for himself, which in many respects mirrored the homes he designed in middle Georgia.[3]

The spacious home now known as *Bankshaven* was built by Pratt around 1828 on the Jones County plantation of John W. Gordon (1797–1868) near the village known as Haddock. Gordon was a wealthy planter owning thousands of acres surrounding the house. Although his plantation was along a stagecoach road connecting Milledgeville and Macon, it was nonetheless remote. However, the home Pratt built for Gordon was as fine or finer than almost any other home on the Georgia Piedmont at that time. Many architectural historians agree that the house Pratt built for Gordon in Jones County, Georgia, and the house he built at *Westover* plantation in Baldwin County, Georgia, were his masterpieces of residential design and craftsmanship. Pratt's design for Gordon included an enormous fanlight transom spanning the entire length of the double doors and sidelights of the entryway. This fanlight transom is the largest transom Pratt designed on any of his homes. Like most of the other Pratt-designed homes, a proportionately perfect two-story portico supported by two Roman Doric columns projected from the central bay of the façade. Its interior was resplendent with faux

Bankshaven's central hallway and stair hall retain their original 1828 faux marble and faux wood graining on its baseboards, doors, and stairs. (Kitchens)

wood-grained doors and wainscoting; and faux marbleized baseboards and stair risers imitating green and gray marbles. Gilt-covered trim pieces highlight much of the exquisitely crafted woodwork and plasterwork. However, the most impressive feature of *Bankshaven* is the oval staircase rising two and a half stories in a continuous spiral to the attic. On entering the mansion one cannot doubt that they are in the home of an important host.

Gordon enjoyed his plantation residence for nearly twenty years, until he sold it in 1848 and moved to vast property holdings he had acquired in Texas. Gordon sold his home in Jones County to Thomas Bowen. Bowen's family occupied the house for the next three decades, including through the tumultuous period of the War between the States. When Sherman's vast army marched from Atlanta toward Savannah in the infamous March to the Sea, a wing of the army marched through Haddock toward Milledgeville. Bowen's home served briefly as the headquarters for Union general Francis Blair Jr., commander of the Seventeenth Army Corps, a division attached to Maj. Gen. George Stoneman's raiding party. Although Stoneman's troops are known to have destroyed many houses and buildings in the area, they spared Bowen's home, but they did not leave the property unmolested. Local newspapers record that "Stoneman's Raid" destroyed over a half million dollars of property in Jones County alone, especially in Clinton and on nearby plantations, including Bowen's.[4] But, at least Bowen's plantation home survived the war.

Bankshaven's present owner carefully furnished this home with pieces appropriate to its construction date, particularly in the parlor with arched niches and exquisite faux marbled mantel. (Kitchens)

The dining room at Bankshaven displays exceptional original wood paneled wainscoting, doors, and mantel. (Kitchens)

In 1880 the Bowen family sold the house and plantation to Thomas's brother-in-law in Macon, James H. Blount. Blount and his family never made the house their full-time residence. Instead, they used it as a weekend getaway and country retreat where they held lavish picnics and socials. Over the years their use of the home became less and less frequent, until finally the home was left virtually abandoned.[5]

By 1940 the plantation mansion was in serious peril since a lumber company was looking to purchase the property and demolish the dilapidated house. However, a professor from Georgia College in Milledgeville considered this house to be an architectural treasure and purchased the home to save it from destruction. It was Dr. Lindsley who also came to own Pratt's other master work—*Westover*—in Baldwin County. Unfortunately, *Westover* was destroyed by fire while Dr. Lindsley resided there and was attempting to restore it. He never lived in the Gordon-Bowen house, but he kept a good roof over it and provided necessary maintenance. Because the house was vacant most of the time he owned it and had been unoccupied for decades before he purchased the home, it is remarkable that none of the interior wood and plaster trim work, mantels, doors, or other architectural features were molested or destroyed. Locals had long recounted stories of the ghosts of several former slaves haunting the old, abandoned home. These ghost stories probably helped to save this early Georgia gem from wanton vandalism and destruction during its perilous years of vacancy and abandonment.

Professor Lindsley took William N. Banks through the Gordon-Bowen-Blount house in the mid-1960s. Banks simply fell in love with the house. After Professor Lindsley died in 1968, Banks and his mother, Evelyn Wright Banks, convinced Lindsley's heirs to sell the house to them. The Banks family had long owned a particularly beautiful property just south of Newnan, Georgia. William Banks conceived of the bold idea to move Pratt's architectural treasure from Haddock in Jones County, one hundred miles away, to their property in Coweta County. Banks consulted with several experts in early American architecture to devise a plan on the best way to transport the home to its new site without compromising the almost three-story spiral staircase or the irreplaceable plasterwork and carved wood trims in the principal rooms of the house. The Banks family ultimately retained noted preservation architect Robert Raley of Wilmington, Delaware, to execute the move, and then reconstruct the house in its new location.

Raley devised a plan whereby the home was divided into several pieces for moving. Its huge front rooms, which include the parlor, front hall, and dining room, were moved by tractor trailer as a single piece in an effort to preserve and protect the unique and irreplaceable original plaster and wood trim crafted in 1828. Perhaps the most difficult part of the move was the three-story spiral staircase, which was removed from the house as a single unit and transported on its own oversized tractor trailer. Raley masterfully planned the move that resulted in the entire house being transported with virtually no major damage or loss of original decorative features. He then oversaw the reconstruction of the home as *Bankshaven* in its new setting near Newnan. The home stands today in virtually the same condition as it stood in Jones County, with minimal alterations to the main block of the house. Banks engaged Raley to add hyphens and service buildings to each side of the house in an effort to replicate the service buildings that once stood near the home on its original site. However, the exact location and appearance of the original service buildings surrounding Gordon's plantation mansion

Presenting one of the most beautiful residential entrances in Georgia is Bankshaven's fanlight extending over the entire width of the double doors and sidelights and opening into the broad hallway leading to the spiral staircase. (Kitchens)

were unknown since they had long since disappeared. Raley designed service buildings at *Bankshaven* that were architecturally appropriate to the design and setting of Pratt's original structure.

The result of all of this effort is nothing less than breathtaking. Banks placed the structure on a rise overlooking a lake in approximately the same spot where his childhood home had once stood. Between *Bankshaven*'s front door and the lake descends a carefully planned green lawn framed on either side by huge oaks, magnolias, and pines. Surrounding the house are over 170 acres of formal gardens, woods, and meadows that purposefully recall those planned by great English landscape designers such as Capability Brown and Humphrey Repton. Garden rooms coax those strolling the grounds from the azalea garden, into the boxwood garden, into the rose garden, and then to the pool house. Marble fountains, statuary, and ancient trees lend to the property the air of permanence and grace.

Bankshaven proudly stands on Georgia soil today just as it did nearly two hundred years ago. More than once its imminent loss has loomed, only for the historic dwelling to be rescued once again. However, the efforts of Dr. Lindsley and William N. Banks to save the house have been worth their tremendous efforts. This gracious and spectacular architectural treasure remains as one of the last remaining homes built by Daniel Pratt in Georgia and perhaps Georgia's finest remaining example of Milledgeville-Federal–style architecture.

CHIEF VANN HOUSE
Unexpected Relic of Cherokee Heritage

9 Murray County, Georgia

The dwelling at *Spring Place* plantation is not one of the largest or most majestic plantation homes built in early Georgia, but this unique home is one of the most important. This 1804 house is one of the earliest brick residences built in the northern half of Georgia. However, it derives its primary importance from the fact that it was built and lived in by Cherokee chief James Vann. Vann's home was the first brick residence in the vast territories held by the Cherokees, and it became known as the "Showplace of the Cherokee Nation."[1]

By the turn of the nineteenth century, the Cherokee Nation thrived with perhaps the highest level of success and sophistication that it had known up to that point. Unlike many other Native American tribes, the Cherokees adopted some of the cultural characteristics of the Europeans who had been interacting with them for the last two hundred years. Centuries before James Vann's time the Cherokees built wattle-and-daub houses, which they called "asi," or stick-and-mud houses that were roofed with thatch. However, toward the end of the eighteenth century and into the early nineteenth century, some Cherokees adopted European home construction methods using logs or wood framing with clapboards. Chief James Vann took it a step further, building for himself a commodious, two-story brick residence with fine Federal features. Vann's residence was basically an I-house with two rooms on either side of a wide central hall, both upstairs and down. The rooms were unusually spacious, particularly compared to the typical log dwellings in which other Cherokees lived at the time. Its exterior brick walls were eighteen inches thick and its interior walls were eight inches thick. Although early twentieth-century histories about Vann's house suggest that the bricks for the house were carted to north Georgia from Savannah, modern research suggests that the bricks were made on or near Vann's plantation. Indeed, even the nails and hinges for the home were made in Vann's blacksmith shop on the plantation.

James Vann was the product of a Cherokee mother and a European father. Scholars have not reached a consensus as to who his father actually was. What is certain is that from a very early age, he was raised by James Clement. Due either to his ambition or rank, James Vann quickly rose to prominence in the Cherokee Nation. He was well educated and wanted other Cherokees to be educated as well. Vann had invited Moravian missionaries to Spring Place, Georgia, the small village adjoining Vann's planation, to provide a formal education to Cherokee children. Some of these Moravians also may have contributed to the building and design of Vann's house.[2]

Vann situated his house along the new Federal Road being constructed to connect Knoxville, Tennessee, with Savannah, Georgia. Vann is believed to have been one of the Cherokee leaders who negotiated the route for this road and used the negotiation to acquire large acreage on either side of the road at Spring Place, Georgia, which had been named for a large, overflowing spring just downhill from the site of Vann's brick mansion. He also erected on his plantation a tavern, store, and ferry, to serve the many travelers who would be traversing the new road. The income derived from these enterprises, along with his planting interests, helped to make Vann very wealthy. His plantation covered over eight hundred acres that were worked by nearly one hundred slaves. Vann became perhaps the richest man in the Cherokee Nation.[3]

In his later years Chief Vann was known to be a brutal man with a drinking problem. With the slightest of provocation, he was prone to fights, including the beatings

The Chief Vann house parlor much as it looked in the early 1800s and showing the mix of bold colors James Vann used in decorating his home. (Kitchens)

The façade of the Chief Vann house stands resplendent today after significant restoration. (Kitchens)

of his wives and slaves. So perhaps it is not surprising that Vann was murdered in 1809 while at Buffington's Tavern. As Vann stood near an open door in the tavern, a shot rang out from outside the tavern's door. Vann fell dead on the floor with a drink in one hand and a bottle in the other. The assassin was never identified or apprehended.

Rather than follow accepted tribal tradition by leaving his home and plantation to either his eldest or youngest child, he instead left it to his favorite child, Joseph Vann. On inheriting the large brick house, Joseph, who later became known as "Rich Joe," hired John McCartney to make some improvements to the house. McCartney was responsible for adding nearly all of the woodwork now seen on the house, including its Ionic columns on the front portico and the floating staircase in the hall. The home's floating staircase is considered by many to be one of the oldest and best examples of cantilevered construction in Georgia. Between 1809 and 1818 Rich Joe continued to make improvements to the house and to decorate it with features more to his liking. Interior rooms were painted in alternating colors of red, blue, green, and yellow, many times with all four colors dominating the same room. White was used only as a filler color. The effect is surprisingly appealing.[4]

The *Spring Place* plantation that Rich Joe inherited included eight hundred acres surrounding the house, a blacksmith shop, forty-two slave cabins, six barns, five smokehouses, a trading post, more than one thousand peach trees, 147 apple trees, and a liquor still. His newly refurbished home developed a reputation for comfort and

refinement uncommon in that region. In 1819 President James Monroe and three other men were traveling from Augusta, Georgia, to Nashville, Tennessee, along the Federal Road. While passing through Murray County, the men decided to spend the night in the town of Spring Place at the Moravian mission, but President Monroe chose instead to seek lodging at the Vann house nearby, which apparently promised more civilized and comfortable lodging. Rich Joe graciously permitted the president a night's lodging in the western guest bedroom upstairs.

Tensions between Georgia's Native Americans and the state's white citizens intensified in the 1820s and 1830s. Laws were passed that made it a crime for any Indian to hire a white person as an employee without a permit. Rich Joe made the terrible mistake of hiring a white man named Howell to work for Vann at his house without first obtaining the requisite permit to do so. Col. William Bishop, an infamously shady character, seized upon the opportunity as an excuse to dispossess Rich Joe from his house by evicting him. At about the same time, Spencer Riley appeared at *Spring Place* plantation claiming possession of the house after allegedly winning it and its surrounding acreage in the 1832 Land Lottery. Caught in an uncomfortable stalemate, both Colonel Bishop and Mr. Riley occupied the Vann house in a contest of wills to claim ownership of the house. In an effort to drive Riley from the house, Colonel Bishop cast a smoldering log onto the landing of the home's wooden stairway, hoping that the smoke would drive Riley from the residence. The ploy worked. Riley vacated the house, but the smoldering log also caused some smoke damage to the

The front of the Chief Vann house in a severely dilapidated condition in the 1950s. (Image courtesy of the Georgia Department of Natural Resources, Parks and Historic Sites Division)

The rear of the Chief Vann house shows broken windows and woodwork in a badly damaged state prior to restoration. (Image courtesy of the Georgia Department of Natural Resources, Parks and Historic Sites Division)

interior of the house and burns to the staircase—a scar that remains visible to visitors today. However, Rich Joe would not cede possession of the house without a fight. Instead, he used Georgia's courts to sue to recover the house. Rather than regaining the house, however, he was awarded monetary damages of $19,605, a sum far less than the house and valuable acreage was worth. Just a few years later, Rich Joe was among the Cherokees driven from Georgia to Oklahoma along the infamous Trail of Tears. He and his family never returned to Georgia.[5]

Over the next ninety years, seventeen different owners occupied this home. Then, in 1920 Dr. J. E. Bradford purchased the dwelling, but over the three decades he owned it, he failed to care for and maintain the historic home. By 1952 when Bradford sold the house to the Georgia Historical Commission, it was in terrible condition. The structure's roof was missing and the elements were destroying its interior.[6] The home was nearly lost for good.

But the Georgia Historical Commission mounted an effort to save this important relic of Georgia's past. After developing a plan and raising the funds to restore the house, the commission embarked on an extensive restoration project in 1958. For six years the commission worked to replace the roof, secure the walls, and restore as many of the original interior elements as possible. Wood was repainted according to its original coloring and the house was eventually saved.[7] Today, the Vann house is administered as a historic tour house and museum by the Parks, Recreation and Historic Sites Division of the Georgia Department of Natural Resources. It is one of the state's most historic and unusual early residential structures telling the fascinating story of Georgia's native inhabitants and earliest settlers.

THOMAS R. R. COBB HOUSE
The Road to Preservation

♀ Athens, Georgia

The *Thomas R. R. Cobb House* stands today less than 200 yards from the spot on which it was originally built. However, the home traveled over 110 miles to get there, making it perhaps the most well-traveled historic home in Georgia. The lengths undertaken by those most interested in its preservation is a testament to the unique importance of the house.

The origins of the house now known as the *T. R. R. Cobb House* are still somewhat murky. No records have been discovered to provide the precise date of its original construction, but it was probably built in the mid-1830s. At that time the home and its surrounding acreage along the Federal Road (now known as Prince Avenue) in Athens, Georgia, was owned by Charles Goodloe McKinley. McKinley built a simple four-over-four plantation-plain–style home lacking in significant architectural adornments. He then sold the house and eighteen surrounding acres in 1842 to Joseph Henry Lumpkin.[1]

Lumpkin was one of Georgia's most prominent lawyers, the first chief justice of the Georgia Supreme Court, and a founder of the Law School at the University of Georgia. Rather than taking up residence in the home that McKinley erected, Lumpkin built a large, column-bedecked Greek Revival mansion on his new property, just yards from McKinley's earlier house. Long a landmark in Athens, Lumpkin's impressive, classically styled mansion still stands along Athens's Prince Avenue. A few years after the completion of his new home, Lumpkin made the older McKinley house a wedding gift to his daughter, Marion, and her new husband, Thomas Reade Rootes Cobb, in 1844.

The substantial but rather plain house that Tom and Marion Cobb were given in 1844 would not remain ordinary. With their family expanding and Cobb's standing in Athens growing, Tom and Marion undertook two rather substantial projects to enlarge the house. Around 1847 they enlarged the house by adding rooms to the back of the residence, including a large dining room, and moving the interior staircase into its own side hall next to the dining room. Then, in 1852 the Cobbs added to the grandeur of the house by building distinctive two-story octagonal rooms on either side of the front

of the structure and a monumental Greek Revival portico between the two octagons. The later addition included massive Doric columns and a second-story balcony embellished with intricate cast-iron railings. A large entablature running across the entire front of the new addition brought the whole into a cohesive unit. The Cobb's newly modified home made it one of the most unusual and appealing homes in a town filled with classical mansions.

Tom Cobb was a brilliant lawyer whose family would become nationally renowned in the two decades leading to the War between the States. His older brother, Howell Cobb, who was also an Athens resident, living just two blocks down the street, was elected to the United States House of Representatives for five terms and presided over that body as the Speaker of the House from 1849 to 1851. He later served in such high offices as secretary of the treasury of the United States under President Buchanan, governor of Georgia, founder of the Confederate States of America, and president of the Provisional Congress of the Confederate States of America.

Tom Cobb did not linger in his brother's shadow. Tom attended the University of Georgia, graduated number one in his class in 1841, and then was admitted to the Georgia bar a year later, at the tender age of nineteen. Cobb authored several legal treatise, but history remembers Tom Cobb best for authoring the Constitution of the

Confederate States of America in 1861.[2] This landmark document, which spans more than twelve feet long when unrolled, now resides in the Hargrett Rare Book and Manuscript Library at the University of Georgia and is proudly displayed to the public each year on April 26, Confederate Memorial Day.

Tom Cobb tirelessly advocated for the education of children. He was the primary force behind establishing a school in 1857 to educate the state's young ladies. The school took on the name "Lucy Cobb Institute," being named after Cobb's fourteen-year-old daughter who died of scarlet fever just before the institution was established. Within a very short time after it opened in 1859, the Lucy Cobb Institute came to be known as one of the finest girls' schools in the state.[3]

At about the time that the Lucy Cobb Institute accepted its first students, Tom Cobb joined with his father-in-law, Joseph Henry Lumpkin, and William Hope Hull to establish Lumpkin Law School at the University of Georgia in 1859. Some of the Law School's first classes were conducted in the library of Tom Cobb's house on Prince Avenue. Because Cobb had one of the most extensive law libraries in Athens, he opened his home library to law students for research and study. Even in years after Tom Cobb's death in 1862, his wife, Marion Lumpkin Cobb, continued to welcome students into her home for legal research.[4]

Tom Cobb was an ardent southern nationalist who would not sit idly by as the North and South rapidly diverged on the issues of states' rights and slavery. When Georgia voted to secede from the Union in 1861, Cobb accepted the mantle of leadership by serving in the Confederate States Congress where he was assigned to committees responsible for handling military affairs and for drafting a constitution for the new Confederate nation. Cobb bears chief responsibility for drafting that constitution.

In the late summer of 1861, Tom Cobb organized a large fighting force for the Confederate army. This force included six hundred foot soldiers comprising seven infantry companies, four cavalry companies, three hundred horses, and one hundred pieces of artillery. The unit became known as Cobb's Legion, with Cobb serving as its colonel. Assigned to the Army of Northern Virginia, the Legion became known across the South for its bravery in battles, such as Lee's campaign into Maryland, the Battle of Sharpsburg, the Seven Days' Battle, and the Battle of Fredericksburg. In November 1862, Cobb was commissioned as a brigadier general, but the commission was not confirmed by the Confederate Congress before he was killed at Fredericksburg while commanding his Legion in defending the now infamous Sunken Road. He suffered a mortal wound in the thigh inflicted by a Union artillery shell. Cobb died on December 13, 1862.

Marion Cobb continued to live in the *Cobb House* for almost a dozen years after her husband's death. She finally sold the house in 1873 to railroad builder Robert Bloomfield. Its demise began in 1913 when the house was moved to the back of its lot so that the church next door could build a larger edifice. For the next fifty years, the *Cobb House* suffered a series of abuses as it leased to renters, twice served as a fraternity house, and then was used as a boardinghouse. The historic residence was rescued from the abuse it suffered from transient occupants when, in 1962, the archdiocese of Atlanta purchased the house to serve as the rectory for adjacent St. Joseph's Catholic Church.

St. Joseph's Church operated a parochial school on the premises. As the school expanded, the church needed to build onto the school and create room for more

The Cobb House just after it had been transported from Stone Mountain Park near Atlanta and was reconstructed on its present site on Hill Street in Athens. (Kitchens)

Oblique view of the Cobb House provides a sense of the size and scale of the huge octagonal wings projecting off of the front of the original 1830s structure. (Kitchens)

parking. As a result, the church decided that the lot that the *Cobb House* occupied was the only place to make these "improvements." The church offered the historic *Cobb House* for sale in 1984 for just one dollar if the purchaser would remove the house from the site. Although Athens historians and preservationists tried to save the house, no relocation plan could be developed and financed. In 1985, the Stone Mountain Memorial Association bought the house and relocated it to Stone Mountain Memorial Park east of Atlanta. Stone Mountain Park features an exhibit called the Historic Square, which features a collection of historic Georgia homes that have been moved to the park for display to the public. To move the *Cobb House*, the home's interior was stripped of its plaster and decorative details. Then the structure was cut into six segments and transported fifty-seven miles to Stone Mountain Park where it was reassembled and

The Cobb mansion's octagonal parlor on the first floor is one of the few rooms of this shape in antebellum Georgia. (Kitchens)

then virtually abandoned. The association intended to refurbish the large house, but funding for the project never materialized. For nearly twenty years the house sat forlorn in a location and surroundings entirely foreign to its historic setting, while insects, water, and the elements worked furiously to devour it.[5]

Fortunately, Stone Mountain Park would not be the final resting place for the home. In 2003 a foundation was established to bring the proud structure home to Athens. The Watson-Brown Foundation, the Georgia Trust for Historic Preservation, and the Athens-Clarke Heritage Foundation partnered to find a lot on which to return the house. They required a location as close to its original site and setting as possible. An acre-sized property on Athens's Hill Street was secured just a stone's throw from Prince Avenue and just a few hundred yards from the original site of the *Cobb House*.

With a new, more appropriate site secured for the house, work began at Stone Mountain Park to again divide the enormous house into parts and transport it fifty-seven miles back to Prince Avenue in Athens. This time the house would be restored to a condition as close to its 1852–1862 appearance as possible. Reconstruction of the house in Athens began in 2004 and was completed by 2006. Though as originally constructed it did not sit upon a basement, a basement was placed under the reconstructed house in order to give it the same sight lines—in terms of height and appearance from the street—as the original house had once enjoyed. Today, the basement rooms are used for a variety of functions, such as storage, office space, and event space.[6]

In 2005 the Watson-Brown Foundation commissioned a microscopial paint and color analysis to determine precisely what sort of circa 1850 colors and finishes the Cobbs used for their home. The results shocked many when it revealed that the 1850s color of the exterior was a pink shade, described as "a moderate yellowish pink," with white trim and green shutters. As a result the reconstructed appearance of the home once again displays pink painted clapboards with stark-white trim.[7]

Today, the Watson-Brown Foundation operates Cobb's former dwelling as a house museum that is opened for tours most days each week. The home is also frequently used by local organizations for events, celebrations, gatherings, and meetings. The road to preservation was a long one, but the *Cobb House* has found its home where it is revered as an object of beauty and a relic of historical significance.

Cobb's library occupied the left octagonal room on the first floor. This room was once filled with a large collection of books and legal treatise. (Kitchens)

GREEN-MELDRIM HOUSE
Gothic Revival Masterpiece

♥ Savannah, Georgia

Savannah is a city filled with imposing houses from its colonial and antebellum history. Tourists from around the globe flock to Savannah by the tens of thousands each year to take in its rich history and southern charm. Many of these visitors take the time to visit at least a few of Savannah's historic mansions in order to gain a sense of the city's richly diverse architectural history. But even in a city laden with architectural treasures, the *Green-Meldrim house* stands out. It is considered by many to be the finest surviving example of Gothic Revival architecture in the entire South. This structure's importance is highlighted by its designation in 1976 as a National Historic Landmark property of national importance in representing the country's heritage.

The *Green-Meldrim house* was designed by noted architect John Norris, who designed several of Savannah's iconic structures, such as the Savannah Customs House, Andrew Low house, and the Mercer Wilder house. Charles Green, an extremely wealthy cotton merchant and shipping factor, commissioned Norris to design for him a Savannah residence befitting his economic success while still tending to his family's desire for comfort. Construction began in 1850 but the home was not completed until 1854.

Charles Green had moved to Savannah from England in 1833 with little more than the belongings in his travel cases. However, through his keen business sense and hard work, he amassed a fortune by 1850, which enabled him to build a unique mansion that in every room would display his financial wherewithal. The resulting red-stone Gothic town house cost the enormous sum of $93,000 to build, and it is believed to be the most expensive residence built in Savannah during all of the nineteenth century.[1]

Once completed, Green's mansion became one of Savannah's showplaces. It was fitted with a number of features, which, if not entirely unique to Green's home, were highly unusual. The front entrance had three sets of doors: an outer set, which would fold into small closets on either side of the entrance; a set of glass panel doors, which allowed a flood of light into the hallway; and a set of louvered doors that allowed for ventilation on hot days. It was also equipped with interior bathrooms featuring

Late 1800s image of the Green-Meldrim house as it originally appeared with a roadway immediately in front of the home. (Image courtesy of the Wardens and Vestry of St. John's Church, Savannah)

Close-up view of the front of the Green-Meldrim house shows its heavy Gothic elements and trim. (Kitchens)

The Green-Meldrim house parlor has layer upon layer of Gothic plaster cornices, niches, and pocket doors opening onto the second parlor. (HABS)

running water at a time when most homes had no interior bathroom and water was carried from a well to the house by bucket. Green's mansion also had a dome capping the wide staircase rising to the upper floors. The dome was built such that during sweltering summer days it could be raised slightly to create a chimney effect, pulling warm air out of the house and creating air circulation that cooled the house considerably. Along the circumference of the base of the dome were dozens of small gas tubes that could be lighted both to provide light to the dome at night and to provide additional updraft to pull warm air out of the house. Finally, Green's home was ornamented with some of the most intricate and extensive plasterwork decoration in the entire city. Gothic plaster cornices, friezes, moldings, and medallions of the parlor are layered in high-relief giving the parlor walls more the look of lacework than of plaster. Green's new mansion was described in 1861 by one Savannah visitor as follows:

> the wealthier classes, however have houses of New York Fifth Ave. character: one of the best of these, a handsome mansion of rich red sandstone belonged to my host, who coming out from England many years ago, raised himself by industry and intelligence to the position of one of the first merchants in [Savannah]. Italian statuary graced the hall; finely carved tables and furniture, stained glass, and pictures from Europe set forth the sitting-rooms; and the luxury of bathrooms and a supply of cold fresh water, rendered it an exception to the general run of Southern edifices.[2]

This 1930s HABS image shows the second parlor mantelpiece and gilt mirror, which hint at the resplendence of the room in antebellum days. (HABS)

All of this comfort and resplendence was too much of a temptation for at least one war-hardened general to pass up. In late 1864, Savannah had been relatively unscathed by the War between the States. However, on November 15, 1864, Gen. William Tecumseh Sherman started the march of his vast army from Atlanta to Savannah, wantonly burning homes and destroying property for over two hundred miles along his path. As he approached Savannah just prior to Christmas with only slight resistance from Confederate troops and militia groups, it became apparent that he would take the city. The ever-savvy Charles Green rode out to visit with General Sherman in an effort to protect his Savannah home and his cotton stores from destruction. Green reminded General Sherman of his English citizenship and neutral position in the present conflict and then invited General Sherman to his Savannah home during his stay there. General Sherman later recounted this exchange as follows:

> While waiting there, an English gentleman, Mr. Charles Green, came and said that he had a fine house completely furnished, for which he had no use, and offered it as headquarters. He explained, moreover, that Genl Howard had informed him, the day before, that I would want his house for headquarters. At first [was] strongly disinclined to make use of any private dwelling, lest complaints should arise of damage and loss of furniture, and so expressed myself to Mr. Green; but, after riding about the city, and finding his house so spacious, so convenient, with large yard and stabling, I accepted his offer, and occupied that house during our stay in Savannah. He only reserved for himself the use of a couple of rooms above the dining room, and we had all else, and a most excellent house it was in all respects.[3]

Almost immediately after occupying the house, Sherman penned his now famous note to President Abraham Lincoln, boasting, "I beg to present to you as a Christmas gift the City of Savannah, with one hundred and fifty heavy guns and plenty of

ammunition, also about twenty-five thousand bales of cotton."[4] Sherman and his army occupied Savannah for slightly more than a month. Unlike other parts of Georgia, Savannah was not significantly damaged and the *Green-Meldrim house* survived the general's residency there, suffering no significant harm.

Once Sherman vacated Savannah, Green's home was returned to him. He continued to reside there until his death in 1881. Green's son, Edward Moon Green, then inherited the house and made it his home until he sold it in 1892 to Judge Peter Wiltberger Meldrim. Meldrim was a Savannah lawyer who was raised in Savannah by his merchant father. He attended Chatham Academy as a young boy, but his father hired private tutors to bolster his education before Peter entered college at the University of Georgia. Meldrim earned a literary degree in 1868 and his law degree in 1869, and then returned to Savannah to begin a law practice. After experiencing professional and financial success, in 1881 he married Frances P. Casey and the couple soon started a family. Within a few years of moving into Charles Green's mansion, the Meldrims had five children to fill its commodious halls. The Meldrim family occupied the house until 1943 when St. John's Church, standing across the street, purchased the mansion for use as their parish house.

To make the house more useful for their purposes, the church converted the buildings formerly serving as the mansion's kitchen, servant's quarters, and stables to suit their need for a church rectory. St. John's Church undertook a complete renovation in 1968, helping to preserve the house for generations to come. It is now used as meeting space for St. John's Church groups, and it is also opened to the public as a museum house.

The Hay House rises five stories
above a high basement and
stands as one of the most
beautiful homes in the South.
(Kitchens)

HAY HOUSE
The Palace of the South

♀ Macon, Georgia

W illiam Butler Johnston (1809–1887) grew up on a small family farm in Putnam County, Georgia, where he learned the value of hard work. When he turned twenty-one years old, he made up his mind that farming was not the life for him. Blessed with substantial mechanical talents, William secured a one-year apprenticeship with the prominent New York jeweler Benedict & Company, where he learned the art and practice of jewelry making. When the apprenticeship ended in 1831, Johnston moved to Macon and opened a jewelry store with his younger brother, Edmund. It took only six years until Johnston's store became the largest jeweler between Charleston and New Orleans.[1]

As Johnston's success as a jeweler expanded, so did his interests in other business concerns. Between the mid-1830s and the early 1850s he became a private banker, an investor in railroads and public utilities, and an organizer of insurance companies. His diverse business dealings, sound business judgment, and wise investments resulted in Johnston being counted among the wealthiest citizens in Macon by 1850.[2]

Around 1850 William met Anne Tracy, who was the daughter of Edward and Susan Campbell Tracy—a prominent Macon family. The Tracy family's high social status and influence would have placed them in the same social and business circles as William Johnston. Indeed, although William was twenty years Anne's senior, the two met, formed a bond, and then married in 1851. Shortly after their nuptials the couple left for an extended honeymoon, making the Grand Tour across Europe, and spending months in Italy alone. When they returned to Macon nearly three years later, they seized upon plans to build a mansion inspired by the architecture that they had so admired in Italy.[3] William ventured to New York City in 1855 to retain Thomas Thomas to design a home that would be one of America's most comfortable and impressive mansions. By the early 1850s, T. Thomas & Son had become one of New York's most successful architectural firms, designing such noted New York landmarks as the Astor Library, the Chemical Bank Building, the Broadway Bank Building, and the Lord &

For the last 150 years, the Hay House has dominated the hill overlooking downtown Macon. (HABS)

Taylor Store.[4] The home that Thomas designed for the Johnstons would live up to, and perhaps add, to the firm's national reputation.

Thomas designed an imposing twenty-four-room, five-story Renaissance Revival residence. The home was the pinnacle of antebellum residential comfort employing a 20,000-gallon tank hidden in the attic that provided both hot and cold running water to indoor bathrooms (an unusual feature in and of itself), the kitchen, and food preparation rooms; walk-in closets in the bedrooms; a speaker tube system to fifteen rooms to enable communication between floors; a huge in-basement kitchen; dumbwaiters to quickly deliver food from the basement kitchen to the main dining room above; a coal elevator to rapidly transport coal to upstairs fireplaces without significant manual effort; a central heating system; and an elaborate ventilation system providing "air conditioning" during Georgia's hot summer days.[5] Few other Georgia houses of the period could boast of even one of these features; Johnston's mansion is possibly the only house in Georgia from the antebellum period to employ all of them.

State-of-the-art air and water systems, however, were not the only design elements that set Johnston's home apart from other Georgia mansion houses. Most of the imposing residences in Macon at that time were built of wood in the ever-popular Greek Revival style. Many of these homes were substantial residences of two and sometimes even three stories containing as many as twelve to fifteen large rooms. Johnston's house was designed as a brick-and-stone residence with twenty-four main rooms and a number of additional ancillary and service rooms, all towering five stories above an exceptionally high basement level. As originally built, the home's brick exterior was stuccoed and then scored to resemble stone blocks, but this exterior treatment was removed by later generations. Once completed, Johnston's in-town residence was perhaps the most imposing dwelling in all of Georgia.

Enormous pocket doors trimmed in three woods and etched glass separate the double parlors from the gallery. (Kitchens)

While the mansion was under construction, the Johnstons resided on the property in a building designed to be the servants' quarters. Due to the sheer size and complexity of the mansion's design, it took five years to complete. Upon completion in 1860, the 18,000-square-foot house reportedly cost the kingly sum of $100,000 to build at a time when even the largest homes of the Johnstons' contemporaries cost between $10,000 and $15,000 to complete. This sum does not include the costs of much of the home's furnishings, which were still being acquired in 1861 when the War between the States broke out. The mansion would not be fully furnished until just after the war.

With or without furniture, Johnston's home was every bit as impressive as he intended. To enter the home, one walks up twelve curved marble steps embraced on either side by massive marble newel posts and balustrades to a Corinthian-columned portico. The floor of the portico is centered by a glass slab that permits light to flood into the wine cellar just beneath the portico. One enters the mansion's main floor through enormous paired doors, each leaf of which is solid walnut several-inches-thick, and weighing five hundred pounds. In the middle of each door leaf is a carved lion's head in high relief, with the wood of the entire door painted to convincingly resemble bronze. The top third of each door leaf is an etched-glass panel through which natural light fills the central hallway.

On either side of the main block of the house are wings standing one story over a high raised basement. Each wing contains a single, expansive room capped by glass monitored roofs. The east wing is home to the dining room, which is trimmed in

Imposing front doors of the Hay House are several inches of solid wood rising twelve feet tall and finished to appear as solid bronze. Each door weighs five hundred pounds, but they open with very slight effort. (Kitchens)

The dining room at the Hay House impresses with barrel vaulted ceiling and carved wood decoration wherever the eye is cast. (Kitchens)

heavily carved solid-walnut paneling and decorative trim work. Its ceiling is nearly thirty feet high, barrel vaulted, and covered in recessed oak paneling. In the ceiling's central panel is a skylight from which a massive chandelier hangs just above the dining room table. Diners were seated at a long dining table and matching chairs, which were smuggled through the Union blockade and into Macon during the war. With the table fully extended the Johnstons could easily seat over thirty guests for dinner. However, the dining room's most notable feature is a stunning Tiffany's stained-glass window depicting a grape vine cascading from the top of the arched window.[6] This unique feature is not original to the house, but was added by later generations.

The west wing served at various times as art gallery and ballroom. It is a single room spanning fifty feet long and thirty feet high. As in the dining room, centered in the ceiling is a skylight from which a pair of enormous Waterford crystal chandeliers dangle. Along its walls are large, arched windows heavily trimmed with carved wood, stained or painted in contrasting light and dark colors simulating graining of expensive and exotic woods. One enters the room through curved, solid-wood doors that disappear as they slide into pockets in the wall. This room is perhaps the grandest and most beautiful room known in antebellum Georgia.

In the main block of the home, the long central hall separates a library and music room on one side and double parlors on the other. The double parlors are noted for their complicated plaster friezes, cornices, and ceiling details executed by stuccadors

which the Johnstons brought from Italy specifically to work on their home. In addition to an enormous basement with summer dining room, kitchen, storage rooms, and numerous utility rooms, the main block of the house has two levels above the main level with bedrooms for family and guests.

The double parlors in the Hay House are laden with architectural details with ceiling medallions and panels, plaster cornice trim, marble mantels, and a window framed by an arched niche. (Kitchens)

To top off all of this glorious resplendence, Johnston's new home had a two-level cupola, or "lantern" crowning its main block. The lantern is octagonal and has its own small balcony. From the lantern one has unparalleled vistas overlooking downtown Macon below and the Ocmulgee River beyond.

William Johnston survived the war with much of his wealth intact. New ownership of his residence did not occur until 1886 when William died and left the house to his daughter, Mary Ellen, and her husband, William H. Felton. William Felton gained prominence in Macon as a judge and legislator. The Feltons occupied and lovingly cared for the house for nearly four decades. Unfortunately, for a long period during the last years of their lives, the Feltons suffered from poor health and were unable to maintain the mansion house properly. It had begun to fall into decay.

Felton family members put Johnston's palace up for sale after William and Mary Ellen passed away in 1925. Prospects for a buyer looked grim. Who could afford to purchase and to maintain such a huge house? Luckily, P. L. Hay, who possessed a substantial fortune through his work with the Bankers Health and Life Insurance Company, purchased the house on a whim. He had not been looking to buy a new house, but once he saw Johnston's mansion, he bought it on the spot. The home was a complete

Perhaps the most awe-inspiring room at the Hay House is its art gallery, which may be the largest room in any antebellum house in Georgia. (Kitchens)

surprise to his wife. The Hays found the house the perfect residence to display their substantial art collections. They undertook an extensive remodeling to modernize the mansion to tastes popular in the late 1920s. They, too, kept the residence in good condition for the next thirty or more years while they occupied it. P. L. Hay died in 1957 and his wife followed him in 1962.[7]

After the Hays died, the fate of the *Hay House* once again became uncertain. During the decade of the 1960s many of Macon's largest and most historic houses, as well as those in countless other southern cities, were being torn down or adapted to other uses, making them unrecognizable. The Hay descendants wanted to avoid having their parents' much-beloved home suffer the same fate, but they could no longer afford to maintain such a huge home on their own. One attempted solution for the family was to open the grand house as a public museum. Though this worked for a while, the income generated was insufficient to maintain the structure.

Finally, in the mid-1970s the burden that the house placed on the family became too great. Their solution to the problem was to convey the house to the Georgia Trust for Historic Preservation along with a small endowment. Since that time, the Georgia Trust has worked steadily to restore the house to its original grandeur.[8] In recent years, the home has been opened for tours, weddings, events, conferences, and even as a movie set. Thanks to the Georgia Trust's efforts, the *Hay House* remains "The Palace of the South," preserved for generations yet to come to study, visit, enjoy, and marvel at its overpowering scale and beauty.

Majestic Lockerly, formerly
known as Rose Hill, stands as
an idealic plantation mansion
commanding a sunny hillside
near Milledgeville. (Kitchens)

LOCKERLY (ROSE HILL)
The Southern Plantation Beau Ideal

♦ Baldwin County, Georgia

The beauty and grandeur of the southern plantation mansion still captivates the imagination of our nation. Impressive southern mansions from Louisiana to Virginia draw visitors from around the globe; visitors anxious to see if all that they have read in novels and seen in movies about the antebellum South is true. What visitors often do not realize until they travel the South is that there was an amazing variety of architectural styles employed in these residences and that these mansions were built with widely divergent sizes and skill sets. However, if any mansion home in the South encapsulates the *beau ideal* of a planter's home that springs to the average person's mind, then it is certainly *Lockerly*, originally known as *Rose Hill*, outside of Milledgeville, Georgia.

Lockerly is built upon the crest of a hill amid an English park-like setting dotted with ancient trees, flowering vines, and fragrant ornamental shrubs. Adding to its commanding presence is the fact that the home towers two stories over an unusually high basement. All of its thick walls are constructed of brick, which was handmade by slaves on or near the property. The façade is dominated by six fluted, Doric columns towering more than twenty-five feet to support a heavy entablature and cornice. The home as it appears today is returned to its original exterior appearance in which the stucco was scored to resemble large blocks of stone. The overall semblance is unmistakably that of an ancient Greek temple, perfect in its proportionality, giving it the appearance of ancient sturdiness while not being overbearing. *Lockerly* is inarguably one of Georgia's greatest architectural treasures remaining from the state's antebellum period.

Georgia established its capital in the frontier town of Milledgeville in 1804. Within a few years, construction commenced on a new Federal-style capitol building. Important and well-heeled citizens began to move from more established cities, such as Savannah and Augusta, to the tiny settlement at Milledgeville to seize upon fresh new lands in the fertile piedmont region surrounding the town and to live closer to the fast-growing state's seat of power. Just a few miles south of Milledgeville, in what could only

View looking from the back
parlor through the pocket doors
into the front parlor at Lockerly.
(Kitchens)

loosely be described as the "town" of Midway (now known as Hardwick), the Presby-
terian Church chartered Oglethorpe University, one of the South's first denominational
colleges, in 1834. The new university constructed several substantial buildings at Midway,
and the college served as one of the preeminent institutions of higher learning in Georgia
during the antebellum period. Set amid lush rolling hills along the banks of the Oconee
River, Midway became a popular location for wealthy and influential families to settle.

One of the early residents of Midway was Richard J. Nichols, who was a prominent
merchant and landowner. Nichols acquired the property now known as *Lockerly* and
in 1839 erected a fine house, which he named *Rose Hill* due to the abundance of Cherokee roses naturally growing on the site. Nichols died in 1849 and his estate placed the
property on the market. *Rose Hill* was purchased by Daniel R. Tucker in 1851.

Daniel R. Tucker was a planter with large acreage in other parts of Baldwin County,
in neighboring Washington County, and in nearby Wilkinson County. He married
Martha Goode, the daughter of Judge Mackiness Goode, and the couple had nine
children. However, just a month after Tucker purchased *Rose Hill*, the home burned to
the ground.[1]

In 1852 Tucker immediately undertook construction of an imposing mansion, built
almost entirely of brick, on the same spot where the original *Rose Hill* had stood. The
resulting structure is the residence we know today as *Lockerly*. His new dwelling was
possibly the most imposing residence in all of the Midway area. One Daniel Tucker
biographer describes his new mansion:

The formal dining room at Lockerly maintains its faux marble baseboards and the beautiful wood panels beneath the huge windows. (Kitchens)

Tucker would build *Rose Hill* amongst a grove of trees and it would grow to be considered by many a perfect example of a plantation home. . . . Daniel Tucker and his wife Martha utilized their fine home to show off to others in the Baldwin County elite, and it would play host to many fine parties that would be talked about by locals for years to come. The most prestigious party to grace the halls of *Rose Hill* was that of the 1853 Inaugural Ball for Governor Hershel V. Johnson, a social event that would surely influence the public's opinion of Daniel Tucker, and only add to Tucker's prestigious reputation.[2]

Although Tucker was a planter with large acreage and numerous slaves, and despite the fact that *Rose Hill* was his primary residence, the land around *Rose Hill* was not cultivated for cash crops. It seems that his planting interests lay across the Oconee River in Baldwin County's Salem District where he probably cultivated cotton. As a consequence, the acreage around his home at *Rose Hill* was used to grow plants used in its kitchens, and for formal and pleasure gardens. In addition to being a planter, Tucker skillfully diversified his financial interests by investing in stocks and bonds in railroads and industrial companies across the South. His business acumen is evidenced by the fact that he owned assets in 1842 comprised of 846 acres in Wilkinson and Baldwin Counties along with fifty-one slaves, but just eight years later, Tucker claimed real estate holdings valued at $521,000 and personal property valued at $95,000.[3] Such holdings counted him as among the wealthiest citizens of an already affluent Baldwin County. This sort of wealth enabled Tucker to furnish his home with the finest furniture and artwork available. It also allowed him to undertake the costs to retain artisans to faux marbleize baseboards, stairway risers, and stair profiles. Interior doors in the mansion are fashioned from solid walnut.[4]

Even after the devastation the War between the States brought to Milledgeville, Tucker was able to retain his *Rose Hill* property along with about one thousand acres in other counties. When Tucker died in 1879, he still owned the ninety acres of land on which his home stood and a half interest in over thirteen thousand acres in Washington County. *Rose Hill* then passed to his daughter, Emma Tucker, who married George R. Sibley. The Sibleys took ownership of *Rose Hill* in 1881, but sold it just two years later to Dr. T. O. Powell, who was then the superintendent of the state mental hospital located just a mile from *Rose Hill*.

In 1886 Dr. Powell sold the house and its surrounding acreage to Baldwin County native George Wiggins Hollinshead. It remained in his care for nearly four decades until it was sold in 1928 to Reginald W. Hatcher. The Hatcher family, who renamed the place *Lockerley,* after the family's ancestral estate in Hampshire, England, took great care to renovate the house and to restore the site's gardens after they had fallen into disrepair in the decades following the war.

Lockerley was well maintained by the Hatchers. But, as the couple aged and as Milledgeville once again experienced commercial growth, the land on which *Lockerley* was built became desirable to developers as a potential site for a shopping center. Its location along US Highway 441 and near the proposed path of a newly planned bypass highway around Milledgeville made it a desirable site for development.

Lockerley's fate grew more and more uncertain until it was finally purchased, and likely saved, in 1963 by E. J. Grassman from Elizabeth, New Jersey. Grassman slightly modified the name of the estate to *Lockerly* in 1965. The grounds surrounding the mansion house had dwindled by that time to just twenty-six acres, but it was enough for Grassman to establish the Lockerly Arboretum Foundation. He used the antebellum residence as a guest house for employees and guests of his corporate interest, the American Industrial Clay Company. He expanded and improved upon the arboretum behind the mansion, which he intended to open to the public.

In 1998 *Lockerly* finally was opened to the public as a house museum. Preservation and care for the mansion continues to be a pressing objective for the *Lockerly* board of trustees, which now oversees the use of the house. In 2005 the trustees adopted a new master plan to guide the further preservation of the site and to direct its future development.[5] *Lockerly*, in combination with other nearby antebellum house museums such as the exquisitely restored Old Governor's Mansion Museum and the Brown-Stetson-Sanford house museum, makes Milledgeville one of Georgia's best cities to visit to gain a sense of the state's historic past.

Lockerly as it appears today as
an arboretum and tour home.
(Kitchens)

VIRGINIA

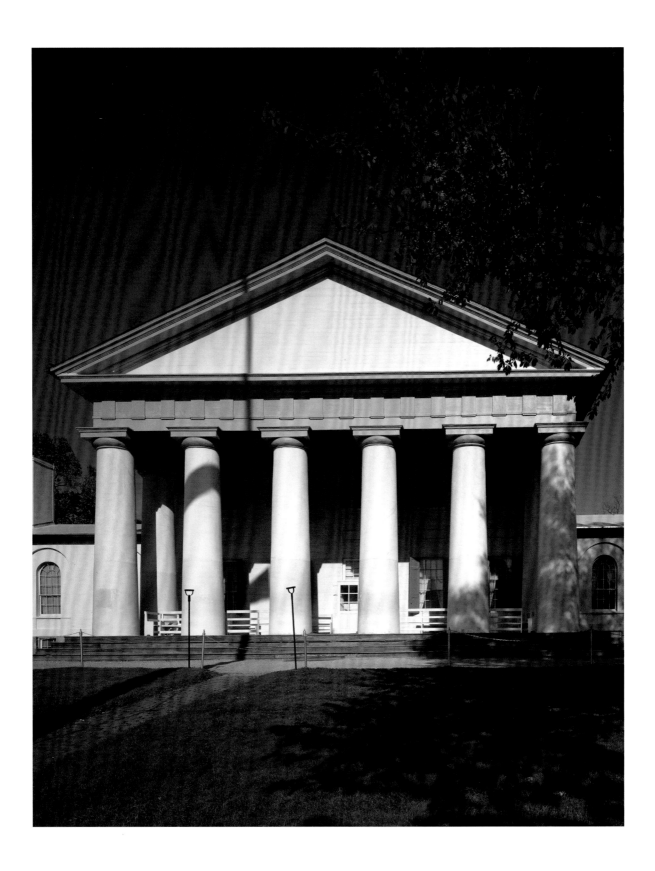

ARLINGTON HOUSE
A Monument to Washington and Lee

♦ Arlington, Virginia

O n the afternoon of April 19, 1861, Robert E. Lee walked beneath the monumental portico at *Arlington House*, his mansion perched on a high bluff along the Potomac River in northern Virginia, and went for a quiet walk in his garden. The weather was fair and the scene peaceful as the aging military leader strolled through his rose bushes, stopping to survey the rooftops and steeples of Washington, DC, in the distance.

Although the setting was serene, Lee's mood was dark and foreboding. Just hours before he had been asked by President Abraham Lincoln to take command of federal troops against the newly formed Army of the Confederate States of America. Lee had declined Lincoln's offer. He knew his decision would forever change his life and alter the course of his family's existence on their ancestral plantation. While Lee had devoted his entire career to the United States military and felt great loyalty to the Union, he could take no part in leading troops against his native state of Virginia or her southern neighbors.

Mrs. Lee later wrote in her diary that after her husband had completed his walk he slowly climbed the stairs to their bedroom. Standing in the parlor below she could hear him pacing the floor. Her journal also records that she could hear him when he knelt beside their bed to pray. Before he left the room Lee had unwaveringly decided to stand with Virginia and the Confederacy offering his services for their defense.[1]

Before the end of the month, both Lee and his wife had relocated one hundred miles to the south to take up residence in the Confederacy's newly fortified capital city of Richmond, Virginia. It is no surprise that a few days after the Lees departed, Union soldiers crossed the Potomac and occupied *Arlington House* to serve as the headquarters of Union general George McDowell. General Lee would never cross its threshold again.

While the principal significance of *Arlington House* lies in its association with Lee, it is also important because of its prior association with its original owner, George Washington Parke Custis, who was the step-grandson and adopted son of George

The plantation home of Robert E. Lee, overlooking the Potomac River and the city of Washington, DC, was constructed in the early nineteenth century for George Washington Parke Custis. Its most distinguishing architectural feature is a monumental portico supported by six Doric columns of stout proportions. The portico was completed in 1818. (Highsmith Collection—Library of Congress)

Washington. The mansion is also noteworthy because it is one of the earliest examples of monumental Greek Revival architecture in this country. According to architectural historian and author Ralph Hammett, who researched the home for the Historic American Buildings Survey in 1940, *Arlington House* was only the third major example of the Greek Revival style in the United States.

"Arlington is one of the finest interpretations of the Palladian style of classic architecture in America," Hammett wrote. "The home's massive proportions and its visibility from Washington, D.C. and the Potomac River, helped introduce temple-form architecture to a much broader audience in this country."[2]

Custis began construction on *Arlington House* in 1803, and placed his home on an eleven-hundred-acre tract that he had inherited from his father, John Parke Custis. George Hadfield, second architect of the US Capitol and designer of Washington City Hall, is credited with designing the Custises' residence. The sprawling eight-thousand-square-foot house is composed of a large, two-story central section flanked by 2 one-story wings. The long axis of the dwelling runs north to south while the main façade faces east. From the beginning, Custis intended his home to be a symbol of his family's contribution to the founding of the nation.[3]

The dwelling's most prominent feature is an iconic portico formed by eight stuccoed brick Doric columns supporting a massive pediment. The portico was completed in 1818. A row of recessed arched windows on the front and sides of the flanking wings adds a measure of sophistication and grandeur to the mansion. The exterior brick walls

Union soldiers and other personnel gathered under the portico and on the front lawn of Arlington House in 1864 during the Civil War. (Library of Congress)

The room known by the Lee family as the "White Parlor" was used for the most formal entertaining at Arlington. It retains original pieces of the Lee family furniture. (Highsmith Collection—Library of Congress)

were covered with stucco, which was incised with grooves to make the surface look like cut stone. Sometime before the 1860s, the stucco on the house and columns was marbleized with a faux painting technique that added even greater classicism to its appearance.

Centered under the portico is a large double door that opens into a long, high-ceilinged hall running to the rear of the dwelling. Another hall located across the back of the home allowed slaves and servants to carry out their duties without having to move through the public spaces of the house.

The central hall is flanked by drawing rooms. The room on the right side of the hall is divided by three open arches that visually divide the space between a family room at the front and the family dining room at the rear. History records that those two spaces were used more often than any other rooms in the house by the Lee family. Lee, a graduate of West Point Military Academy, and his bride, Mary Ann Randolph Custis, had been married beneath the arches in 1831.

The large formal space to the left of the main hall is known as the White Parlor. That name was chosen by Mrs. Lee because of the room's white walls and the pair of matching white mantelpieces carved with an oak leaf design and specially purchased for the room by Robert E. Lee in 1855. The room adjacent to the White Parlor in the

The family parlor was used by the Lee family on a daily basis. The portrait above the mantel is of Nellie Parke Custis, who had been reared at George Washington's Mount Vernon. (Highsmith Collection—Library of Congress)

The "White Parlor" took its name from the painted white walls and white marble mantels found in the space. Traditionally, red damask upholstery materials and drapes have been used in the room. (Highsmith Collection—Library of Congress)

The family dining room was used for everyday meals and entertaining. The portrait above the Italian marble mantel is of George Washington Parke Custis, the home's original owner. (Highsmith Collection—Library of Congress)

south wing was used as a formal dining room and later as a painting studio for George Washington Parke Custis. Following his death it was used as a workroom by Mrs. Lee. A smaller room nearby was used as an office by Robert E. Lee during his ownership.

Two small bedrooms and a schoolroom in the north wing were used by the Custis and Lee children. Four larger bedchambers, including the room used by the general and his wife, as well as smaller dressing rooms fill the second floor of the home. Access to the uppermost story is obtained by a staircase located in a hall just behind the bedrooms.

Many of the furnishings at *Arlington* had been originally used at *Mount Vernon*, the home of George Washington. Following Washington's death in 1799, and Martha Washington's demise three years later, many of their personal belongings were acquired by their heirs. Wagonloads of items made the ten-mile journey from *Mount Vernon* to *Arlington* in the early nineteenth century.

"There is a direct link between *Mount Vernon* and *Arlington* house that makes the Custis-Lee home even more important to the American story," says Civil War historian Michael Hardy. "And that connection doesn't just come from the material items in

The bedroom of General and Mrs. Robert E. Lee contains original Lee family furniture. The bed hangings are copies of those used in the room at the time of the Civil War. (Highsmith Collection—Library of Congress)

the home and its powerful architecture. At *Arlington House* you have a resident family related closely to the nation's greatest leader of the American Revolution, and also to the most respected southern military commander of the War between the States. You get a great sense of how the issues of state loyalty and slavery that existed at the founding of the Republic eventually brought about the tumult of the Civil War."[4]

Like many plantations across the South, the Civil War brought great change to *Arlington House* and to the landscape of Lee's estate. The transformation of the property began with the destruction of major stands of trees as the grounds were lined with trenches and battlements for Union soldiers. Several roads were built across the property to supply federal troops with much-needed equipment.[5]

Although *Arlington House* was occupied by Union troops almost from the start of the war, commanders in charge of the house saw themselves as caretakers of the mansion until the war's conclusion. At that time, they felt the home would be returned to its original owners. However, Edwin M. Stanton, Lincoln's secretary of war, had more vindictive plans for the estate. Stanton was determined that General Lee should never again enjoy his family home at *Arlington*. On its grounds he established a "Freedman's Village" to house runaway slaves in 1863. Then in 1865, Union general Montgomery Meigs, Secretary Stanton's quartermaster general, instructed that a cemetery be located as close to the house as possible. The first graves in the new cemetery were dug just feet from the home's front doors. The cemetery quickly expanded and became Arlington National Cemetery, now considered among the most revered ground in the nation.[6]

While the house itself was spared destruction during the Civil War, life would never be the same again for the Lee family on the plantation. Several pieces of furniture were destroyed or damaged during the Union occupation and many of the family's personal possessions, art treasures, portraits, and irreplaceable heirlooms from George Washington were lost or stolen throughout the war. The heavy traffic of military boots scarred the staircase treads and the parlor floors.

But, even greater changes were still to come. In May 1863, Congress levied a tax on all confiscated properties, including *Arlington House*, requiring that owners personally appear to make payment. A relative attempted to pay *Arlington*'s taxes for Mrs. Lee, who was ill and behind Confederate lines, but that payment was rejected. The plantation and mansion were put up for sale for nonpayment of taxes, and in January 1864 it was purchased by the US Government.[7]

In 1877, General Lee's oldest son, George Washington Custis Lee, filed a lawsuit against the US Government and successfully regained the property. He subsequently sold it back to the US Government for $150,000. For much of the next fifty years the house was used as the cemetery office, and groundskeepers and the cemetery superintendent lived in the rooms earlier occupied by the Custis and Lee families.

Throughout that period many of the interior rooms were painted a stark white, including stained woodwork, and many of the home's original chandeliers were removed. During that era functionality took precedent over historical integrity on the property.[8]

In 1924, the United States Congress, realizing the historical significance of the property and considering the wealth of sentiment felt for Robert E. Lee throughout the nation, empowered the secretary of war to restore *Arlington House* to its pre–Civil War appearance, and to secure as many original Lee family furnishings as possible. The work to restore the home was conducted by the United States Army under the guidance of the quartermaster general.[9]

Despite the enthusiasm for the project, however, the War Department, largely at the insistence of the Commission of Fine Arts director Charles Moore, decided to furnish and interpret the home to its earliest days before General Lee's ownership. The decision was based, in part, on the popularity of the Colonial Revival movement that had held the country's imagination since before the turn of the twentieth century. As a result, the home was restored to the period of George Washington Custis's occupancy, and no furniture crafted after 1830 was used in the home's decor.[10]

That decision drew heavy complaints from historians and thousands of concerned citizens who felt the property should reflect Lee's tenure and legacy. Financial constraints of the Great Depression followed by World War II, however, made it impossible to make changes in the home beyond necessary maintenance. All the while the house continued to be visited by tens of thousands of tourists every year. It was transferred from the Department of the Army to the National Park Service in 1933.[11]

Spurred by a grassroots movement of citizens calling for acknowledgment of Lee at the historic site, in 1955 Congress passed legislation that designated *Arlington House* as a permanent memorial to Robert E. Lee. In time, the house was furnished and interpreted to the period of the 1850s, during the final years of Lee's ownership.

The refurnishing of the house was greatly aided by generous gifts from lineage societies and heritage organizations, including the United Daughters of the Confederacy, the Sons of Confederate Veterans, and the Daughters of the Old South (DOS). More than twenty-five additional pieces of Lee family furniture were returned to *Arlington* in the late 1950s, and conservators were employed to replicate original wallpapers and fabrics used to upholster furniture and to create window treatments. In time, more than thirty-three hundred pieces of furniture, decorative objects, books, and personal items belonging to the Lee family would be housed at *Arlington*.

In 1960, the National Park Service reported that approximately 450,000 people visited the home annually. Those numbers continued to climb in the coming decades. Extensive exterior renovation projects were conducted in 1967 and again in 1974.[12]

Then in 2006, a massive restoration and preservation campaign was launched by the nonprofit organization, Save Arlington House, Inc., with funding from a Save America's Treasures grant. At the same time, federal funding was secured to accomplish much-needed upgrades including fire suppression technology, climate management systems, and museum-quality showcases for displaying archival materials to the public.

In the summer of 2014, the National Parks Service announced that a $12.35 million donation had been made by Washington, DC, philanthropist, David Rubenstein, to restore and improve access to *Arlington House*. Rubenstein's gift was designated not only to aid the restoration of the mansion, but to improve the interpretation of the surviving slave quarters. The gift also funded technology improvements on the property and upgraded mobile and web assets, including both audio and virtual tour capabilities.

Today, *Arlington House* portrays the family life of the Lee family, as well as the contributions and role of African American slaves on the property. Three outbuildings, including an original slave cabin, have been restored, and much emphasis has been placed on returning appropriate plantings used during the nineteenth century to the gardens surrounding the home.

BERRY HILL PLANTATION
A Doric Temple in the Old Dominion

📍 South Boston, Virginia

Virginia is known by many superlatives. It was the home of more of America's Founding Fathers than any other state. It lays claim to the first permanent settlement by Europeans on this continent, Jamestown. It contains more Revolutionary War and Civil War battlefields than any of its neighbors, and high on its list of credentials is an extraordinary number of fine historic homes.

The mansion at *Berry Hill Plantation*, located in Halifax County, in southern Virginia just a few miles from the North Carolina border, is set apart from many other historic homes in the state. In a region that long favored red-brick and frame structures, *Berry Hill's* grand edifice, sheathed in stucco and stone, looks like a temple lifted from the Greek countryside and gingerly dropped in the rolling hills of the Old Dominion.

The distinguishing feature of *Berry Hill's* impressive façade is a great octastyle pedimented portico supported by eight fluted Doric columns that stretches across the entire front of the home. The massive twenty-four-foot granite columns support an entablature ornamented with a continuous band of ribbed molding crafted into limestone. Temple-form houses, with full-front pedimented porticoes running across a gable end, are uncommon in Virginia and her border states. They can be found in greater abundance in the Deep South.

A series of seven stone steps, sixty feet wide, rises from the gravel drive to the base of the portico. Visitors entering the home step through a wide double door topped by a nine-light transom and surrounded by bold granite trim.[1]

Flanking the drive that leads to the main house are twin, single-story buildings that originally served as the plantation office and a schoolroom. In later years they were used as a billiards room and a *garçonniere*. Those buildings are also temple form in style and have tetrastyle Greek Doric pedimented porticoes.

The most important interior feature of the seventeen-room mansion is the entrance hall, twenty feet wide and forty-four feet long, with its grand cantilevered staircase rising in separate flights to meet at a central landing before continuing to the floor

The entrance hall of the mansion contains a grand, cantilevered staircase that rises in twin flights before meeting on a central landing. The staircase is similar to one found at Staunton Hall Plantation in Charlotte County, Virginia. (Levet)

A view of the main stair hall looking toward the double front doors. (Levet)

The seventeen-room mansion at Berry Hill Plantation was built between 1842 and 1844 for planter and businessman James Coles Bruce. It was designed by fellow Halifax County, Virginia, planter John Evans Johnson. (Levet)

above. The staircase is similar in design to one found at another estate, *Staunton Hall Plantation*, in Charlotte County, Virginia. Other lavish interior elements at *Berry Hill Plantation* include mahogany doors, silver-plated locks, hinges, and doorknobs, and ten Italian marble mantels. The rooms on the first floor have eighteen-foot ceilings. The ceilings are slightly lower on the second floor.

To the left of the main hall is a pair of drawing rooms, both having deep Greek Revival–style crown moldings ornamented with water leaf moldings. The mantels in those spaces are Empire in style and feature caryatid supports. An interesting feature of the house is a glass-enclosed conservatory to the rear of the second drawing room. That room, designed with large floor-to-ceiling windows that flood the space with natural light, is documented as one of the earliest conservatories in America built within the central part of a dwelling.

The mansion's dining room is entered beneath the point where the staircases meet. That room was originally adorned with silk damask wallpaper and fashioned with a silver closet and a dumbwaiter that allowed chilled wine bottles to be brought to the room from the cellar below.

Built between 1842 and 1844 for James Coles Bruce, heir to a mercantile fortune, the home was designed by a fellow Halifax County planter, John Evans Johnson, and erected by a local builder named Josiah Dabbs. Johnson, who had studied engineering and architecture at West Point Military Academy, was a close friend of the Bruce

An 1850s square grand piano graces the southwest parlor at Berry Hill Plantation. (Levet)

family. Johnson built the new structure around an existing Georgian-style home that had been erected in 1770 and lived in by Bruce's parents, James and Sarah Bruce.[2]

The younger Bruce had asked Johnson to create a columned mansion for him that was similar to Philadelphia banker Nicholas Biddle's home on the Delaware River, known as *Andalusia*. Biddle was an enthusiastic supporter of the Greek Revival style of architecture and was one of the first Americans known to have traveled to Greece to visit ancient ruins.[3]

Erected with slave labor at a cost of more than $100,000, the mansion was a showplace that exceeded the scale and style of most other homes in the Virginia Piedmont. For many years after the home's construction, the Bruce family entertained lavishly and welcomed many guests including local, state, and national politicians.

According to Halifax County historian Leland Luck, commissioning such a grand structure was no struggle for Bruce, whose fortune was estimated to be more than $6

The mansion's double parlors are divided by heavy pocket doors. Each of the rooms displays elements of period trim work including plaster moldings, paneled ceilings, and marble mantels. (Levet)

The bold ceiling medallion in the mansion's southwest parlor. (Levet)

million, not only in land, slaves, and tobacco in Virginia, but in thousands of acres of frontier land in Iowa, Wisconsin, and Nebraska. Bruce had attended college at Harvard and the University of North Carolina before obtaining a law degree from the University of Virginia. He married Eliza Wilkins in 1838, and the couple had three children.[4]

Although it is said that Bruce opposed the South's secession from the Union, once Virginia had joined the Confederacy he paid to equip two companies of southern troops. He later lost his son, Charles, at the Battle of Malvern Hill. Bruce himself died just a few days before Gen. Robert E. Lee's surrender at Appomattox on April 9, 1865.

Luck gives tours of the mansion and shares many stories not found in history books. He also revels in describing the period furnishings of the mansion. "Much of the original furniture in the home came from Philadelphia and was brought down to the James River and then carted overland to this plantation," says Luck. "No expense was spared in making this one of the grandest homes in Virginia."

Luck is also attuned to the many stories associated with the construction of the home and the architectural elements that survive today. "It is said that the windows in the mansion were copied from designs used by Thomas Jefferson at Monticello," remarked Luck. "The sashes come all the way down to the floor so that you can raise them up and walk outside."

"The mansion's floors are all cherry wood," Luck explains. "Mrs. Bruce wanted a fireplace in all the principal rooms and she wanted marble baseboards throughout the first and second floors. It has long been said that the marble came from the same mine in Italy that supplied Michelangelo with the stone for his statue of David."[5]

In the years following the Civil War, much of *Berry Hill Plantation*'s agricultural land returned to forests, but the plantation remained in the Bruce family until 1950. The property was then bought and sold many times, and even sat vacant for more than eleven years. Finally in the 1990s, at the urging of preservationist and historian Richard Hampton Jenrette, the mansion and surrounding property was purchased by AXA, a French financial services company, and completely restored at a cost of more than $19 million. AXA turned the plantation into a corporate retreat and built a large hotel adjacent to the historic mansion and opened the house to the public. Since that time, the property has been owned by three different private owners who have also operated *Berry Hill Plantation* as a resort destination.

"Virginia has a fascinating history and has been home to a lot of important people who lived in beautiful homes," says Luck. "There are many, many important homes in this state. But, none of them has the grand appearance and bold architectural style of *Berry Hill Plantation*. The mansion here is a treasure all its own."[6]

MONTICELLO

Rescuing Thomas Jefferson's Masterpiece

⚐ Charlottesville, Virginia

Thomas Jefferson (1743–1826) is remembered for numerous accomplishments during his lifetime. In addition to authoring the Declaration of Independence and serving as the third president of the United States, he also served as vice president of the United States, governor of Virginia, minister to France, America's first secretary of state, founder of the Library of Congress, and architect of the University of Virginia. He is also credited with establishing the US Military Academy at West Point.

Beyond that impressive resume, he was a man of many refined talents and varied interests. Americans of all ages know of his endeavors in architecture and agriculture. Many are also aware of his deep intellect, his ability to engage in enlightened conversation, his curiosity of the natural world, his love for history and classical literature, and his appreciation for good food and fine wine.

One aspect of his life that is not well known, however, is that when he died at age eighty-three on July 4, 1826, he was more than $104,000 in debt. That debt greatly jeopardized his Virginia plantation and set it on the path to an uncertain future.

The financial burdens that Jefferson left for his heirs eventually caused his beloved home, *Monticello*, to be sold, and its contents auctioned to the highest bidder to satisfy creditors. Even before his descendants relinquished ownership of the home, the mansion had slipped into a serious state of decay, and the surrounding gardens, fields, and pastures showed signs of significant neglect. At later times in its history, Jefferson's mansion came perilously close to ruin.[1]

Debt was not the personal legacy that Jefferson envisioned or hoped for his daughter, Martha Jefferson Randolph, and her children. The prospect of poverty for his heirs concerned him deeply and caused heavy shadows to fall over his final days. Eyewitnesses recorded that Jefferson agonized over his financial situation even while lying on his deathbed.[2]

More than fifty pieces of art, including landscapes and portraits, adorned the walls of the main parlor at Monticello. (HABS)

For years he had lived well beyond his means hoping that profits from future crops and the sale of livestock from his plantation would offset his personal indulgences. But it was not to be. Purchases of art treasures and a collection of books, such as those belonging to Jefferson, would have bankrupted many planters. At the time of his death, Jefferson's personal library consisted of more than four thousand books, and no less than fifty portraits and landscapes hung throughout his mansion. Imported wines filled his cellars, and the dwelling's pantries, cupboards, and tables were laden with silver, fine china, and stemware.

As was the custom of the time for planters and statesmen, Jefferson entertained lavishly. A parade of dignitaries, including the Marquis de Lafayette, James Madison, James Monroe, Benjamin Franklin, and George Washington, once sat at Jefferson's

table. It was not uncommon for more than forty guests to be invited to the home at a time. Dozens of other uninvited guests often appeared at *Monticello*'s doors just for a chance to meet Jefferson and to step inside his home.

Jefferson loved *Monticello* and saw it as a symbol of all that was important to him and his role in the founding of the nation. He once wrote to a friend while visiting Paris, "I am savage enough to prefer the woods, the wilds, and the independence of *Monticello* to all the brilliant pleasures of this gay capital."[3]

The love he felt for his Virginia plantation and the dwelling that sat at its heart was manifest in a single statement that he made nearly two years later. "I am happy no where else and in no other society, and all my wishes end, where I hope my days will end, at *Monticello*. Too many scenes of happiness mingle themselves with all the recollections of my native woods and fields, to suffer them to be supplanted in my affection by any other."[4] Wherever Jefferson was in the world and whatever role he was fulfilling, it was the simple pleasures of country life and his mansion that he loved best.

The famed home, which sits atop a small mountain just outside Charlottesville, Virginia, was designed by Jefferson, who began construction of the dwelling when he was twenty-six years old. It was transformed and enlarged over the course of the next fifty-seven years to satisfy his whims. It was an indigenous structure, with the bricks made on site and the wood for construction coming from Jefferson's own forests. The nails and other hardware needed for construction were also manufactured

Jefferson often referred to the space beneath the dome at Monticello as the "sky room." During his lifetime it served many purposes including bedchamber and playroom for his children and grandchildren. (Highsmith)

by blacksmiths on the plantation, while other craftsmen cut stone and created plaster moldings to be used throughout the interior of the dwelling.

Jefferson's house was based on the neoclassical principals outlined by Italian architect Andrea Palladio. It is a three-story structure with a total of thirty-five principal rooms, including twelve rooms in the basement. The dominant feature of the home is a dome that crowns the garden or west front of the structure. The room under the dome is octagonal in shape. Historically that space has been referred to as a ballroom, but Jefferson referred to it as the sky room because it was lit by eight large oculus windows looking out over his plantation.

The main entrance into the home is through the portico on the east front. Glimpses of Jefferson's character can be seen throughout the house. The spacious entrance hall reveals Jefferson's love of classic design. His inventive genius is also displayed in a seven-day clock located above the center door. The clock, designed by Jefferson, is automated by the weight of cannon balls on a chain. A balcony looks over this room from the floor above.

Between the entrance hall and the main drawing room are double glass doors that open at the touch of a hand. They are operated by a hidden mechanism underneath the floorboards. The drawing room showcases incredible parquet flooring, said to be the

The entrance hall is well lighted by three arched openings. The room was used by Jefferson as a display space for his burgeoning collection of natural and historical artifacts including maps, sculptures, and paintings. (HABS)

first of its kind in America. A dumbwaiter, designed by Jefferson, allows wine bottles to be easily transported to the dining room from the cellar below.[5]

The absence of a grand staircase in the main hall has long been discussed by architectural historians. During his extensive remodeling of the home in 1793, Jefferson removed the principal staircase and placed two smaller ones in each of the flanking wings. They rise from the basement floor to serve each level of the home.

The main floor not only contained a series of public entertaining rooms and guest bedchambers, but also a private suite including Jefferson's bedroom, and adjoining study and library that open onto a conservatory. In addition to the ballroom, or "sky" room under the dome, the second floor of the home also contains several bedchambers and storage closets.

"An architectural masterpiece, *Monticello* is one of the best examples of classic revival style, of which Thomas Jefferson was the first exponent," once wrote historian Randle Bond Truett. "It is a superlative document, displaying the taste and skill of the first architect of the Republic."[6]

Despite Jefferson's attempts to improve his financial situation and Martha Jefferson Randolph's hopes of keeping the house, within a few short years of her father's death she had to sell the property. It was purchased on November 1, 1831, by a local

Jefferson had his bed positioned between two rooms in its own niche. (HABS)

pharmacist, James T. Barclay, for $7,000. The burden of maintaining the home soon became too much for Barclay and his family, and they vacated the property and advertised it for sale. During their absence, the home was visited by William Barry, postmaster general of the United States, who wrote following his pilgrimage to *Monticello* that "all is dilapidation and ruin from the ceiling to the floor."[7]

According to historian Henry N. Ferguson, the stately home had become a victim of rampant neglect. "The roof fell in, and the columns, once graceful, lost their stately appearance. The splendid drawing room where Jefferson had entertained a procession of notable visitors was used for a granary; its exquisitely inlaid floors littered with corn."[8]

In 1836, the mansion and 218 acres was sold by Barclay to US naval officer Uriah Levy for $2,700. Levy, of Jewish ancestry, was inspired to purchase the estate because of his deep admiration for Jefferson, and out of respect for the Founding Father's advocacy for religious freedom and human rights.

When Levy purchased *Monticello* he began a lengthy and costly program of restoration. He focused considerable attention on repairing the cherry and walnut parquet flooring throughout the home. He replaced numerous panes of broken glass, repaired a

This small sitting area adjoining Jefferson's bedroom served as his study or "cabinet." He penned many letters and other documents in this room. (Highsmith)

badly leaking roof, and stabilized the east portico, which had begun to collapse. All the while Levy was scouring the countryside for furniture and paintings originally used at the mansion by Jefferson, and he successfully acquired dozens of books that once lined Jefferson's shelves.

He also busied himself in rehabilitating the gardens and grounds surrounding the home. He employed gardeners to restore the immediate landscape in accordance with the elaborate plans left by Jefferson. In 1837, Levy purchased 960 additional acres, and then added 1,542 more acres in 1838. For more than two decades the estate was properly managed. But, there were dark days ahead.[9]

Levy's death during the Civil War set in motion a series of events that nearly destroyed his hard work and his desire to preserve Jefferson's home as a shrine to the former president. Despite the Levy family's contributions to the home, numerous trials and tribulations befell the clan, perpetuating a cycle of loss that undermined their good intentions and jeopardized their investment in the property. Although the plantation was commandeered by the Confederate government during the war, and for a while mistakenly became the property of an absentee owner, it was eventually returned to the Levy family.

For more than fifteen years after Uriah Levy's death, his heirs contested the will and fought for control of the property. Throughout that time the estate was managed by a caretaker who proved to be a poor steward. Once again the estate fell into ruin. Rainwater poured through rotted shingles causing considerable damage to the home's floors and walls. While it seems unimaginable, it was during that time that Jefferson's own gravestone was destroyed by vandals, and cattle were allowed to be stabled in his once grand home. Vegetation grew so thick on the front lawn that the main entrance door could not be seen from a short distance.

Then, on March 20, 1879, Jefferson Monroe Levy, a nephew and former congressman from New York, acquired full ownership of the home at auction for $10,500. He promptly undertook to repair the dilapidated structure and its neglected gardens, and engaged a scholarly engineer, T. L. Rhodes, to supervise the restoration of the estate. Levy invested a considerable sum in the project. He made several trips to Europe and across the United States to gather furniture, wallpaper, and rugs used in the home during Jefferson's time. When originals could not be secured he had copies made from earlier sketches and photographs. Under his ownership, *Monticello* became one of the finest house museums in America during the early twentieth century. Levy's dedication to scholarship was emulated by other owners of historic properties, and his quest for authenticity was applauded by museum experts and historians alike.

Jefferson Levy continued to care for *Monticello* as long as he could. In the days following World War I, however, he lost much of his fortune and was eventually forced to sell *Monticello*. In 1923, he sold the mansion and 223 acres to the Thomas Jefferson Memorial Foundation for $500,000, and the foundation opened the estate as a public attraction the following year.[10]

From the beginning, the foundation's primary goal was to return the estate to a condition resembling, as close as possible, the *Monticello* of Jefferson's time. The foundation also sought to operate the estate as both a house museum and educational site devoted to advancing awareness of Jefferson's legacy, his family's story, the contributions and role of subsequent owners, and the story of the diverse community of people once living on the plantation.

In its more than ninety years of existence the foundation has greatly increased *Monticello*'s functions and holdings. Its stewardship now consists of approximately twenty-five hundred acres, of which more than fourteen hundred acres are held under protective easements. The organization strives to build on the successful work of the past and to preserve the historical integrity of the estate. While much of the modern-day work focuses on the installation and operation of mechanical services, the heart of its restoration and preservation activities still involves the structure, maintenance, and ornamentation of the mansion and the appropriate display of its gardens, lawns, and grounds.

Monticello now appears much as it did in the summer of 1809 when workmen on the plantation completed the final addition to the mansion to meet Jefferson's specifications. More than 500,000 visitors make the journey to Jefferson's mountaintop estate each year. The foundation estimates that since 1924, more than 27 million people have walked through *Monticello*'s doors.

The east front of the mansion, while less familiar to many Americans, served as the principal entrance into the home during Jefferson's lifetime. (Lattimore)

The property not only holds designation as a National Historic Landmark in the United States, but also has the distinction of being, along with the academical village of the University of Virginia, which was designed by Jefferson, named a United Nations Educational, Scientific and Cultural Organization (UNESCO) World Heritage Site in 1987. That honor recognizes the plantation as vitally significant to the history and heritage of all people worldwide.

"It is amazing how many times *Monticello* has been rescued from ruin during its history," says educator Risa Ryland, who visited *Monticello* often during her student days at the University of Virginia in Charlottesville. "In so many ways *Monticello* represents the ideals of democracy set forth by Jefferson. I think he would be proud to know that his estate serves as such an inspiration to people around the world and engages a global audience in a dialogue with his ideas."[11]

The unique, eight-sided, brick mansion
built on the Mountain View Plantation
near Marion, Virginia, once contained
some of the South's most elaborately
detailed interiors. Today, the structure,
known locally as the "Octagon House," sits
in a great state of deterioration awaiting
a full-scale restoration. (Bush)

MOUNTAIN VIEW PLANTATION
Rescuing an Octagonal Gem

◉ Marion, Virginia

When Derek and Deborah Orr purchased the historic *Octagon House* on the property originally known as *Mountain View Plantation* near Marion, Virginia, at public auction in 2003, the dwelling could not be seen from the country road at the edge of its gently sloping front lawn. The unique, eight-sided, brick mansion, long noted for having one of the South's most elaborately detailed interiors, was veiled in a cover of poison ivy, Virginia creeper, and other indigenous vines that clung to its exterior walls and wrapped around the chimneys that rose from its rusted tin roof. A deep growth of scrub trees, bushes, and invasive weeds made it difficult to approach the home's front doors that barely hung from broken hinges.

Having grown up near the antebellum home and having made numerous visits to the vacant structure throughout his childhood and young adulthood, Derek Orr knew what lay hidden behind the jungle of vegetation. He had often climbed through the mansion's open windows into shadowy rooms littered with broken plaster and glass, and strewn with splintered wood and ornamental trim ripped from graffiti-filled walls by vandals and vagrants. Each visit drew him deeper into the home's story fueling in him a passion for its history and architecture, and eventually a fervent hope for its restoration.

"My family says that I've talked about buying this house since I was a little boy," states Orr. "I think that I always realized, even when I was very young that this house is very special. It is not just its unique shape, but the incredible amount of elaborately painted ornamentation and faux finishes found throughout the home, not only in the grand public rooms, but in the more private spaces, as well that charm me. I was mesmerized by the size of the rooms inside the home and wondered how the original owners had used each of the spaces. When you step into this house you know that you are entering a time very different from today."[1]

The home's location, on a small knoll with a panoramic view of the Rye Valley and the South Fork River, caused the original owners to name their estate *Mountain View Plantation*. To the south rises the Iron Mountain Range, and from the mansion's front

This photo of the Octagon House from 1894 shows remnants of the original porch that wrapped around three sides of the front façade. The railing from the upper gallery, however, is missing. (Library of Congress)

The rear of the dwelling originally opened onto a brick patio that was bordered by ornamental shrubs and perennials. Most of the windows in the structure are badly deteriorated and have been boarded over. One of the mansion's exterior brick walls collapsed in the mid-twentieth century and was replaced (visible at left) with concrete blocks. (Bush)

windows can be seen Mount Rogers, the highest peak in Virginia. Due to the structure's unique shape, however, few people referred to the dwelling by its geographically inspired name, and chose simply to call it the *Octagon House*.

Built for wealthy planter and industrialist Abijah Thomas and his wife, Priscilla Scott Thomas, in 1858, the home was originally a showplace that displayed Mr. Thomas's love for European-inspired decoration and his penchant for fine furniture, oil paintings, expensive china, glassware, and sterling silver. On the eve of the Civil War, the Thomases owned more than forty tracts of land consisting of several thousand acres, an iron foundry, two woolen mills, twenty-seven slaves, ten horses, one hundred cattle, and three carriages. The couple had twelve children, eleven of whom lived to adulthood. Tradition says that the family entertained lavishly with sumptuous meals and dance balls that lasted late into the night.[2]

But the Thomases glory days were not to last. The dilapidated condition of the *Octagon House* began early in its history. After the Civil War destroyed the family's finances and Abijah Thomas died in 1876, Mrs. Thomas held on to the property for another nine years, and then her heirs sold the house to William K. Brooks of Abingdon, Virginia, in 1888. Many of the home's fine furnishings were auctioned or sold at that time. For many years afterward, the dwelling was the private residence of a succession of owners, none of whom ever maintained the house in good repair. By the late nineteenth century it displayed many signs of neglect.

During the Great Depression of the 1930s, the house was transformed into a tenement property with apartments for several families. When the last tenant moved out in the early 1940s, the structure was converted into a tobacco barn and a storage building for apple boxes, bales of hay, and farm equipment. At some point in the early 1960s, a major portion of one of the rear brick walls collapsed and extensive repairs were made with cement blocks.[3]

During its many years of decline, large sections of the main floor began to sag significantly, which in turn caused several areas of the second floor to separate from the interior walls that were anchored to the ceiling above. The shifting of the interior walls and ceilings, and the stress on those surfaces, caused much of the plasterwork to crumble leaving only traces of the original ornamentation.

It is fortunate that much research and documentation has been performed through the years by architectural historians and others interested in the mansion. According to information gathered in the 1940s for the Historic American Buildings Survey (HABS) and held by the Library of Congress in Washington, DC, the interior of the Abijah Thomas house is divided into seventeen spacious principal rooms and numerous closets and storage areas. The use of each of those rooms is also noted in the inventory.[4]

The floor plan of the 6,556-square-foot house is complex. The first floor contains eight principal rooms, including a "best" parlor, drawing room, dining room, and plantation office, as well as two bedrooms, six closets, and the enclosed hall for the grand staircase. The second floor is divided into eight bedrooms, two halls, a large storage area without windows known as "the dark room," and four closets.[5]

Eight brick columns originally supported a single-story porch on the front of the house that was accessible from the double doors on the second floor. A wrought-iron railing originally surrounded the upper deck. In the 1890s, the original veranda was replaced with a wooden-frame porch with sawn millwork. That structure survived for only a few decades and is not seen in later photographs taken of the house in the 1920s.

The principal entrance into the home on the west façade was through double, six-paneled doors flanked by multipaned sidelights and topped with a transom. A similar door opened onto the promenade deck or gallery above. While only portions of the space remain today, the home was originally designed with a triangular-shaped entrance vestibule of such small proportions that it belied the spaciousness of the rooms beyond.

Baseboards throughout the home were painted with elaborate designs and accented with faux marble trim. (Bush)

An original mantel survives in the room once known as the home's "best parlor." The walls and floors in this room, and throughout the house, are in need of complete restoration. (Bush)

Much of the home's original millwork has been stolen or removed through the years, including the spindles from the main staircase. (Bush)

Surviving remnants of plaster ornamentation and painted details can be seen on the walls and ceiling of the "best parlor." Much research has been conducted to document the original ornamental designs of this room so that they can be replicated by professional restorers. (Bush)

Despite its small size, the foyer was painted with faux marble blocks and the space above each door in the room contained a painted landscape in bold colors. Only fragments of those paintings survive today, but documentation of the elaborate murals can be found in a series of photographs taken by historian David Greear in 1941. Several of those photos appeared in local newspapers and books through the years, but the whereabouts of the originals is not known.[6]

All ceilings on both floors of the home are eleven feet high, and the heart pine floorboards are different widths. The two-part baseboards seen in most of the principal rooms vary in width from twelve to fourteen inches. They are composed of a lower marbleized board and an upper board that is either painted a complementary color or stenciled with flowers, vines, and acanthus leaves. A few chair rails remain, and where they can be found they are painted the same color as the upper baseboard.

The six mantelpieces on the first floor were marbled or stippled to match the bottom of the baseboard in each room. The mantel in the "best" parlor was also decorated with glass insets with eglomise ornamentation. While that mantel survives, most of the other originals have been stolen or lost to time.

Unlike many homes constructed during the 1850s, the *Octagon House* features a main staircase completely enclosed in its own room. Because the space, which rises from the first through the second floor, lacks a cupola or oculus window above, it is poorly lighted. Seven steps ascend to the first landing, six more to the second, and seven more climb to reach the upper hall, which is closed from all adjoining rooms by doors. While little of the stair hall's original trim survives today, it is apparent that three balusters were mounted in each tread and capped by a cherry handrail. A simple wooden scroll design survives on several of the risers. The paneling around the walls of the staircase is faux-grained to resemble tiger oak. The baseboards in the stair hall are painted rose at the top with a marbled design below.

The home originally contained thirty-four single doors and three sets of double doors of different styles and sizes. All of the door frames are alike, however, and are constructed with cyma (curved) molding and square corner blocks, some of which are marbled. Every door in the house was stippled or feather painted to give the impression of fine or exotic wood. Many were fitted with pressed-glass or Bennington porcelain knobs, manufactured in Bennington, Vermont.[7]

Many of the walls throughout the home were originally painted ivory, except those in the "best" front parlor, which were painted to resemble blocks of rose marble. The ceiling in that space was painted blue-gray and embellished with an octagonal design around a circular medallion ornamented with oak leaves and scrollwork. An imported French chandelier hung from the center of the medallion and matching gilt torcheres flanked the fireplace mantel.

Restoring the home to its original state will take a Herculean effort and the Orrs are aware of the challenges ahead. To accomplish the tasks, they formed the Octagon House Foundation in 2013, a nonprofit organization led by a board of directors, to coordinate all necessary fundraising, planning, and restoration work.

Due to the excessive deterioration of the home's interior beams and support structure, it has been decided that the dwelling will be gutted to its brick walls and all significant wood trim, moldings, and flooring will be numbered and stored for use when the interiors are reassembled using architectural plans preserved at the Library of Congress. Plans are also in place to replicate the original front porch and the brick terrace once found at the rear of the home.

"Our concept for restoration is very similar to what was done at the *White House* in Washington, D.C. in the 1940s," says Orr, who is intimately familiar with the architectural drawings of the *Octagon House* held by the Library of Congress. "Once a new interior support structure is in place, we can return as many of the original interior materials as possible."[8]

Because many significant pieces of trim and ornamentation have been stolen or lost to neglect and deterioration over the past 150 years, expert artisans and craftsmen versed in historic restoration will be employed to replicate what cannot be found or salvaged.

"I have spent much of my life thinking about this house and safeguarding it and its history," Orr says with determination. "I will see this project through to completion. I want to see this property returned to its original state because it means so much to the history of Smyth County and the State of Virginia."[9]

Following the lead of many historic homes owned and managed by nonprofit foundations, Orr says that supporters of the *Octagon House* feel that the property can become an important economic stimulus for the surrounding community. They envision that the restored house, opened to the public and available for special events, can become both an educational and a commercial property that provides jobs for several local people.

"There is a lot of hard work ahead for us," Orr believes. "But, I know we can make this happen. We can preserve and restore this house and make it a viable economic resource for this area of Virginia."[10]

The mansion known as the "White House of the Confederacy" is today dwarfed by the towering hospital complex of the Medical College of Virginia and other office buildings, in Richmond, Virginia. In its earliest years the home had a view of the James River in the distance. (Bush)

WHITE HOUSE OF THE CONFEDERACY
Caught in Time

♀ Richmond, Virginia

I
n the minds of many southerners, time stood still at the corner of East Clay and 12th Streets in Richmond, Virginia, the moment Jefferson Davis left the home on Sunday evening, April 2, 1865, to escape approaching Union troops, who inevitably ransacked the city and took possession of the dwelling that had come to be known as the *White House of the Confederacy*.

In reality, time has not stood still. The home, which once looked down across a wooded hillside to the banks of the James River, is now dwarfed by the towering hospital complex of the Medical College of Virginia and located only a few feet away from a branch facility of the American Civil War Museum. As a result, the mansion appears out of place in a modern, urban landscape that resembles many cities in America.

Time does slip away, however, when stepping across the threshold of the mansion into rooms that are steeped in history. Due to a successful restoration project in the early 1980s that returned the home to its 1865 appearance, visitors are indeed visually transported back to that spring long ago when the Davis family still resided in the mansion and the South was a separate nation.

The story of the gray stuccoed neoclassical-style mansion began many years before its principal role in the Civil War. It was built in 1818 for John Brockenbrough, who was then serving as president of the Bank of Virginia, for $20,000. Located two blocks north of the Virginia Capitol Building, the dwelling was designed by master architect Robert Mills, who designed many important structures in America including the Washington Monument and the United States Treasury building, both in Washington, DC.[1]

Mills's design for the Brockenbrough home produced a grand two-and-one-half-story, 14,000-square-foot dwelling with vastly different front and rear façades. A pair of fluted, Ionic columns support a simple porch over the main Clay Street entrance. In contrast, Mills designed a monumental portico with four pairs of Doric columns stretching across the entire expanse of the home's garden front. An uncovered porch

The Clay Street façade of the mansion. (Bush)

leads from that space down the east side of the home providing a sheltered entrance to the service floor below.

Sold by the Brockenbrough family in the 1840s, the mansion then passed through a succession of owners, including prominent individuals such as US congressman and future Confederate secretary of war James Seddon. In the 1850s, the dwelling was purchased by Lewis Dabney Crenshaw, who added a third floor and made significant improvements to the service floor, as well as decorative enhancements to the main living spaces. At the start of the Civil War, Crenshaw sold the house to Richmond city officials for $42,894.97, and they in turn rented it to the Confederate government for use as the official executive residence of President Davis, his wife, Varina Howell Davis, and their children.[2]

When the Davises moved into the mansion in 1861, the family consisted of President and Mrs. Davis, six-year-old Margaret, four-year-old Jefferson Davis Jr., and two-year-old Joseph. The two youngest Davis children, William and Varina Anne "Winnie," were born in the White House, in 1861 and 1864, respectively. Sadly, Joseph died at the home in the spring of 1864 when he fell fifteen feet from the mansion's east portico onto a brick path below.[3]

The Clay Street entrance into the mansion. Confederate president Jefferson Davis addressed the citizens of Richmond from this small portico in 1863. This was the same entrance used by Abraham Lincoln in April 1865 when he toured the residence. (Bush)

A portico supported by four pairs of monumental Doric columns can be seen on the mansion's garden façade. (Bush)

A portrait of Jefferson Davis painted in 1863 hangs over a marble mantel in the center parlor. Also shown are reproductions of the first and second national flags of the Confederacy, and examples of prisoner-of-war art made by Confederate soldiers during the war. (Highsmith Collection—Library of Congress)

Despite that tragedy, there were many happy days for the Davises in the role as the First Family of the Confederacy, and they entertained many important guests, including Generals Thomas J. "Stonewall" Jackson and Robert E. Lee. Mrs. Davis explained the family's use of the home's many spaces to one Richmond resident, saying, "The basement of the mansion was occupied and used as a breakfast room and children's dining room, the first story as drawing, reception rooms and state dining room, the second story as bedrooms, one of which Mr. Davis used as a private office."[4]

In the final days before Richmond fell in 1865, Davis sent his wife and children to a safer location farther south. Within twelve hours of his departure, Union soldiers seized the mansion. Two days later it was toured by US president Abraham Lincoln, who stayed in the home for three hours, conducting meetings with his military officers.

Following the war, the dwelling was used as a federal military command center for five years between 1865 and 1870, and then served as a school for twenty years. The restored *White House of the Confederacy* today, however, shows none of those uses. Historians and preservationists have focused their attention solely on the structure's role as

an executive mansion, and on how the home was decorated and furnished when used by the Davis family.

Beyond his structural improvements and additions, it was Crenshaw's updated 1850s interior decoration of the home and purchase of fine furniture, wallpapers, carpets, and fabrics, as well as the addition of gilt gas-burning chandeliers and intricate plaster moldings and ceiling medallions in 1858, that gave the home its mid-Victorian style and look when it became the *White House of the Confederacy*. Fortunately, much documentation has survived outlining Crenshaw's many purchases for the mansion. Those records have been invaluable to restorers in their efforts to return the home to its mid-nineteenth-century appearance.[5]

It was also fortuitous that sketches were made of several of the interiors by Richmond artist Virginia Armistead Garber in the early 1890s, more than twenty-five years after the close of the war. Those drawings, along with recorded memories of both Varina Howell Davis and her daughter Varina "Winnie" Davis, provide many clues to the past and allow current-day curators to present the rooms of the mansion in much the same fashion as they would have looked during the Civil War years.[6]

Garber's sketches were created at a time when the city of Richmond was planning to demolish the structure to build a new school. The sketches were used by the newly created Confederate Memorial Literary Society (CMLS) to raise necessary funds to help purchase the home. The city transferred title of the property to the CMLS on June 3, 1894, and the home opened as a Confederate museum in February 1896.[7]

While the focus of the museum was the procurement of Confederate military artifacts and items belonging to principal Confederate figures, in time the museum's collection grew to include a significant amount of furniture, glassware, paintings, and personal items used by the Davis family during the war years. By the 1960s, the collection of original items was so large that several period rooms were opened to the public, and for the first time the mansion took on the look of a house museum.

When a new museum building, known originally as the Museum of the Confederacy, was opened adjacent to the mansion in 1976, all of the military collections were transferred to that facility, and the CMLS began planning to return the Executive Mansion to its wartime appearance. The three-phase project took more than a decade to complete. Much emphasis was placed on retrofitting the structure with wooden trim and other architectural elements removed when the interior of the house was sheathed in "fireproof" materials in 1896. Historians had long assumed that the changes had taken away key architectural features that could never be reconstructed.

According to a newspaper article written in 1988 at the conclusion of the extensive restoration project, "with the help of restoration architects Paul Buchanan, who worked at Colonial Williamsburg, and Charles Phillips, who has worked at Old Salem, it was possible to find evidence of certain architectural features thought to have been destroyed. The discoveries allowed the missing features to be reinstalled with an accuracy that had previously been thought impossible."[8]

Coinciding the restoration of the mansion was the conservation and restoration of its contents. Of special note, many upholstered pieces of original Davis furniture were covered in reproduced fabrics based meticulously on surviving remnants of fabric used in the home in the 1860s. Careful analysis of surviving woodwork in the home produced valuable evidence about interior paint colors. Wallpaper fragments from the 1860s were discovered when mantels and door and window casings were removed for restoration. The restored mansion was opened to the public in June 1988.

"Without question the restoration of the *White House of the Confederacy* represents one of the finest such projects to have ever been attempted in this country," says noted Civil War historian and author Michael C. Hardy. "The extent to which that home was returned to its 1860s appearance shows the magnitude of respect that proud Southerners have for their ancestors and for the leaders of the Confederacy. It is a home that everyone should tour."[9]

In November 2013, the Museum of the Confederacy was merged with the American Civil War Center at Historic Tredegar, site of a former ironworks in downtown Richmond, and in January 2014, it was announced that the combined institution would be known as the American Civil War Museum. The *White House of the Confederacy* remains a crucial part of the institution and is open to the public.

NORTH CAROLINA

The mansion at Creekside Plantation
in Burke County, North Carolina, was
completed in 1836. It has the distinction
of being the finest Greek Revival–style
antebellum home in the western
portion of the state. (Bush)

CREEKSIDE PLANTATION
One Family's Architectural Legacy

♀ Morganton, North Carolina

Like all family histories, the story of the Waltons of Burke County, North Carolina, is filled with elements of joy, sorrow, success, failure, and the seemingly infinite details of everyday life. While the majority of their neighbors were sheltered in modest log and frame structures in the days before the Civil War, the Walton clan lived their lives against the backdrop of an imposing brick mansion that has long been considered one of the finest Greek Revival–style homes in the state.

Since it was completed in 1836, the mansion at *Creekside Plantation*, facing Table Rock Mountain in the Catawba River valley, has been lived in by seven generations of the Walton family. Its drawing room, dining room, and library have witnessed events that have shaped the history of the region, and its bedchambers and hallways have heard the hushed whispers and secrets of its occupants' hopes and dreams.

While passersby and visitors rightly surmise that living in the 7,000-square-foot dwelling offers many rewards, few understand the excessive work and dedication required by its stewards. Owning the house provides many challenges. Keeping it in good repair and safeguarding its treasures requires constant attention and care.

"This is truly a great house," says Louisa Emmons, a great-great-granddaughter of the original owner. "I have so many wonderful memories of growing up here and being in each of the rooms with my extended family. But at the end of each day, there is always the reality that this house requires all of the energy and funds we can muster to keep it in good repair."[1]

Built at a time when dozens of servants and slaves could be engaged in the mansion's upkeep and tasked with maintaining the home's gardens and grounds, the daily care of *Creekside* was originally not so daunting a responsibility. Today, however, those jobs fall on the shoulders of Emmons, as well as her husband, Kirk, their son, Alex, and Emmons's mother, Mary Alexander. Each member of the small family carries out specific tasks that are necessary for making the house livable and keeping it from falling

A window with delicate tracery ornaments the mansion's portico. (Bush)

into an advanced state of decay as has been the fate of so many other historic dwellings throughout the South.

"I have so much respect for my ancestors and truly appreciate the contributions that they have made to our history here in North Carolina and across the South and nation," says Emmons, who counts a signer of the Declaration of Independence and many other statesmen among her forebears. "*Creekside* is a treasure for my family. But it is a blessing that comes with a price. The reality is that homes like this were made possible because of the wealth that came from the land and from cash crop production. But those days are long gone."[2]

Originally, vast fields and pastures surrounded the mansion. A documentary photograph taken in the late nineteenth century shows the home nestled in a grove of trees with a number of rail fences running through the property. Shocks of hay are seen in the foreground with timbered hills providing the backdrop to the pastoral setting.

Today, only two and a half acres remain in the family's possession. The mansion sits in the corner of a busy intersection, including a four-lane highway. Commercial establishments, fast-food restaurants, and a manufacturing plant are located on the site of the former slave cabins and kitchen garden. The view from the mansion today is vastly different from the way it would have looked for its builder.

Planter Thomas George Walton was one of the richest men living in western North Carolina before the Civil War. He owned thousands of acres spread across five counties. The 1860 census documents his ownership of more than 160 slaves. Those African Americans worked not only the four plantations under his rule, but also provided the labor and skill necessary to build and maintain Walton's home.

With the erection of the mansion at *Creekside Plantation*, Walton set a new standard of construction for the backcountry region of the Carolinas that placed his

A view of the mansion's staircase framed by the tall arch that divides the front and rear center halls on the main floor. (Bush)

monumental home in a rugged landscape of mountains and swift-flowing rivers. While other plantation homes were built in the vicinity of *Creekside*, none could compare to the refinement of its architecture and its impressive scale.

Tradition says that Walton was inspired to build such a grand dwelling by the homes he had seen while traveling through Virginia. Other tales say he felt compelled to build the mansion to impress his bride-to-be, Elizabeth Murphy. Whatever the source of his inspiration, he indeed gave North Carolina an architectural gem.

In the book, *The Early Architecture of North Carolina*, published in 1937, noted architectural historian Thomas T. Waterman, who researched and documented hundreds of properties for the Historic American Buildings Survey, praised *Creekside's* style and presence. He wrote, "the dwelling is the most monumental mansion in the Piedmont."[3]

Waterman stated that *Creekside* is both grand and graceful. The face of the mansion is dominated by a heroic tetrastyle portico upheld by four Doric columns. The portico's pedimented gable is ornamented with a half-round window with delicate tracery. Brick pilasters are fashioned into the side walls of the home and give the impression that they

support the structure's wide entablature, which runs continuously around all four sides of the mansion. Its classical portico is ornamented with a frieze of carved stone blocks detailed with stylized oak leaves.[4]

A departure from many of the bold, exterior Greek Revival details seen throughout the home is the elegant fanlight and sidelights of the main entrance door, which harken back to the Federal style that was the preferred architectural style in the decades before *Creekside*'s construction. The sidelights have splayed diamond panes of both ruby and clear glass. Circular panes of colored glass also ornament the fanlight above.

The door opens into a spacious center passage that is divided by an elliptical arch of fluted molding. Most of the hall's ornamental features, including heavy chair rails, wide doors with corner blocks, roundels, and Greek key designs, are Greek Revival in style. The stairway, however, which rises from the rear of the main hall in two flights, is characteristically Federal, with slim balusters, a rounded handrail, a slender newel post, and delicate vernacular foliate bracket beneath each tread.

The principal rooms on the main floor display bold trim work, including exceptional mantels, stylized with fluted columns, and pedimented shelves with molded Greek key designs. In the main drawing room, a pair of niches flank the fireplace and feature trompe l'oeil paintings, dating to 1840, that show scenes from classical Athenian history.

A pair of trompe l'oeil niches flank the Greek Revival–style mantel in the mansion's main drawing room. This image was taken for the Historic American Buildings Survey in 1937.

A portrait of planter James Walton hangs above the mantel in the mansion's drawing room. The room's walls retain their original yellow paint from the nineteenth century. (Bush)

"The paintings in the drawing room are among my favorite features of the house, because they represent an affinity for classical literature and art," Emmons muses as she glances past those murals to gaze at the portraits of her ancestors hanging nearby. "But, I guess I'm like so many other people who love Southern history and the architecture of the Old South. It really is the grand portico and massive columns that I love best. I have been charmed by them my whole life. In my heart they are the symbol of my family and of this home's survival through the Civil War and Reconstruction."[5]

As the family historian and author of *Creekside: Tales from a Civil War Plantation*, Emmons is intimately aware of events that brought the War between the States across the mansion's threshold and into the rooms that her family still uses today. She is astonished that her ancestral home survived the tumultuous raid by Union troops in the spring of 1865. "It really is incredible that the home is still standing," exclaims Emmons. "I really can't explain why it was not burned to the ground after being used to shelter Union Major General Alvan Gillem and more than 20 of his men. I guess we were just lucky."[6]

At *Creekside*, Gillem was met on the front portico by an aging Col. Thomas Walton. Emmons says he greeted the Union officer with the words, "On your honor as a gentleman, I entrust my home and family to your care, sir." She feels it is likely that Walton's deference to General Gillem may have spared *Creekside* the fate of being destroyed like many of its neighbors.

Despite Walton's kind words and good will, however, the intentions of the marauding troops soon became obvious. They smashed much of the furniture and used pieces as firewood. The dining room table was carried out onto the lawn and used by General Gillem and his men to review maps and plan strategy. They filled their pockets and saddlebags with items from the home and ransacked the larder and smokehouse. The troops stayed on the property overnight and the upstairs bedrooms were all commandeered for their use.

Tradition says that a Walton slave buried several pieces of sterling silver tableware and family jewelry on the plantation just prior to the arrival of enemy troops to keep those treasures from being stolen. Today, a few of those items survive and are displayed throughout the mansion alongside other precious objects that remind the family of the collective history of their ancestors and the trials they once faced.

"Once you have stared down an enemy, you know where your strength lies and what kind of stock you are made of," Emmons feels. "I think a part of what keeps us committed to this house today is the knowledge that it was once violated by men who had no respect for its owners or their property. The fact that my family survived those dreadful days and kept going inspires me today."[7]

While the presence of enemies is long ago in the past, what does confront *Creekside's* current residents on a daily basis is the chore of keeping the home in good order. Within the past decade the Emmons have had to make significant repairs to one of the four columns to keep it from collapsing. They have had to replace rotting window frames and stabilize sinking hearth stones. There have been occasional chimney fires that have occurred, and properly maintaining the roof always represents a challenge.

"Age is a tremendous factor in caring for any old house," says Emmons. "It doesn't matter how well a house is constructed. In time the roof will leak and masonry and plaster will begin to fail. On top of that there are always plumbing and electrical issues and the constant struggle to heat and cool a house such as this one that has 14-foot ceilings, and exceptionally large windows."[8]

Maintaining a property like *Creekside* is a monumental task says Ted Alexander, historian and western regional director of Preservation North Carolina, the state's leading nonprofit agency that assists owners of historic structures. Alexander and Emmons are cousins, and he knows firsthand the challenges faced by his relatives. In his work he visits dozens of historic properties each year. While there are success stories, Alexander knows that a significant number of antebellum and colonial structures in North Carolina are in dire need of attention to preserve them for future generations. Many of those buildings will eventually be lost.

"Aside from the incredible architecture at *Creekside*, one of the most amazing aspects of its story is that it still belongs to descendants of the original owner. That is very rare today," says Alexander. "Although the antebellum home is an architectural gem that all North Carolinians can celebrate, in reality the burden of history and care falls squarely on the shoulders of its owners. I have to applaud them. They have been faced with many challenges, and yet the mansion is still there. And we are all richer because of the architectural legacy of this one family."[9]

Unlike many owners of historic homes who have made the choice to abandon or sell their properties in exchange for more modern accommodations, Emmons says that she cannot imagine surrendering *Creekside* to another's care. "We fully intend to keep it in our family as long as possible. It means too much to me to ever let it go."[10]

FOX HAVEN PLANTATION

Surviving Earth's Fury

⦿ Rutherford County, North Carolina

O n the evening of August 31, 1886, the most powerful earthquake in recorded history to strike the southeastern United States caused considerable damage throughout the Carolinas. While the epicenter of the quake, estimated to be between 6.6 and 7.3 on the Richter scale, was located near the city of Charleston, South Carolina, the effects could be felt from Maine to Florida and as far west as Texas. Thousands of homes and public buildings were destroyed or damaged and ninety-one deaths were recorded.

The majority of the residents of North Carolina's foothills region had already gone to bed for the evening when the ground began to shake at 9:51 p.m. Over the course of seven minutes more than one hundred jolts rattled the countryside, including three major wrenchings that resulted in considerable damage to both man-made structures and the natural landscape. A series of aftershocks continued for weeks.

During the tumult, known historically as the "Great Charleston Earthquake of 1886," the ground was ripped open at numerous places throughout the region, and the courses of rivers and streams were changed. Centuries-old trees were toppled and acres of young pine forests were leveled. Flames shot from caverns in the North Carolina mountains emitting smoke that covered the region for days, and residents frequently heard great rumbling noises that sounded like thunder even when there were no clouds in the sky.[1]

At *Fox Haven Plantation,* near Rutherfordton, North Carolina, the two-story portico that originally spanned the entire front façade of the mansion was torn from the home and collapsed onto the wide brick porch below during the quake. The force of the rumbling earth caused more than twenty cracks to appear in the home's masonry walls. The tremors were so severe that many of the home's solid stone lintels above windows and doors were shattered. The plantation's kitchen, a single-story masonry building located behind the main house, was completely leveled.

Descendants of the John Morris family who had owned the plantation for more than one hundred years rushed from the house into the front yard to escape a home

Magnolia trees and boxwoods flank the brick-lined path leading to the front porch at Fox Haven Plantation, near Rutherfordton, North Carolina. (Bush)

The Great Charleston Earthquake of 1886 caused the two-story veranda at Fox Haven to collapse. This photo from 1920 shows the single-story shed porch that replaced it. (Lattimore)

they felt was sure to collapse. They were met on the front lawn by servants and tenant families who were equally alarmed and concerned about their own houses. The events of that evening and subsequent days were something they would remember for the rest of their lives.

The effects of the earthquake have had a lasting impact on the lives of the plantation's owners for more than 125 years. Each owner has had to remain vigilant and sensitive to the challenges resulting from immediate and residual damage. Evidence of the quake is still being discovered as restoration, preservation, and other structural improvements are necessary to care for the venerable dwelling. Since 2003, an extensive restoration project has been undertaken by the current owner to ensure that the home will stand for many generations to come and that it remains as sound as the day it was built.

"Keeping this home in good repair and preserving it is challenging," says owner Delphine Jones, a veteran of several restoration projects of historic properties throughout the nation who works tirelessly to ensure quality craftsmanship on each project she tackles. "There is something very special about a place that has endured great tragedy and trials. I think *Fox Haven* survives for a reason. I can't think of anything more rewarding than taking care of this home and preserving it. I'm grateful that it was never abandoned or razed because of the damage caused by the earthquake in 1886. My goal is to make sure that it is as sturdy and beautiful as the day it was completed nearly 200 years ago."[2]

Repairs to the home were immediately necessary following the earthquake. Fearing that the mansion would collapse, several large bolts were inserted through the brick walls into the heavy pine timbers that framed the interior spaces. Because the brickwork on the home's east wall was severely compromised, a large wooden beam was positioned in the attic to anchor the cracked brick and mortar on the north and south walls. Workmen climbed ladders to fill open cracks with new mortar, and inside the home much of the plaster had to be repaired, particularly in the great east room on the main floor.

While the precautions taken were difficult to orchestrate and accomplish, the owners only had to look to some nearby estates to judge the importance of such measures. At *Cross Keys Plantation* in Union County, South Carolina, a major portion of the front brick wall of the main house collapsed into the yard during the earthquake, leaving bedchambers and other living spaces exposed to the elements.[3] Both of the tall brick exterior chimneys at *Meridian Plantation* located a few miles south of the North Carolina state line in York County, South Carolina, were shaken from their fieldstone foundations, leaving jagged holes in the home's side walls. The damage was never repaired and the home was never lived in again.

While no known documentary photographs exist to reveal *Fox Haven*'s appearance before the earthquake, a photo taken about 1920 shows the long, single-story shed porch with tin roof that replaced what surely was a much more imposing veranda. The replacement porch partially obscured the main entrance door and its Greek Revival–style trim. Close inspection of the photo shows that rustic timbers were being used as porch posts at that time, which greatly diminished the elegant appearance of the home.

The fact that *Fox Haven* remained standing through such powerful seismic activity is testament to its solid construction and to the integrity of the materials used. Constructed in 1823 on a small hill overlooking the Broad River, the mansion is an exceptionally fine example of late Federal-style architecture. The two-story dwelling was built for planter James Morris II. It contains some of the best examples of period millwork and mantels to be found in the region, and was also one of the first brick houses to be erected in western North Carolina.

The first floor consists of a wide center hall with two rooms to the west and a large drawing room to the east that extends the entire width of the house. The second floor mirrors the same plan. The home's attic is lit by matching fanlights on the gable ends. A string stair rises along the east wall of the main floor's central hall to the rooms above. At opposite ends of the main hall are impressive Greek Revival–style doors with multipaned sidelights and transoms. Original brass locks are still in use on the home's exterior doors.

Three chimneys serve the home with six fireplace openings. Tradition says that the collection of finely crafted mantels ornamenting each opening were made in Charleston, South Carolina, and brought to the plantation with furnishings and other decorative arts when the Morris family took up residence in the home.

The plantation estate is much older than the mansion. Early records indicate that John Morris, who supported the Patriot cause during the American Revolution, was granted the first 200 acres of the plantation along Broad River on March 2, 1775. In 1780, he added 340 acres. When John Morris died in 1783, the estate was inherited by his son, James Morris I. James Morris I and Elizabeth Grant were married on January 8, 1783, and added acreage to the plantation.[4]

Their son, James Morris II, was born on the plantation in 1785. It was James Morris II who built the existing plantation mansion. In addition to his role as a planter, he was the first clerk of superior court for Rutherford County, North Carolina, a position he held for twenty-five years. James Morris II died on May 11, 1855. His son, James Bryan Morris, was born on the plantation on April 28, 1831. He served as an officer in the Rutherford County Home Guard during the Civil War. James Bryan Morris married

The main entrance into the home is through a paneled door surrounded by multipaned sidelights and topped with a transom. Greek Revival moldings and other trim can be found in this space that also features the home's principal staircase. (Bush)

Heavy box locks with brass keys that still function properly can be found on both the home's front and rear entrance doors. (Bush)

The mansion, circa 1989, before the current restoration project of the structure was started. The dwelling was built in 1823, and is documented as one of the earliest brick houses in western North Carolina. (Lattimore)

Martha Gaither McEntire, a daughter of Dr. John McEntire of Rutherfordton, North Carolina. Their son, Thomas McEntire Morris, was the last member of the original family to own the estate. More than ten members of the Morris family are buried on the plantation within an enclosed graveyard a few hundred yards east of the mansion.[5]

While the Morris family cultivated the fields along the river, one of their primary occupations was raising thoroughbred horses. For many years a racetrack existed near the home. Wealthy families from as far away as Savannah, Georgia, and Baltimore, Maryland, came to the plantation to attend high-stakes races and to select horses for purchase.

The 1850 United States Census records the Morris family's ownership of thirty-one slaves. Those African Americans resided in a row of cabins that stood below the main house along a creek that flows into the Broad River. Those men, women, and children helped produce crops of cotton, corn, and wheat on more than 400 acres of cultivated fields that were a part of the plantation's overall expanse of 630 acres.

The plantation's name comes from an event that occurred in the eighteenth century, before the present mansion was built. Tradition says that the estate was named for a Native American known as "the Fox," who warned white settlers of an impending raid by a band of Cherokee Indians in the 1770s. The Morris family gave the young brave shelter, and he remained on the property eventually marrying a slave girl. Soon thereafter, the name *Fox Haven* appeared on property maps and other documents.[6]

The plantation remained in the Morris family until 1941, but was intermittently lived in by tenant families for much of the first decades of the twentieth century. In the early 1940s the estate was owned briefly by the Thomas Keeter family. In 1946, the plantation mansion and its remaining 344 acres were purchased by Ben and Fran Sumner, who launched a major restoration project on the home. One of their first tasks was to reinforce several sections of broken masonry dating to the earthquake in 1886, and to construct a new porch. While the couple did not endeavor to replace the two-story veranda that had been on the house originally, they did erect a smaller porch in keeping with the style of other North Carolina plantation homes of the period.[7]

The Sumners filled their home with antiques, including a square grand piano that had belonged to the Morris family before the Civil War. The couple hosted many parties and social events, often as fundraisers for the local historical society and chapters of the Daughters of the American Revolution and the United Daughters of the Confederacy. Mr. Sumner served as a state senator in the 1950s and 1960s, and was also a trustee of the University of North Carolina at Chapel Hill.

It was during the Sumners' ownership that the home was first wired for electricity and a telephone was installed. The Sumners added a small bath at one end of the upstairs hall and converted one of the principal rooms on the first floor into a kitchen. Until that time all meals prepared on the plantation had been cooked over an open flame in the separate kitchen building located behind the mansion.

The couple also worked tirelessly to ensure that the development of neighboring properties and the cutting of large tracts of nearby timberland did not impact the integrity or appearance of the plantation. It was through the efforts of the Sumners that *Fox Haven* was nominated and listed on the National Register of Historic Places in 1972.[8]

The mansion's stately appearance and location on a hill looking over vast bottomland was what first attracted its current owner, Delphine Jones. She vividly recalls driving down the winding approach road and seeing the house across a broad expanse of green pastures bordered by oak and walnut trees and dotted with glossy magnolias. It was springtime and the front lawn was covered with thousands of daffodils that were radiant in the bright morning sun.

"It took my breath away," exclaims Jones, a native of Georgia. "I knew the minute I saw this house that I wanted to live here. I knew nothing of its history when I first stepped through the front door. Since that time I've really tried to immerse myself in the story of this plantation and the people who once lived here. I consider it an honor to now be a part of the plantation's history and to play a role in making sure that it is saved for the future."[9]

Extensive restoration work by the current owner has returned the home's interior to its nineteenth-century appearance. An open pergola was added to both sides of the front porch in 2015 to support trailing wisteria. (Lattimore)

A view of the mansion at Green River
Plantation from the old carriage drive.
Two ornamental lagoons border the
home's front lawn. (Cantrell)

GREEN RIVER PLANTATION

Belle of the Carolina Backcountry

♀ Polk County, North Carolina

A gracious welcome for guests has always been a dominant theme of southern hospitality and nowhere is that welcome greater than at *Green River Plantation*, near Rutherfordton, North Carolina. Travelers from many walks of life have made their way to the estate for more than two hundred years. And the stories and tales of the planter families once ensconced there reveal many of the rich cultural traditions of the Old South.

When visitors enter the carriage gates today, they witness the enticing sights and sounds of an era long past against the backdrop of an early nineteenth-century home. Winding through towering oaks and ancient boxwoods, they first glimpse the plantation's twenty-seven-room mansion across an expansive lawn bordered by tranquil lagoons. Ellen Clayton Cantrell saw that same view more than sixty-five years ago when traveling to western North Carolina to visit relatives. She was enchanted by the magnitude of the main house and the beauty of its surroundings. It was then as a little girl that she first dreamed of owning the plantation.

That dream was realized in 1987, when Ellen, her husband, William E. Cantrell, and the couple's daughter, Amanda Cantrell, purchased the estate and its remaining 372 acres to serve not only as a private home, but also as a historic site open to the public for tours. The opportunity to purchase the plantation, however, came at a time when the main house had been abandoned for a number of years and the dwelling and surrounding gardens were in great need of restoration.

The once manicured lawns and famed boxwood gardens ornamenting the approach to the house were all but lost to the ravages of neglect. Fallen limbs and other debris littered the grounds, while briars and weeds had grown thick in old paths and roadways. The plantation's ornamental ponds were choked with thick vegetation and the surface of their black waters was stirred frequently by rodents and snakes sliding quietly out of view.

English ivy grew thick around trees and shrubs, and not only trailed high into tree limbs but also climbed its way up the porches and walls of the house, latching itself into mortar joints and rotting timbers. Closer inspection showed that the main veranda was near collapse. The interior of the mansion fared no better. The dwelling's sagging roof had been leaking water onto 180-year-old paneling and rotting away floorboards that had been fashioned by slaves.

"A lot of damage can happen to a house that has not been properly cared for through the years," says Ellen Cantrell. "It was hard work, but very rewarding to bring this house back from the very serious state of decline that existed here. A few more years and it is possible that it would have been beyond saving."[1]

Amanda Cantrell vividly recalls the physical labor that went into restoring the venerable structure. She worked alongside her father and grandfather carrying lumber and other supplies into the house to make repairs while sweating through summer months on a ladder painting rooms and removing old wallpaper from moldy plaster walls. Hundreds of panes of glass were reglazed and cleaned. Similarly, basement and attic spaces were cleared of mounds of debris and materials left by former owners.

Most importantly, the Cantrells corrected structural problems with the mansion's foundation, chimneys, and porches. Large fieldstones that had been hauled to the mansion from more than a mile away during the early antebellum period were repositioned, and hundreds of crumbling bricks were repaired or replaced. Many of the large timbers supporting the verandas and upper floors were reinforced, and one of the oldest porches was enclosed to create a tea room for guests to the plantation. That porch, which originally served as the main entrance to the mansion, provided a view of the Green River in the distance, from which the plantation took its name. Changes and later additions to the home saw the main entrance opened from another porch.

Discoveries were made along the way that revealed many stories of the past. Hoof marks were found on the heart pine flooring in the drawing room confirming tales that Union soldiers had stabled their horses in that grand space during the Civil War. Signatures were discovered etched into the wavy, hand-blown glass in the dining room windows from brides on their wedding days long ago. Boxes of nineteenth-century china and stoneware used by the original family were found underneath the house, and letters, journals, and receipts came spilling out from the walls when mantels were moved for restoration and baseboards loosed for repairs.

"*Green River* is an incredible old house," Ellen Cantrell tells each visitor to the home. "Every room has the wonderful feeling of the families that lived here before we became the stewards of its history. I'd like to think that old Mr. Carson himself, who started this plantation when Thomas Jefferson was the president of the United States, would find himself at home if he were able to step back from the grave and stand in these gracious old rooms."[2]

Begun in 1807, the rambling three-and-a-half-story home was constructed during three architectural periods of the nineteenth century. The earliest portions of the dwelling consisted of a Federal-style, frame structure perched high on brick piers with a wide, two-story veranda opening from the front and rear façades. No interior staircases existed in that first construction. Instead, the upper floors were accessed from staircases located on the porches. In 1830–1831, a brick, Greek Revival–style addition of equal proportions was constructed to the rear of the original dwelling. The veranda between the two houses was then enclosed just before the Civil War and became the site of a

The drawing room is the largest space in the mansion. Many special events, including balls, weddings, and christenings, were held in this room during the decades before the Civil War. (Cantrell)

grand staircase serving both sections of the home. In time, many additional porches were added and then enclosed. The largest room in the house is the main drawing room, which measures 24 x 24 feet, with twelve-foot ceilings.

Tradition says that the collection of sixteen mantels in the home were handcrafted in Philadelphia and shipped to Charleston, South Carolina, before being loaded onto flatboats for journey into the interior of the state and then off-loaded onto wagons for transport to the plantation in the foothills of North Carolina.[3] One of the mantels bears a landscape painting of an English country scene rendered by noted artist Jacob Marling in the 1840s. Marling painted at least one portrait while visiting *Green River*,

and it is likely that he rendered the landscape at that time.[4] Throughout the home exceptional Greek Revival–style trim, including rondels and corner blocks, can be seen on the window casings and door trim.

The plantation was established in the first decade of the nineteenth century by Joseph McDowell Carson, a lawyer and planter, who had married his first cousin Rebekah Wilson, of Tennessee. Carson chose the site of the plantation because of the fertile bottomland that existed along both sides of the Green River. The couple had ten children, and while they were raising their family, they were also increasing the size

The dining room contains one of sixteen mantels shipped from Philadelphia in the 1830s for use in the mansion. The plaster ceiling medallion was handcrafted in Washington, DC. (Cantrell)

Several of the home's bedrooms, including this room in the oldest portion of the mansion, are furnished with nineteenth-century antiques and decorated with fabrics and wallpapers appropriate to the period. (Cantrell)

While it has been used as a library for more than one hundred years, during the antebellum period this room was used as the home's main dining room. The walls retain their original color of "Williamsburg" blue. (Cantrell)

of their landholdings. At Carson's death in 1860, the plantation consisted of seventeen hundred acres and was worked by 124 slaves. For a number of years the plantation was also the home of Carson's younger half-brother, Samuel Price Carson, a United States congressman and senator who left North Carolina in the late 1830s, eventually becoming the first secretary of state for the Republic of Texas.[5]

After the Civil War, the plantation became the home of Joseph McDowell Carson's granddaughter Mary Mills and her husband, Col. Franklin Coxe. Coxe was a railroad baron and real estate magnate who is credited with helping develop Asheville, North Carolina, into a resort city in the 1890s.[6]

Coxe family heirs owned the home until 1958, when the house was sold and the entire contents of the mansion sold at public auction. For the next two and a half decades, the home was owned by a succession of different persons until it sat vacant for a number of years in the late 1980s. That is when the Cantrells discovered it was for sale.

While the Cantrells brought a measure of authenticity to the restoration project, they also realized that the home would have to accommodate modern living. A kitchen with modern appliances and several bathrooms with contemporary amenities were fitted into spaces that had once served as rear porches on the home. The greatest challenge of the restoration project was upgrading electrical and plumbing systems, and the addition of a security network without destroying the craftsmanship of earlier years.

"Most historic homes have evolved through the years," reminds Amanda Cantrell. "It is rare for older homes to survive without the alterations imposed by daily living. Sometimes older homes are more interesting precisely because of their evolution over time. I think that is one of the main reason that I love this house so much. It represents the deep history of an important family across more than 150 years of time."[7]

Mrs. Cantrell's choices for interior decoration included replicating many of the original paint colors that existed in the home before the Civil War, and also applying wallpapers from the historic collections of some of this country's leading manufacturers. In choosing furnishings for the rooms, she selected antiques and period reproductions and anchored many of the rooms with woolen rugs. In addition, special emphasis was placed on incorporating exquisitely detailed, handmade window treatments throughout the principal rooms.

The house opened for tours on a regular basis in December 1990. The initial opening was met with fanfare and media coverage that highlighted one very important fact— that very few historic properties are open to the public in western North Carolina. By opening their home, the Cantrells enabled the general public to glimpse what life was like for a prosperous family living in the Carolina foothills during the nineteenth and early twentieth centuries.

"The *Green River Plantation* house is one of the premiere residences in the western part of this state," says Ted Alexander, regional director of Preservation North Carolina, a nonprofit organization that solicits buyers for endangered historic homes and buildings. "It is also one of the best places in North Carolina to see fine architectural details of the Federal and Greek Revival periods. Allowing the general public to tour the main house and the surviving plantation kitchen affords many people an opportunity to see the incredible craftsmanship and styles from before the Civil War. The restoration

At more than 17,000 square feet, the mansion at Green River Plantation is one of the largest antebellum homes in North Carolina. Its twenty-seven principal rooms have been meticulously restored by the Cantrell family. (Cantrell)

of this great house has made a valuable contribution to the preservation of this state's architectural heritage."[8]

Each year since 1990, thousands of people, including hundreds of school-age children, have toured the *Green River Plantation*. In addition, several historical associations and preservation societies have traveled for long distances to visit the home and grounds. Often, individuals claiming an ancestral connection to the plantation have come for a tour. One such event occurred in the summer of 1997 when more than 150 African Americans with direct lineage to the plantation's former slaves, and to the Carson family, held a reunion on the plantation and toured the house and grounds where their ancestors once labored.

"It seems odd, as a black person, to claim *Green River* as my ancestral home," said Connie Carson, who is descended from former slave Harvey Carson. "But this plantation is the one piece of geography that I can definitely say was home to my ancestors. I can see the fields surrounding this house and know that they lived, worked and died here. It is with strong emotions that I stand on this soil."[9]

HOPE PLANTATION
Restoring the Home of a Statesman

◉ Windsor, North Carolina

The 1960s will always be remembered as a time of great tumult in this country, when many of the traditions and beliefs of the past were challenged and changed. It was also a time, however, of renewed interest in America's history and when great strides were made toward the preservation of some of this country's greatest architectural treasures.

Inspired by First Lady Jacqueline Bouvier Kennedy's landmark restoration of the White House in Washington, DC, historical societies, heritage groups, and private individuals across the country launched a myriad of preservation projects that saved thousands of important historical homes and other buildings. Many of those structures were nearly beyond saving but were dramatically snatched back from the brink.

In North Carolina, successful efforts by Jeanelle Coulter Moore, wife of Gov. Dan K. Moore, to save the state's executive mansion from demolition helped fuel a movement of preservation in the state. Mrs. Moore urged her husband to call for legislation creating the North Carolina Executive Mansion Fine Arts Committee. Like Mrs. Kennedy, Moore took particular interest in furnishing the state's executive mansion with authentic pieces of nineteenth-century antiques including a vast collection of items belonging to former governors.[1]

Excitement over the preservation efforts in Raleigh could be felt in many other communities across the state where local citizens knew that too many significant structures were being neglected or lost. From the Appalachian Mountains to the coast people began looking at older structures with greater appreciation and sought the resources necessary to save them from distress and ruin. Nowhere was the determination and excitement greater than in rural Bertie County, located approximately one hundred miles inland from the Atlantic Ocean, where preservation efforts saved one of the South's most important architectural treasures.

Anyone driving west out of the little town of Windsor, North Carolina, in the fall of 1964, would most likely have seen a decaying mass of rotting lumber, crumbling chimneys, and sagging porches amid the lush green landscape of tobacco and corn fields. It was a view that middle-aged John E. "Jack" Tyler had seen since he was a little boy riding with his father out to visit farm families in an old Model-T Ford during the Great Depression.

What Tyler saw was the former home of North Carolina governor David Stone. The decaying mansion had been built in 1803, and for more than 150 years had served as a landmark in the community; a physical symbol of Stone's political career and his contributions to the people of North Carolina. Tyler had been charmed by the house and its history for as long as he could remember.

Sadly, the structure had fallen so far into decay that many people, including historians and preservation specialists, felt that the dwelling would soon collapse. The condition of the home was so dire that Dr. Christopher Crittenden, respected and capable director of the North Carolina Department of Archives and History, stated, "The house at *Hope Plantation* is hopeless. I fear that the end is very near for this significant structure."[2]

Excited by the work being conducted in Raleigh and Washington, Tyler was convinced that something could be done. He launched an effort with his wife, Margaret, and several of their neighbors and friends to acquire the home from Dr. and Mrs. J. E. Smith, of Windsor. After a few months the group of dedicated citizens legally formed the Historic Hope Foundation, which was incorporated by the state on February 2, 1965.

Early the following year, the foundation employed one of the state's most outstanding craftsman, Wilbur M. Kemp, to begin a project of restoration. Tyler served as chairman of the restoration committee. He was assisted by A. L. Honeycutt, a representative from the North Carolina Department of Archives and History, who was engaged in the project due to the importance of the home's architecture and the original owner's connection to the history of the state and nation.[3]

Stone, a man of many talents and aspirations, was the son of a successful merchant. He began acquiring property at an early age. Following his graduation from Princeton University with a medical degree in 1788, he was elected to the North Carolina House of Representatives seven times and to the state senate once. He served two terms as a superior court judge, one term as governor of North Carolina (1808–1810), and also single terms as a US congressman and US senator. Stone also had the distinction of serving as a delegate to the state convention of 1789, which ratified the US Constitution, and also for serving as one of the original trustees of the University of North Carolina, a position he held from 1795 until his death in 1818.[4]

The house built by Stone was exceptional in its style and ornamentation. It has the distinction of being one of North Carolina's finest Georgian-style mansions from the early nineteenth century. Documented evidence shows that Stone used a popular eighteenth-century architectural manual by Abraham Swann, *The British Architect*, to design his house.

In her landmark book *North Carolina Architecture*, historian Catherine Bishir states that between 1780 and 1830, families in the wealthiest plantation communities built far more elaborate residences than had been seen in the state before. For the first time,

Hope Plantation as it appeared in 1957 before a complete restoration was conducted on the dwelling. The mansion was built in 1803 for planter David Stone, who would later serve as governor of North Carolina, and as a US congressman and a US senator. (Library of Congress)

This rear view of the house in 1957 shows a shed porch that was later removed during restoration and replaced with a replica of the original. Notice an automobile parked under the sagging porch, and the severely decayed chimneys on the mansion's west side. (Library of Congress)

a significant number of rural houses, like the mansion at *Hope Plantation*, followed formal plans and presented prominent exterior ornamentation in the classical style.

"The most formal of these residences were concentrated in eastern North Carolina where the plantation culture developed more fully," writes Bishir. "They (planters) built and furnished their homes with a fashion-conscious blend of regional and urban elements . . . Working with local or regional artisans, including many who traveled from one area to another, planters incorporated into their houses a dynamic blend of stylish models, imported items, customary forms and various personal styles." Despite the growing number of fine homes in the region, Bishir relates that few homes could rival the importance and style of *Hope Plantation*.[5]

Built on a raised basement of stone and brick, the upper two frame stories portray a basic Palladian design with some neoclassical elements. The five-bay façade features a pedimented double portico built on brick piers and supported by slender Tuscan-inspired columns. Pairs of tall brick chimneys laid in Flemish bond flank the house and rise higher than the captain's walk that crowns the structure. The captain's walk is surrounded by a Chinese-Chippendale railing that mirrors the design of railings on the front and rear porches of the home.

The basement of the home contains a warming kitchen and two large storage rooms. A primary kitchen was originally housed in a separate structure located just east of the main house. Providing many of the necessary ingredients for meals for Stone, his wife and ten children, as well as a myriad of guests, was an expansive vegetable garden and the plantation's dairy and smokehouse, all located within sight of the mansion.

The front and rear doors of the main floor above open into a wide hall that is divided into unequal sections by an elliptical archway supported by fluted Doric pilasters. The home's principal staircase rises from a side hall located left of the main entrance. A secondary stair, one of very few built in early nineteenth-century North Carolina, extends from the basement to the upper floor, permitting privacy in the public rooms, while allowing servants greater freedom to do their work.

Heart pine flooring was used throughout the home on both levels. The first floor contains a dining room and three bedchambers, including Governor and Mrs. Stone's room. The main bedroom not only provided private quarters for the master, but it also provided Mrs. Stone a workplace. From that room she directed the work flow of the main house, supervised her children, and gave instruction to her house servants.

Unlike many contemporary houses, Stone relegated his family life to the main floor and focused his role as a statesman and planter on the second floor. The home's two main rooms, the drawing room or ballroom, and the library are located upstairs. The library is furnished with floor-to-ceiling bookcases on two walls with glazed doors above enclosed cabinets. In Stone's lifetime, the bookcases held more than fourteen hundred volumes, including law books, histories, governmental studies, science manuals, and religious texts. The drawing room, measuring 20 x 30 feet, is the largest room in the house. It contains original raised panel wainscot and a dentil cornice. The drawing room mantel is Federal in style and consists of a facing of imported Italian marble. Other mantels in the home were crafted of red stone from Newark, New Jersey.

The Stone family sold *Hope Plantation* in 1838, and the governor's descendants left North Carolina. After a succession of live-in owners, the house eventually became the

The restored single-story porch on the rear of the mansion replicated original details including dentil moldings and Chippendale trim and stair balustrade. (Bush)

domain of tenant farmers in the early twentieth century until it was completely abandoned during World War II. Documentary photographs taken in the early 1950s show the house nearly in ruins, with few remaining signs of the estate's grandeur.

The restoration of the home is remembered as a Herculean feat. In 1966, the Historic Hope Foundation hired Richard W. Iobst, a professional historian, to research the plantation, Governor Stone's personal papers, and the estate inventory. Iobst found the inventory, which was conducted at the time of Governor Stone's death, to be invaluable in his nationwide search to acquire items originally belonging to the Stone family.[6]

Restoration team members used Stone's estate inventory, a fifty-page document that records dozens of pieces of principal furnishings and the titles of the books in Stone's library, to furnish the mansion. The inventory helped to identify particular pieces of furniture and provided clues as to their placement throughout the home.

In addition to the inventory, scholarship was applied to every aspect of the restoration. According to historians Wayland Jenkins and Eric Hause, "the Foundation consulted with numerous restoration specialists to ensure an authentic restoration, and they applied the techniques available at the time to painting the exterior what was thought to be the original colors: yellow and green. Since that time, paint analysis experts have discovered that linseed oil from the original paint (on which the exterior colors were based) had separated and yellowed, giving false test results to the original restorationists."[7]

Continued scholarship has revealed other earlier misjudgments. Gregory Tyler, current curator of the property and daughter of Jack and Margaret Tyler, discovered in 2010 that some of the pages of Stone's estate inventory were out of order and that mistakes had been made in identifying the original use of some of the rooms in the mansion.

With the corrections made, two rooms in the house now more closely resemble the way they would have looked in Stone's time. The new interpretation allows visitors to more accurately see which rooms were used directly by the Stone family, which were the domain of servants, and which spaces represent the areas where all of their lives intertwined.[8]

Tyler has now devoted more than three decades of her own life to *Hope Plantation*. She follows the example set by her late parents while embracing new opportunities to expand the educational and historical experience of visitors. Her focus is always one of scholarship and improved interpretation of the plantation's story.[9]

When the home was opened to the public in the 1970s, the primary goal was to present the life of David Stone and his family. Today, the interpretation of the mansion and surrounding plantation is expanded to also show the daily life of the slaves and servants on the estate.

Historian David Serxner, who has contributed to the continued restoration at *Hope*, says that showing the role of the servants and slaves adds greater historical integrity to the property as a first-rate historical site. "We have this unfortunate tendency to ignore parts of our past," muses Serxner. "What we are now doing here (at *Hope*) is helping people remember that there wasn't just one family here. The family in the big house was two families, the Stone family, and the family—the network—of servants who supported them."[10]

During the past forty-five years, *Hope Plantation* has been visited by hundreds of thousands of visitors who marvel at the home's architecture and its burgeoning collection of fine decorative arts from the eighteenth and nineteenth centuries. More than twenty original pieces of Stone's furniture can be found in the dwelling, and the Historic Hope Foundation has acquired originals or period copies of more than 90 percent of the books once found in his library.

Tyler is continuing the work of her parents and assists with planning future maintenance and restoration projects that will hopefully preserve the home for generations to come. "This house reminds us that everything special must be guarded and cared for, or it could be lost," says Tyler. "The miracle of this plantation is that it was restored. If the home had sat for even a few more years without intervention it would have been lost forever."[11]

SIDNEY VILLA PLANTATION
Hanging by a Thread

♥ Spindale, North Carolina

I t is hard to imagine today, amid the noise of street traffic and the flow of pedes-
trians, that the white-columned building standing at the corner of Tanner and
Main Streets in the textile town of Spindale, North Carolina, was once the seat of
a prosperous backcountry plantation surrounded by fields of cotton, corn, and rolling
pastureland.

Three generations before the first bolt of cloth and spool of yarn was manufactured
in Spindale a house was built on the headwaters of Stonecutter Creek that in time
would become the symbolic heart and geographic center of the mill community. Francis Sidney Coxe, the original owner of the home and surrounding plantation, was the
son of Tench Coxe Sr. of Philadelphia, one of the wealthiest men in America during
the late eighteenth and early nineteenth centuries.

Tench Coxe was the assistant secretary of the United States Treasury from 1789 to
1797, during the presidency of George Washington. He also served as a paid advisor to
the secretary of state during the Adams and Jefferson administrations. A vast collection
of letters and journals held at the time of his death reveal a close association with just
about every prominent political figure of the time from Washington and Jefferson to
Benjamin Franklin and Henry Knox.[1]

In addition to his governmental career, Coxe was a land speculator who purchased
hundreds of thousands of acres of land in western North Carolina in hopes of reselling
at a higher price. That endeavor steered his son, Francis Sidney Coxe, to the state's
foothills region in the early decades of the nineteenth century. Francis Sidney Coxe was
heir not only to his father's fortune but also to the world of responsibilities and work
that it took to maintain and manage such riches. It was his desire for a country home
that led to the creation of one of western North Carolina's most important antebellum
landmarks.[2]

A two-page contract dated June 25, 1849, shows that Francis Sidney Coxe and his
wife, Jane McBee Alexander Coxe, contracted with J. H. Wilkins, of Rutherfordton,

The planter's cottage built for Francis Sidney Coxe in 1849, near Rutherfordton, North Carolina, was originally surrounded by hundreds of acres of cotton. This photo from 1880 shows the dwelling and former slave cabins in the distance. (Rutherford County Historical Society)

A rare image of a young African American girl spinning cotton into thread on the porch of Sidney Villa Plantation in the late nineteenth century. (Rutherford County Historical Society)

North Carolina, to build their plantation home in exchange for 334 acres further down Stonecutter Creek. Coxe was meticulous in his record keeping as the house began to take shape in a grove of oak and walnut trees two and a half miles east of the Rutherford County Court House. Field slaves and a few hired craftsmen were engaged in building the house.[3]

Construction details of the home's staircase, banisters, shutters, windows, and flooring, as well as the cost of needed materials, were recorded by Coxe. The bricks for the plantation home were manufactured on Cleghorn Creek in the nearby town of Rutherfordton and hauled to the site on horse-drawn wagons. The lumber needed for construction was felled and sawn on the property by Coxe's slaves.[4]

While the dwelling was small in comparison to other plantation mansions across the South and belied the Coxe family's wealth and influence, it gave the family the requisite home necessary for entertaining in style. It was a one-and-a-half-story, brick structure with four principal rooms on the first floor and two rooms above. The first floor faced a single-story veranda running the entire length of the home's front façade.

On the main floor a well-appointed parlor and dining room originally flanked a wide center hall. Those rooms were ornamented with fine millwork, including mantels, window trim, and door casings. To the rear of those spaces was a library and bedroom, both of which opened onto the back loggia. The kitchen was a separate structure located behind the home.

The plantation house faced the main road running through rural Rutherford County, and was surrounded by a collection of support structures including slave cabins, a stable, a smokehouse, and barns. As was the custom of the time, when the house was complete the Coxe family gave the home a name, *Sidney Villa*, in tribute to its plantation master.

While no inventory survives to indicate how the home was furnished, there are receipts among the Coxe family papers that give insight into the lifestyle of the family. Purchases for the Coxe household in the late 1840s and early 1850s include English china, sterling silver serving pieces, clocks and watches, gilded mirrors, a sideboard and eight matching chairs, bedsteads, music boxes, a cellaret (wine cooler), chamber porcelains, and a spinet (piano). In addition, numerous lengths of expensive fabrics were ordered for the home including silk damask, velvets, and lace.[5]

At the time of the home's construction, Francis Sidney Coxe had been a resident of Rutherford County for more than twenty years. Two of his sons, Franklin Coxe and Tench Charles Coxe, were born in Rutherfordton. The family's reputation was strong throughout the region. In addition to land sales, Coxe was a successful merchant. Surviving ledgers from the 1830s and 1840s show that many of the prominent families of Rutherford County kept open accounts with the Coxes and depended on their mercantile to order supplies from faraway places like Philadelphia, Boston, and New York.[6]

Francis Sidney Coxe was not able to enjoy his new home for long. Two years after its completion he succumbed to tuberculosis, which had plagued him for years, and he died on April 8, 1852. He was buried in the Rutherfordton City Cemetery. An estate inventory conducted following Coxe's death indicates that the plantation consisted of seven hundred acres and twenty-five slaves.

Mrs. Jane Coxe continued to live on the plantation for much of the next two decades. In the late 1850s, the management of all farming operations on the plantation fell on her shoulders while her sons were attending Furman University, in Greenville, South Carolina.

A letter written by Mrs. Coxe in December 1859 reveals that the plantation had produced more than sixty bales of cotton during the previous autumn, and more than eighty hogs had been raised that year for slaughter. Agricultural production would soon come to an end on the estate with the coming of the Civil War. During the war years Mrs. Coxe stayed at neighboring plantations with relatives and friends.[7]

After the war the house became the possession of Col. Franklin Coxe, who had served in the Confederate army, and who had returned from the war to take charge of his family's business endeavors with even greater skill and tenacity than his father. Colonel Coxe had married Mary Matilda Mills, of the *Green River Plantation*, near Rutherfordton, North Carolina, in 1861.

The coming of the railroad to Rutherford County in the late 1880s brought changes to the landscape around the plantation. In 1887, a line of the Charleston, Cincinnati & Chicago (CC&C) Railroad was completed from Charlotte to Rutherfordton. Later, the Carolina Central Railroad followed the same route and crossed the tracks of the CC&C Railroad in front of the old plantation home. This resulted in the community surrounding the house becoming known as "Coxe's Crossing." In time, the railroads would become the Southern and Seaboard Airline Railroads.

After Colonel Coxe's death in 1903, the home was used by his wife's aunt, Matilda Carson Thruston, until 1908. After Mrs. Thruston died, the home sat vacant and then was leased by the Coxe family during World War I, before it was operated as an inn in the 1920s. The home was purchased by textile magnate S. B. Tanner Sr. in 1922, and donated to the newly formed Town of Spindale for use as a community meeting hall and recreation center the following year.

At the time of Tanner's gift the old plantation house was remodeled by architect Martin E. Boyer Jr., and a portico upheld by four Doric columns was erected on the front of the structure replacing the earlier wooden porch. Alterations made to the home during the 1920s and 1930s greatly diminished the original character of the interior spaces leaving very few clues of the structure's plantation past.

Without concern for the architectural or historical integrity of the building the main rooms on the first floor were converted into offices for town personnel. The dining room was refitted for use as a public library and the town's police department was located in the former master bedroom. The two upstairs bedrooms were converted into a suite to serve as the residence of the town's athletic director and his wife.

Those alterations were minor compared to the changes that were soon to come. In an effort to provide amenities and recreational opportunities to mill families, the town council soon began the construction of a full gymnasium, and later a bowling alley, that opened directly from the rear of the original plantation home's main hall. In the years following World War II, a commercial kitchen and 250-seat dining hall were added above the gym's locker rooms on the ground floor. On a weekly basis thousands of local citizens streamed through the old plantation home that had been transformed into a multipurpose community center.

In the 1920s, the brick plantation home was acquired by a textile executive who greatly expanded the structure to serve as a community building for his employees. A new portico was added at that time. (Rutherford County Historical Society)

Outside the home the changes to the landscape were equally dramatic. After the Town of Spindale was incorporated in 1923, seven manufacturing plants were constructed directly across the main road from the old plantation home. Stores and restaurants, a bus station, theater, automobile garages, churches, schools, and hundreds of homes soon lined a grid of streets encircling the antebellum landmark.

For generations now the façade of the home has served as a beloved symbol of the town. But, much of its antebellum appearance has been lost or is covered by twentieth-century elements. While the home's two front rooms, the original parlor and dining room, survive to give some semblance of their earlier use, the quality of those spaces has been greatly diminished due to the installation of acoustical tile ceilings with recessed lighting. The bedchambers above have become a maze of air cooling ducts and electrical conduit making it difficult to imagine how the spaces would have looked before the Civil War.

While much of the home's architectural significance has been lost, there have been several positive developments made in preserving its history. Beginning in the 1980s, a group of concerned citizens began gathering Coxe family memorabilia and furniture to display in the home's original parlor in an effort to create a heritage room for the community.

Coxe family descendants donated an American Empire sofa, square grand piano, Eastlake-style fainting couch, and a pair of ornamental sconces originally used in the home as anchors of the heritage collection. Complementing those pieces was a collection of framed family portraits and a landscape photograph of the home from 1909 that was hung over the

These aerial photographs from 2015 show how the textile town of Spindale, North Carolina, eventually engulfed the old plantation home. The house can be seen (with white columns) facing its surviving front lawn. (Medford)

This Greek Revival–style mantel with fluted trim is the only original piece of millwork to survive in the structure. It still graces the home's east parlor. (Lattimore)

mantel in the parlor. The Greek Revival–style mantel, original to the home's construction, is one of only a few remaining pieces of millwork to survive from the 1840s.

"So much has been lost here in respect to the architectural history of the home," says Spindale mayor Mickey Bland. "But, the people of this town love the story of this house and what the Coxe family meant to our community. Our town can't afford to go back and undo the alterations that were made to this property more than 90 years ago. But, there is a strong desire to preserve our history, and the town is committed to saving what remains of the original portions of the old Coxe plantation house."

In the fall of 2016 the Spindale Town Council approved a new logo for the municipality that features the façade of the old plantation home. At the same time town employees began the process of having the original Coxe family furniture restored and upholstered pieces covered in period-appropriate fabric. The two surviving front parlors will be decorated appropriately to the 1850s era, and discussions are being held about improving the bedchambers on the second floor.

"The antebellum portion of the Spindale House is an amazing survivor," says Ted Alexander, regional director of Preservation North Carolina. "While it is a shame that so much of the historical integrity of the property was compromised when it was converted into a community center in the early twentieth century, it is encouraging to know that local residents remain committed to saving the original brick walls of the house and making sure that what remains of [the] original millwork is protected. There is still so much to celebrate about the old house."

SOUTH CAROLINA

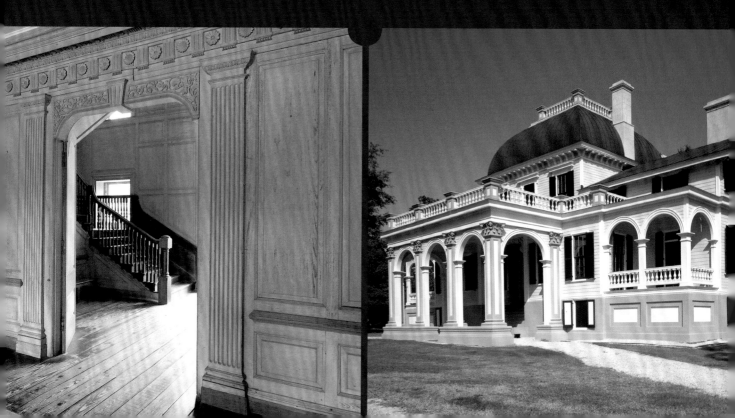

A variety of window and door pediments can be seen on the river façade of Drayton Hall. The structure was once flanked by matching dependencies that contained a laundry and kitchen. (Levet)

DRAYTON HALL
Time Capsule on the Ashley River

♀ Charleston, South Carolina

When Miss Charlotta Drayton died in the fall of 1969, a small group of her relations and old friends gathered at the family's ancestral home on the banks of the Ashley River, near Charleston, South Carolina, to pay their respects and to spend time in rooms that had sheltered the Drayton family since colonial days. The old home, known for more than two centuries as *Drayton Hall*, had only been lived in a few weeks each year since the early twentieth century, and its interiors had remained virtually unchanged since the dwelling was completed in 1742.

It was a time capsule like few other historic homes in America. The Draytons had never disturbed the interiors by adding electricity, plumbing, or central heating. And most of the rooms had never been updated with faddish wallpaper or paint in keeping with changing tastes and trends.

While family members cherished the home and their association with one of the nation's greatest architectural treasures, no one was willing to make the dwelling their primary residence or to take full responsibility for its maintenance and protection. Although located a mere thirteen miles upriver from Charleston, the isolated location of the home and its lack of modern amenities made it impractical for daily living.

When Miss Drayton's estate was settled, the home was inherited by her adult nephews, Charles and Francis Drayton, seventh-generation members of the family. The men had grown up visiting the estate each summer, swimming in the river, hunting in nearby swamps, and playing games in the shadow of the great house. It was an idyllic time in their young lives that seemed as if it would last forever.[1]

In their adulthood, however, things changed and careers and family responsibilities often took the men far from Charleston. "It became evident that we had to do something to preserve it or it would go," Charles Drayton once said of the manor house and surrounding property, recognizing that it could not continue to sit uninhabited and unprotected. "And I think we did the right thing. It was a hard decision to make, but I still think it was best for everyone concerned. There was a lot of soul-searching. It had been in our family for so long."[2]

The decision made by the Drayton heirs in 1974 was to sell the estate and its magnificent manor house to the National Trust for Historic Preservation. Three factors weighed heavily in their decision. A property reassessment at the time sent taxes soaring, the maintenance costs of the property continued to rise, and random acts of vandalism and theft had begun to plague the old home.

The National Trust was an obvious choice for ownership of *Drayton Hall*. It is a property that is best described with superlatives. Built between 1738 and 1742, it is considered to be the finest example of early colonial architecture in America. It is the only plantation house on the Ashley River to survive the Civil War intact, and it was the first property in South Carolina to achieve National Landmark status. Beyond that, it is the ancestral home of one of South Carolina's most prominent families and has played host through the years to some of the nation's most important leaders in government, business, education, and the arts.

"The depth of what is known about architectural design and interior ornamentation during the early colonial period is greatly enhanced by the presence of *Drayton Hall*," says architectural historian Jay Phelps, of Charleston. "The house is the oldest surviving example of Georgian-Palladian architecture in the entire South. It certainly outshines most other buildings of its age in America."

The mansion was erected for John Drayton, a young planter who came from Barbados to the Carolina colony in 1738. While the name of the architect or master builder responsible for the mansion's design is unknown, its style mirrors the most fashionable building trends sweeping Britain during the same period. Georgian architecture is characterized by the classical use of strict symmetry and bold details. The main residential block was once flanked by matching dependencies (no longer standing) that housed the kitchen and laundry.[3]

Like many homes of the period, the front and rear façades of the home are not identical. The façade facing the river, considered the main entrance in the eighteenth century because most travel to the home was by boat, displays a pedimented central doorway reached by flanking staircases that rise in two flights to a central landing. The rear façade of the home, looking out over a broad lawn bordered by centuries-old live oaks draped in Spanish moss, boasts an impressive, two-story portico supported by eight columns of different orders. It is believed to be the first of its kind in America.

The floor plan at *Drayton Hall* is similar to many English manor houses of the period. The entire structure is perched on a raised basement that originally housed a warming kitchen and slaves' quarters. Massive stones line the floor in much of that space and arched brick piers support the weight of the rooms above. Some of the rooms on the basement level have exposed earthen floors. Interestingly, numerous pieces of limestone, including unused shafts of columns and matching capitals, survive in this space, which may indicate that the original builder had plans to erect a monumental portico on the river side of the home that was never constructed.

Both of the upper floors feature large rooms that were conducive to entertaining on a grand scale. On the first floor the main entrance opens into a great hall. The designs of the mantel and overmantel found there are copied from illustrations found

The dominant architectural feature of the mansion's land side is a two-tiered, Palladian portico that is thought to be the first of its kind in America. (Levet)

in pattern books published in England in 1727. Pairs of smaller drawing rooms, ornamented with wooden carvings and plaster embellishments, flank the great hall.[4]

The principal access to the spacious second floor is by way of a grand double staircase with richly carved mahogany spindles and brackets. Rising through the center of the home is a hidden, circular stair originally designed to be used by servants.

Many of the interior spaces on the second floor feature exuberant displays of ornamental trim and millwork. The principal drawing room on that floor boasts a rare ornamental ceiling, the designs of which were shaped in wet plaster. Classical decorations found throughout the room include carved wooden Ionic pilasters, and an elaborate cornice featuring candlewick-and-dart, bead-and-reel moldings, as well as plaster medallions embellished with acanthus leaves.

A number of the mahogany and yellow poplar carvings throughout the home were left natural to contrast with painted cypress paneling. Cypress wood was ideal for construction in the damp and humid environment along the Ashley River, because it is nearly impenetrable by insects and vermin, and is highly resistant to rot and decay.

Drayton Hall has been the witness to many historic events. It served as headquarters for British commanders Lord Cornwallis and Banastre Tarlton during the American Revolutionary War (1775–1783). During the Siege of Charleston in 1780, Patriot and British forces camped in the swamps all around the property, and cannon fire, although not directed toward *Drayton Hall*, rattled the thick masonry walls and broke windowpanes.[5]

Throughout the four years of the Civil War (1861–1865), the manor house was occupied by both Union and Confederate troops. When the war began, the banks of the Ashley River around *Drayton Hall* were lined with palatial plantation mansions along

The grand staircase at Drayton Hall rises in separate flights that meet on a landing leading into the upper drawing room. The elaborately carved mahogany spindles and brackets are original to the 1740s. (HABS)

both sides of the river. However, by the time marauding Union troops had done their damage and Union gunboats on the Ashley River had shelled many of the plantation homes, only *Drayton Hall* and two other once grand homes had survived the war. Tradition says that the home may have been spared because the Drayton family posted flags around the property identifying the house as a smallpox hospital.[6]

The great house and its surrounding gardens have not been lucky, however, when it comes to natural disasters and storms. During the Great Charleston Earthquake on September 1, 1886, the northeast dependency, thought to have contained the laundry, was destroyed. The sister dependency was leveled by a hurricane in 1893. A tropical storm in 1923 uprooted more than fifty trees in close proximity to the house that had been standing from before the Revolution.[7]

Safeguarding the great house and preserving its history was no easy task when the National Trust took ownership in the 1970s. Decisions made more than forty years ago still impact how the home is presented to the public today. The ultimate goal was to provide a rich cultural experience like none other in the United States.

Rather than restore the house to reflect a single historical period, the National Trust made the bold decision to preserve the site as it was received from the Drayton family in order to provide a timeline showing change and continuity through three centuries. Early efforts centered on research, as a team of preservationists began studying how the great house was constructed and to determine when alterations were made. They focused much attention on architectural features and historical surfaces in order to prioritize restoration projects over the first few years.

During the late 1970s and 1980s, the trust's primary objective was to stabilize the structure, improve the foundation, and replace a badly deteriorated metal roof. To strengthen the floor system in the upper great hall, engineers bolted angle irons on each side of every joist. To reattach falling pieces of the great hall's cast plaster ceiling to the lath above, conservators installed a system of wire mesh and plaster of Paris to secure the original handiwork created at the time of the home's construction.

The designs of the mantel and overmantel in the great hall were copied from an English pattern book. A carved fox head can be seen in the center shell medallion of the broken pediment. (Levet)

Paneled walls, carved cornices, and pilasters crafted from cypress are hallmarks of the grand interior ornamentation found at Drayton Hall. (Levet)

The oval ceiling medallion in the great hall was carved and applied in wet plaster in the 1850s. (Levet)

Looking from the great hall into the stair chamber on the mansion's river side. (Levet)

Of equal importance were their efforts to preserve original paint colors and remove generations of the dirt and grime that had accumulated on walls, ceilings, and floors over centuries of use. Paint experts have now spent decades studying the earliest layers of paint and varnish in the home to make sure that they appear today the way the manor house would have looked in the early eighteenth century.

Since 2006, a major project of restoration has been conducted on the home's masonry walls and the limestone and sandstone elements of the dwelling's iconic portico. The original limestone steps had cracked significantly and required much attention. Also, many of the stone tiles on the portico's floor had separated or shattered. Each tile was removed, repaired, and replaced with mortar appropriate to the early eighteenth century.

Visitors to *Drayton Hall* today are often surprised to find its rooms unfurnished. Many expect to see its interior spaces stuffed with art treasures, furniture, and other Drayton family heirlooms. During the course of each tour, docents explain the choices made by the National Trust and preservation experts in leaving the rooms void of material objects. Most guests leave with a greater appreciation for the home as one of this country's finest preservation projects.

"Walking into *Drayton Hall* is an incredible experience," says cultural historian Todd Lavender, of North Carolina. "Your eye is drawn to the remarkable artistry and craftsmanship of the structure itself. Keeping the rooms free from furniture and other decorative elements gives one a true sense of the space inside the home and the size of each room in relation to its function. I am captivated by the home. Each time I visit, I come away with a greater appreciation for its preservation. Thanks to the very wise planning of the National Trust *Drayton Hall* sits in an unchanging state. It is only my perspective that changes as I learn more about its amazing architecture."

Lavender says he is a purist when it comes to historic homes and artifacts. "While restoration is often a necessity in the case of buildings with compromised structural integrity, preservation is so much more desirable when possible," Lavender believes. "It provides a unique snapshot in time which allows us the unique opportunity to experience a property in its original or 'found' state."

Visitors to *Drayton Hall* since the 1970s have had an opportunity to witness preservation in progress. They have frequently interacted with conservators and have seen firsthand the work they are conducting to keep the home in excellent repair. Educational programs, lectures, and workshops are often conducted by staff of the National Trust for Historic Preservation and by other noted architectural historians and preservationists from across the country for the benefit of both the public and scholars engaged in research.

"The preservation of a National Landmark property like *Drayton Hall* is something that really has no end," once remarked George McDaniel, former director of the property, when asked if the work on the property will ever be complete. "Individual preservation projects have a timeline for completion. The overall preservation of this magnificent property will never end. It is too valuable to our national history and to our understanding of the colonial era in this country to ever stop the work required to protect and preserve this property for all time."[8]

Homestead House, the dwelling
of the prominent Bratton family
of York County, South Carolina, as
seen across its broad front lawn
bordered by walnut, magnolia,
and oak trees. (Bush)

HOMESTEAD HOUSE

Historic Brattonsville's Shining Jewel

♥ York County, South Carolina

I n the early 1970s, as Americans were preparing to celebrate the nation's bicentennial, a wave of patriotism and pride swept the country. Historical societies, grassroots preservation organizations, and individuals endeavored to accomplish Herculean tasks in an effort to preserve the nation's past, often with very little money or resources. But with sheer will and hard work these groups realized an astounding degree of success for which current generations will ever be indebted.

Few of the challenges were more daunting than the efforts required to rescue and restore the once grand home known as *Homestead House* at Historic Brattonsville, in the undulating countryside of York County, South Carolina. The antebellum mansion had once been the domain of the prominent Bratton family, who had earlier played a significant role during the independence movement of the late eighteenth century in the Carolina backcountry. By the last half of the twentieth century, however, the home was in deplorable condition. Its rooms were used by teenagers for late-night parties, and its lawns and gardens were trampled by cows and strangled by brambles and underbrush.

"Time had not been kind to that beautiful home," recalls Wade Fairey, who glimpsed the structure for the first time as a young boy in 1959 while visiting the property with his father. "When I saw it that summer the grand front porch was missing and many of the windows had rotted away. Rain poured into the home around each chimney and a major portion of the wall on the east gable end, near the roof, was open to the elements."[1]

Decades of occupancy by tenant farming families had resulted in much neglect. Even with close neighbors keeping an eye on the property while it was unoccupied, nature still took its toll. A tornado in 1920 had torn the main porch away from the house, and falling tree limbs from nearby oak and walnut trees had damaged the rear of the home.

Luckily, unlike so many other historic structures located in isolated farming communities, the *Homestead House* had not been robbed of its mantels, doors, and decorative

The mansion as it appeared in 1900. (Courtesy Culture & Heritage Museums, York County, SC)

By the early 1920s, Homestead House showed its age. The original portico collapsed during a tornado in the 1950s and had not been replaced, and many of the windows needed to be replaced. (Courtesy Culture & Heritage Museums, York County, SC)

millwork. It is fortunate that faux finishes on the home's baseboards, doors, and plaster walls had not been marred by graffiti. While some rooms had been painted over to comply with styles and fashion changes, in many places the original work of nineteenth-century artisans and itinerant painters survived untouched.

"I fell in love with history and architecture because of *Homestead House*," muses Fairey, a native of York County, who credits his long career in preservation and curatorial science to his early experiences on the Brattons' plantation. "I knew from a very early age that I wanted to help save incredible pieces of the past that were being lost at an alarming rate."[2]

In the 1960s and 1970s few colleges and universities, particularly in the South, had dedicated academic programs that trained aspiring preservationists and architectural historians. For Fairey it was numerous "hands-on" experiences at *Homestead House* that gave him the base knowledge to begin his career. His prior training and apprenticeship as a furniture maker also gave him the patience and the eye for detail necessary for genuine restoration work.

Each summer and during long school holidays while in college, Fairey visited *Homestead House,* often to document the dwelling's architectural details and take measurements of each room. He made sketches of the scrollwork that ornaments the stair risers, and scraped layers of paint away from original decorative surfaces and finishes. His efforts laid the groundwork for future preservation and restoration that would be required to open the house to the public.

"As I learned more about architecture and preservation in college, I developed an immense appreciation and respect for the home's original owner, Dr. John Bratton, a physician and successful planter. I knew his plantation house was the exception rather than the rule. He was well educated and familiar with refined architecture," says Fairey. "So many plantation homes throughout the South are basically rambling structures that display a vernacular interpretation of classic styles. But at *Homestead House,* the architecture is symmetrical and deliberate. There is a definite plan for order and balance."[3]

While no architect has ever been identified for the home, written records reveal that the builder was local carpenter Henry Alexander (1772–1845). Alexander built several important homes in the area and was paid approximately $1,500 for his work on *Homestead House*. Lesser amounts were paid to other artisans who painted and plastered the dwelling. Construction began on the central block of the Federal-style, four-over-four frame home in 1823. Two, single-story brick wings were added in 1826, and a wide double porch was added sometime in the 1840s. These successive additions give the home a more palatial appearance.[4]

It was its evolution over time that eventually transformed *Homestead House* into a Greek Revival–style home that had few equals in the upstate of South Carolina, particularly during the early antebellum period. In its final form the home contained twelve rooms and four chimneys with seven fireplaces.

According to historian Michael C. Scoggins, one of the *Homestead House*'s unique features is a large brick dining room wing extending from the rear of the main house and connected by a covered breezeway. That structure was constructed at the same time as the home's side wings. Relatively few such spaces are known to have existed in the American South before the Civil War.

The main floor of that impressive space, measuring more than forty-two feet long and twenty feet wide, was used by the Brattons for dining and entertaining. The room is entered through an impressive doorway ornamented with sidelights and a fanlight above, and the opposite wall is anchored by a wide fireplace flanked by storage cabinets for silver and porcelain. Journals kept by Bratton family members reveal that the room was occasionally used for recitals and dances, particularly in the 1840s and 1850s when an academy for girls was operated on the plantation. A deep cellar underneath the space, lit by windows at ground level, was used for food storage and for weaving.[5]

The majority of the plantation home is raised on rock piers, including the wide double porch, which is upheld by chamfered posts and lined with simple balusters. The dwelling is entered on the main floor through a paneled door topped with a simple transom. The door looking out onto the upper porch is much more elaborate. It is surrounded by sidelights and a transom ornamented with Chippendale-style fretwork. Inside the home, Adam-style mantels ornament the principal rooms, while less decorative mantels service the bedchambers.

Scoggins has documented much of the genealogy and history of the Bratton family and their Scots-Irish ancestry. The family came early into the backcountry region of South Carolina. Initially, the family lived in a single-room log cabin that was, in time, enlarged to contain four rooms, including a large room on the upper half-story.

The patriarch of the family, Col. William Bratton, a local militia commander, fought in the Battle of Huck's Defeat on July 12, 1780. That battle was a small-scale confrontation that gave the Patriots a psychologically important victory over Loyalists and British forces during the Revolutionary War. Colonel Bratton had begun his fledgling plantation with just two hundred acres in 1766.[6]

This side view of the mansion shows how it is connected by an open passage to a brick structure that served principally as a dining room. (Bush)

The estate was situated at the intersection of several important colonial roads, and the location would serve the family well for generations to come. The growing assemblage of buildings and agrarian support structures surrounding the Bratton home, including smaller cabins used by other members of the Bratton family, soon became known as "Brattonsville," a name that grew in importance when an academy, post office, and store were operated on the property in the early nineteenth century.

The Brattons began planting cotton in the 1810s, and within a decade their wealth had increased substantially. John S. Bratton, a son of Col. William Bratton, was educated as a physician and became affluent through the practice of medicine and cotton farming. As a young planter, John Bratton lived with his bride, Harriet Rainey Bratton, in the frontier cabin of his parents. By 1820, however, it was clear that the young Brattons wished for a home that was more in keeping with their standing in the community and more reflective of the architectural styles of the day. Soon, a substantial frame home would be constructed for the couple within sight of the earlier log cabin.

"The house that was built for John and Harriett Bratton is representative of their wealth and their position in society," says Scoggins. "During the early antebellum period the Bratton Plantation became one of the most important agrarian estates in upstate South Carolina. Few neighboring planter families could rival the Brattons' wealth, and an even smaller number of plantation families could boast owning a home as nice as the *Homestead*."[7]

At the time of Dr. John Bratton's death in 1843, the plantation had grown to more than six thousand acres worked by 139 slaves, and the farming complex consisted of more than twenty structures encircling the Bratton's plantation mansion. Mrs. Bratton continued to manage the estate with much success following her husband's death. She was aided by her sons John S. Jr., Samuel, and James, as well as by her brother, Samuel Rainey. Between 1845 and 1861, many slave cabins, barns, an overseer's home, and a cotton gin were added to the property.[8]

The Civil War, however, destroyed the family's fortune and removed the necessary labor force required to run a large estate. Mrs. Bratton continued to live in the plantation mansion, but the halcyon days were over. While the family continued to maintain an interest in the property, they increasingly turned to operating the plantation with tenant labor. It was during that time that the deterioration of *Homestead House* and surrounding support structures began. By the 1950s, the entire plantation complex of more than fifteen structures was in poor condition.

Despite obstacles and challenges, several York County citizens felt the plantation mansion should be preserved. It was through their efforts that on August 19, 1971, the home was listed on the National Register of Historic Places as a part of the Brattonsville Historic District.[9] Shortly after that time, Dr. James Rufus Bratton, of Florence, South Carolina, a great-great-grandson of the plantation's original owner, agreed to lease *Homestead House* and a few surrounding acres to York County for potential restoration. That move opened a window of opportunity for the York County Historical Commission and local heritage organizations to pool the necessary resources to accomplish a successful restoration.

Over the course of three years, restorers and day laborers endeavored to return the home to its 1840s appearance. The most dramatic work included the construction of

a double veranda on the front of the home, and the addition of a new shake shingle roof that replicated one that had been on the dwelling during the nineteenth century. Locals and travelers from across the globe visited Brattonsville during the restoration process and were amazed at the home's transformation.

When the physical work was complete on the structure, historians and dedicated volunteers helped fill each room with period antique furniture, window treatments, and other decorative arts that conveyed the lifestyle of the Brattons during the decades leading up to the Civil War. *Homestead House* opened to the public for tours in 1976 in celebration of the nation's bicentennial. In the late 1990s, the Sony Pictures film, *The Patriot*, starring Mel Gibson and Heath Ledger, was filmed on the estate with major scenes shot inside *Homestead House*.[10]

"Brattonsville and *Homestead House* would be gone today if it had not been for many dedicated people in York County and across South Carolina," says Fairey, who served as executive director of the York County Historic Commission, Archives and Museums from 1979 to 1998. "The people of this county are to be commended for their efforts in saving *Homestead House* and a host of other structures at Historic Brattonsville. Saving

The main drawing room at Homestead House is today decorated with many original pieces of furniture that once belonged to the Bratton family. (Bush)

Handcrafted details can been seen throughout the home including this scroll trim on the staircase that rises from the second floor to the attic. (Bush)

that property has been very important to the history and heritage of South Carolina, and to the South."[11]

Today, *Homestead House* sits at the heart of a complex of more than twenty-four structures and 240 acres of fields and pastures that serve as a living history museum. As with many heritage sites and house museums, the work of restoring and maintaining the property will continue in perpetuity. "Helping restore *Homestead House* has been a major part of my life," says Fairey. "There will always be enough work here for anyone who wants to protect this property in the future. Preserving the past is a task that should never end."

Millford's grand façade is dominated by six massive Corinthian columns. Its monumental presence reflects a certain purity and simplicity, hallmarks of Greek Revival architecture of which Millford Plantation is considered by many to be the finest surviving example in the American South. (CAHPT—Schwarz)

MILLFORD PLANTATION
Grande Dame of the South

♥ Pinewood, South Carolina

The mansion at *Millford Plantation* is breathtaking. It is without question the grandest home constructed in South Carolina during the antebellum period. Many architectural historians consider it to be the South's most outstanding Greek Revival–style plantation home to survive into the modern age.

Beyond the home's rich architectural style and impressive scale, *Millford Plantation* is revered today for its authentically preserved and restored period interiors, as well as its connection to one of the nation's leading preservationists, Richard Hampton Jenrette. Jenrette, a native of North Carolina, has been a leader in the historic preservation movement in this country for more than fifty years. Historic properties associated with Jenrette include six immaculate homes that he has owned personally, including *Edgewater* on the Hudson River in New York; *Roper House* and *Millford Plantation*, both in South Carolina; *Ayr Mount* in North Carolina; the *Baker House* in New York City; and *Cane Garden* in the US Virgin Islands.

Ensuring that the future of each of his beloved properties will be secure, Jenrette created the Classical American Homes Preservation Trust (CAHPT) in 1993. The not-for-profit foundation will eventually own each of his properties and open them to the public. Three of his houses, including the mansion at *Millford Plantation*, are already owned by the CAHPT. The foundation's board of directors and staff are committed to seeing that each of the properties is preserved and maintained properly for all time.

In addition to the physical structures, the foundation is also charged with the care of each property's collection of decorative arts. The trove of furniture and art objects at each home is tightly focused. At *Millford Plantation* the collection of furniture includes numerous masterpieces by New York furniture maker Duncan Phyfe, who is considered America's leading cabinetmaker of the early nineteenth century. In addition to upholstered and case pieces, *Millford Plantation* showcases an important collection of crystal chandeliers and other lighting fixtures, mirrors, clocks, and porcelains.

The detail and craftsmanship of the cast-iron capitals atop Millford's row of Corinthian columns can be seen in this vintage photo taken for the Historic American Buildings Survey. (HABS)

In his award-winning book, *Adventures with Old Houses*, Jenrette recounts how his fascination and appreciation of historic homes began during his early childhood and how rewarding it has been to play a major role in the preservation of so many important structures across the South and the nation. Jenrette writes, "I am nothing more than a caretaker and feel grateful for the years I have been given to watch over and enjoy these beautiful places, preserving them for the future as a part of America's architectural heritage."[1]

Of all the homes owned and preserved by Jenrette, he says that *Millford Plantation* is his favorite. He calls it his own personal "Taj Mahal."[2]

The double parlors are filled with classically styled Duncan Phyfe chairs, couches, and benches made for Millford. In the center is a unique set of four Corinthian columns with a pair of movable mirrored partitions used to separate the two spaces on occasion. The mirrors above the elegant Philadelphia mantels and between the tall windows at either end of the room were shipped from New York to Charleston, then up the Santee River to Millford. (CAHPT—Schwarz)

Erected between 1839 and 1841 for John L. Manning, who later served as governor of South Carolina, the mansion at *Millford Plantation* has no equal in the southeastern United States in terms of its pure Greek Revival architectural style and detail. When first built, the mansion was called "Manning's Folly" by locals and others across the Palmetto State because its location was so remote. The house is situated on a small hill in a pine forest in the center of Sumter County, South Carolina, in the heart of the state's piedmont region. Swamps and marshes surround the property beyond its manicured lawns, gardens, and groves of ancient trees draped with Spanish moss.

The entire structure, from its grand colonnade and flanking wings to its exquisite interior plasterwork and carved cypress trim, was meant to impress. Nathaniel Potter, of Rhode Island, is credited as the builder of the mansion, although no architect has ever been confirmed. Jenrette feels that Potter was most certainly influenced by the design of the Charleston Hotel, designed by Charles Friedrich Reichardt, in Charleston, South Carolina, in the early 1830s. That hotel burned in 1838, but was rebuilt along the same lines by Potter at the same time that he was commissioned to build the mansion at *Millford Plantation*.[3]

Millford's six gigantic, stop-flutted Corinthian columns, twenty-eight feet tall, dominate the front of the home and support a massive architrave topped by a gently sloping pediment adorned with acanthus leaves. Classical symbols, including laurel wreath appliques, ornament opposite sides of the home's entablature. A strong dentil molding

The dining room, oval-shaped at one end, is furnished with the original Duncan Phyfe dining table, twelve chairs, serving tables, and cellaret. (CAHPT—Hall)

The balustrade of Millford's grand staircase ends with an S-curved newel post related in design to the scrolled ends of the Phyfe sofas and recamiers in the mansion's double parlors. (CAHPT—Schwarz)

runs continuously underneath the eaves on all four sides of the main house. The main entrance into the home is through wide mahogany doors crowned by a heavy entablature topped with scrolled trim supported by pairs of fluted Corinthian columns and pilasters.

Bricks fired on the plantation were used in the construction of the home's two-foot-thick outer walls. The granite used to sheath the house was brought from Rhode Island. The central block of the home is flanked by smaller service wings, connected to the main house by loggias supported by smaller square columns. One wing was used originally as a kitchen, the other as a laundry.

The interior of the mansion is ornamented with exceptional plasterwork that appears above many of the windows and doors and on the ceilings of the principal rooms on the first floor. One of the most striking features of the home is a two-story, domed rotunda that boasts an imposing circular staircase rising in forty-four steps to the second floor. A stained-glass oculus caps the circular dome over the staircase.

The twenty-foot-wide main hall traverses the house for nearly seventy feet from the front door to the foot of the grand staircase in the rear of the home. A screen of Corinthian columns divides the home's high-ceilinged double parlors. Both parlors feature open fireplaces ornamented with a pair of custom-made matching marble mantels crafted in Philadelphia. They are topped with expansive gilt-frame mirrors made in New York about 1840. A similar mirror hangs above a black marble mantel in the mansion's dining room.

Governor Manning and his wife, Susan, were leaders of South Carolina high society during the halcyon days before the Civil War, and many of the balls and parties they hosted at *Millford Plantation* are said to have lasted until dawn. They furnished the mansion in the fashionable Grecian style. Unlike many historic homes, much of the Manning's personal collection of furniture, paintings, and tableware survives in the house today.

The Manning family owned *Millford Plantation* until 1902, when it was purchased by Mary Clark Thompson. Inheriting the estate from her was a nephew, Emory W. Clark. Clark's son, W. E. Reeve Clark, later owned the estate. The property was purchased by Jenrette in 1997.[4] Jenrette, a collateral descendant of Susan Hampton Manning, donated the home to the Classical American Homes Preservation Trust in 2008.

Like many plantation homes across the South, *Millford* had begun to show the frailties of its age when Jenrette took ownership. While much emphasis was placed on making sure that the structure itself was secure and stabilized for decades to come, equal attention was given to ensure that the home's interiors retained the integrity of the period in which they were first used. Stylistically the home faithfully bears the hallmarks of period design in the 1840s and 1850s.

Jenrette, eighty-six, visits the home often and enjoys entertaining friends and colleagues there. In addition to the home's public and private spaces, Jenrette also takes great interest in the gardens that surround the mansion. They are planted with many heirloom plants, shrubs, and trees that were typical of pre–Civil War gardens in South Carolina.

In describing his affection for the mansion at *Millford Plantation*, Jenrette penned these words, "*Millford* sits in pristine state today—my dream house with big columns on the hill, down south, overlooking acres of green lawn and moss-draped live oak trees. It is a great place for reading and writing. With thousands of surrounding acres in swamp and park land you are not disturbed by the noise and traffic of man, only the sounds of nature, which are divine, especially at night when the bobwhite quail are calling, and the frogs and crickets are singing."[5]

The home was listed on the National Register of Historic Places in 1971 and designated as a National Historic Landmark two years later. It is regularly opened to the public.

Millford's grandeur is revealed in
this view from the carriage drive.
(Kitchens)

The mansion at Kensington
Plantation, near Columbia, South
Carolina, is considered one of
the finest antebellum Italianate
structures in the entire South. It
was completed in 1854. (Highsmith
Collection—Library of Congress)

KENSINGTON PLANTATION

A Planter's Palace

📍 Eastover, South Carolina

The mansion at *Kensington Plantation*, located in the heart of South Carolina, is an architectural gem. It sits in regal splendor surrounded by thousands of acres of timberland and cotton fields stretching for miles along the Wateree River. What makes the antebellum dwelling so special is its unique style, which sets it apart from other grand houses in the Palmetto State that have followed more traditional forms. Its appearance has been described by one architectural historian as a mixture of "Renaissance Revival excess and Greek Revival classicism perched like a wedding cake in the midst of verdant fields and forests."[1] A love for European architecture is said to have inspired the well-traveled original owners who commissioned their home to resemble an Italian villa.

The two-story frame structure, gleaming white under a brilliant red tin roof, is situated on an elevated brick basement with shuttered windows on each of the home's four sides. It is surrounded by arcaded porches and features a central entrance pavilion adorned with Corinthian pilasters. The porte-cochère was designed with sufficient width to allow a two-horse carriage to pull beneath allowing passengers to unboard in any weather.

From the covered porch visitors ascend a flight of stone steps into a small vestibule before entering a two-and-one-half-story domed hall rising forty-two feet from the floor to the ceiling with leaded and stained-glass skylights above. A second-story balcony, enclosed by an elaborate iron baluster with a classical motif of Athenian scrolls and acanthus leaves, encircles the center hall. Intricate plaster moldings and carved cypress trim adorn this space as well as other areas of the home.

The hall opens through arched doorways into a number of rooms used for varying purposes, including a drawing room, dining room, library, ballroom, and bedchambers. Four bedchambers and two small dressing rooms exist on the second floor.

The dining room features a barrel-vaulted ceiling with delicate plasterwork similar to that in the hall. The dining room wing extends off the rear of the home and contains

The mansion's impressive forty-two-foot-high center hall is surrounded by a gallery ornamented with elaborate wrought-iron railings. The space also exhibits elaborate plasterwork on the ceiling and walls. (Highsmith Collection—Library of Congress)

windows that look across an expansive back lawn down to the banks of the Wateree River in the distance. The wing is surrounded on three sides by a deep, wrap-around porch supported by arched colonnades.

When completed in 1853, the home was a marvel of technology not seen in many places in the South. Several of the bedrooms had marble basins supplied by warm water for bathing drawn from a ten-thousand-gallon cistern on the brick-paved basement floor that was heated by a wood-fired boiler. The home also featured a system of call bells for servants and a speaking tube from the main floor to the service basement below.[2]

The design of the home was rendered by Charleston, South Carolina, architects Francis Lee and Edward C. Jones, who drew their plans in direct consultation with the owners. The mansion was built around an existing Georgian-style frame dwelling with the help of slave labor and the work of skilled craftsmen brought to the site from Philadelphia. Construction took nearly two years to complete.[3]

While the mansion was the aspiration and dream of Matthew Richard Singleton, a wealthy and influential planter, it was never to be his home. Singleton died a few weeks before the house was completed. His wife, Martha Rutledge Kinloch Singleton, moved

This view of the mansion shows the arched porte-cochère that allowed visitors to step from their carriages and enter the home unhindered by inclement weather. (Highsmith Collection—Library of Congress)

into the dwelling with the couple's three children and lived there for many decades to come. New generations of the family were born on the plantation and the house continued to serve as a social hub before and after the Civil War, which amazingly left the home unscathed despite the near ruin of Columbia, South Carolina, by Union troops in 1865.

The family's influence and connection to many of the nation's leading politicians and lawmakers of the early nineteenth century is seen best in Matthew Richard Singleton's sister, Sarah Angelica Singleton, who married Maj. Abram Van Buren, son of US president Martin Van Buren. President Van Buren was a widower and chose his daughter-in-law as his official hostess at the *White House* in Washington, DC. Sarah Van Buren's portrait still hangs in the presidential mansion today, and is considered one of the finest paintings in the entire *White House* collection.[4]

The four-thousand-acre plantation, one of many owned by the Singletons, had originally been known as the *Headquarters*. It was Matthew Richard Singleton who chose the name *Kensington* to honor Mrs. Singleton's childhood home in Georgetown County, South Carolina. The new *Kensington Plantation* mansion became not only a landmark in the local community, but also was well known throughout South Carolina and the region for its unique architectural style and its gracious interiors.[5]

Documentation of life on the plantation before the Civil War can be found in the memoir *My Life in the South*, by Jacob Stroyer (1848–1909), published in 1879. Stroyer was born a slave on *Kensington Plantation* and spent many of his adult years after the Civil War living in the community near the estate. He was one of approximately 240 slaves living at *Kensington* at the beginning of the war.

Elaborately detailed ceramic tiles line the firebox of the chimney in the mansion's best parlor. The tiles were made in Europe and acquired through a merchant in Charleston, South Carolina, in the 1850s. (Highsmith Collection— Library of Congress)

Ownership of the dwelling and its sprawling agricultural fields and forests changed hands several times after the turn of the twentieth century. The plantation remained in the Singleton family until 1910 when it was sold to Robert Pickett Hamner. His son Robert Cochran Hamner inherited the house in 1922. He lived there with his wife, Jane Porcher DuBose, and their family until 1941, when the property was sold to an agricultural company known as Palmetto Farms. It was later owned by the Lanham family, who built a modern home on the property and abandoned the aging mansion and allowed it to be used for agricultural purposes.[6]

Although *Kensington* had been added to the National Register of Historic Places in 1971, by the time that International Paper (formerly Union Camp Corporation) acquired the property in 1981, the mansion had been unoccupied for more than forty

By the 1970s the home sat in an advanced state of deterioration. This photo taken for the Historic American Buildings Survey shows the mansion surrounded by a chainlink fence. Several of the windows are boarded over and several sections of exterior trim are missing. (HABS)

years and was in a serious state of advanced deterioration. In the 1950s through the 1970s, it had even been used to store farm equipment, fertilizer, and feed for livestock.

Sensitive to the concerns of the many history-minded citizens who were interested in the mansion's preservation, International Paper launched an extensive restoration of the home. Work began in June 1983 and was completed fourteen months later. When workers arrived at *Kensington* in the summer of 1983 the mansion required extensive work on its interior and exterior surfaces, as well as on its foundation and roof. In addition, each of the chimneys were rebuilt from the roof up.[7]

While the company salvaged as many original architectural elements as possible, some pieces had to be replaced, including much of the original exterior wood siding and many of the window frames. Several pieces of exterior trim, such as shutters and balustrades, were deteriorated beyond use or were missing entirely.

Approximately 90 percent of the wooden sills that rested on the foundation and supported much of the weight of the house had to be replaced. That task required workmen to raise all four corners of the house with hydraulic jacks to hold the structure's weight while the work was accomplished.[8]

According to information kept by International Paper, none of the original metal roofing material was salvageable. It is fortunate that the same company that supplied the original roofing material in the 1850s was still in business and still manufactured the same type of sheet metal used to sheath the unusual roof.

The interior of the home had been a victim of both neglect and decay. The skylights located high in the ceiling of the center hall had broken and allowed rainwater to pour onto the heart pine flooring below. Several of the plaster walls had major cracks that exposed the lathe underneath. While much of the original plaster details survived, in several areas of the home birds, honey bees, and wasps had built nests in its delicate designs.

When the restoration was complete and the home opened to the public in 1984, the work done by International Paper was met with a fanfare of accolades from the local community, as well as preservationists and historians from around the nation. In 1996, International Paper partnered with a nonprofit foundation to open the house to the public on a regular basis. The foundation was responsible for furnishing the home with period antiques and window treatments, and for hosting special events that celebrated and honored the Singleton family and the lives of the enslaved African Americans who once worked the plantation.[9]

In 2014, a major ice storm hit the piedmont region of South Carolina, which resulted in considerable damage to the mansion at *Kensington Plantation*. Following that event, tours were halted. In addition, the home was cleared of its furnishings and other decorative arts to protect them from damage. Many of those items belonged to the foundation. Other pieces were on loan from local citizens.

Today, the house sits quiet and still with its windows shuttered and its doors locked. The vacant rooms of the great house are rarely visited, and the laughter and music of previous years have faded into the past. But a new day may be on the horizon for *Kensington*.

Representatives from International Paper have stated that repair work is scheduled on the home and that it will be secured and protected from future harm. "Our intention is indeed to make repairs to the mansion and to work with the community-at-large in planning the future of the plantation," said Kim Wirth, senior communications manager with International Paper. "Obviously, we have a tremendous respect for the home's history and for its architectural significance. That has been shown through our commitment to the property in the past, and it will certainly continue in the future."[10]

Michael Bedenbaugh, executive director of the Palmetto Trust for Historic Preservation, South Carolina's leading, statewide, nonprofit preservation organization, expresses hope that the home can indeed be opened to the public again. He also has great hopes that planned work on the property can take it to a level of restoration that was not accomplished in the 1980s, when the majority of the interiors were simply painted white.

"We have a tremendous interest in the *Kensington* mansion as well as the surviving slave dwelling on the property," says Bedenbaugh. "We are so pleased that the corporate owners have expressed a desire to stabilize and repair the home. But, we feel that even more emphasis should be placed on restoring original paint colors inside the home and enhancing some of its original faux finishes. It would be a true coup for the community if a more genuine and authentic restoration could be accomplished."[11]

ROSE HILL PLANTATION
Survivor of Wars

⚲ Union County, South Carolina

While the American Civil War forged a place in history for the antebellum mansion at *Rose Hill Plantation*, located in the piedmont of South Carolina, it was a war fought thousands of miles away from the South that nearly spelled the dwelling's doom. Fortunately, the great house survives today to reveal many stories from the past, including its brief tenure as the state's executive mansion, and how it first was refurbished in the 1940s and then meticulously restored two decades later.

Despite the mansion's once grand appearance, by the early twentieth century it sat dilapidated and uninhabited. Descendants of the original owners had deeded the plantation, including the twelve-room mansion, to the United States Government in 1932. The historically important property soon became a part of the Sumter National Forest, complete with a Civilian Conservation Corps (CCC) camp that was home to five hundred men. With the coming of World War II in the 1940s, the property was used by the United States Army as a training facility and the plantation mansion was slated to become a bombing target for test pilots of the United States Army Air Corps.[1]

When word of the planned test-bombing made headlines in newspapers across the South, local historians flew into a state of panic and began a campaign to save the structure. The answer to their prayers materialized in the form of Mr. Clyde T. Franks, a South Carolina businessman who made a successful bid to buy the antebellum dwelling and its immediate forty-four acres from the government for the sole purpose of preserving the mansion.[2]

"Mr. Franks' purchase of the *Rose Hill Plantation* is one of this county's most amazing stories," says Ola Jean Kelly, president of the Union County Historical Society. "He made it possible for others to get involved with the plantation's restoration, and in a very short time it became a shining jewel of our local history. So many heritage groups and lineage societies, including local chapters of the Daughters of the American Revolution and the United Daughters of the Confederacy, helped him acquire many pieces

The east portico as it appeared
when the house sat in near ruins,
circa 1940. (Library of Congress)

of furniture and decorative objects that had belonged to the original owners and had
been used in the mansion before the Civil War."[3]

Upon taking ownership of the historic site, however, what Franks first discovered at
Rose Hill must surely have been disheartening. The gardens, which were once the pride
of the entire upstate of South Carolina, had been reduced to a field of briars, and the
main driveway had eroded to the point that it was not passable by passenger vehicles.
Giant boxwoods and one-hundred-year-old magnolias completely obscured the view
of the dwelling.

Anyone visiting the house would have seen that the rear portico was in danger of
collapse. Inside the mansion, squirrels and other rodents ran rampant through the

The east façade of the mansion at Rose Hill Plantation, located near Union, South Carolina. The mansion was built in the 1830s and enlarged in the 1850s by planter William Henry Gist, who served as governor of South Carolina from 1858 to 1860. (Bush)

drawing rooms while honeybees built massive hives within the walls that dripped amber goo onto the floors of the elegant second-story ballroom.

The home's isolated location deep in a pine forest along the Tyger River had made it a prime spot through the years for teenage shenanigans and other debaucheries, including serving as a gathering place for bootleggers and a hangout for vagrants and other ne'er-do-wells. During that time, vandals carried away pieces of the home's millwork, stole the sterling silver hardware from doors, and carted away furniture from the home's spacious rooms.[4]

Adding even more shame to its derelict condition, many of the home's windows were broken, with shards of splintered glass strewn about the premises. One local resident said that the smashed windows and ragged curtains blowing in the breeze made the front of the home look like "the sad face of a broken doll."[5]

Franks set about to accomplish a complete refurbishment of the property that aimed to stabilize the mansion and return it to some semblance of its antebellum appearance. He completely replaced the front and rear verandas and replicated their original wrought-iron balusters. He removed stepped gables along the roofline and, most importantly, covered the red brick exterior walls with stucco to replicate the look of the home's original appearance during its ownership by planter and statesman William Henry Gist.

A paneled door surrounded by sidelights and a fanlight greets visitors stepping onto the west portico of the mansion. (Bush)

Historians have long stated that Gist began building the home about 1828 with bricks that had been imported from Europe. The house was designed in the Federal style with strict symmetry that reflected classical architecture. The home took four years to complete and was constructed entirely with slave labor. Tradition says that it was named *Rose Hill* by Gist's first wife, Louisa Bowen, because of her love for roses and the numerous varieties of the plant that the family collected from around the world to ornament the home's formal gardens.

Some of the home's most important architectural features are the semi-elliptical fanlights that crown each of the main entrances. The mantels in both the main drawing room and the dining room showcase fine detail work and feature flanking pairs of columns that support a molded shelf above. In 1860, Gist's plantation consisted of 6,500 acres with 178 slaves, and had an estimated value of $75,000. The primary crops grown on the estate were cotton and corn.[6]

Gist was born in Charleston, South Carolina, on August 22, 1807. He attended South Carolina College and was admitted to the state bar in 1830. Gist represented the

The main drawing room of the mansion has been recently restored with painted finishes that replicate the nineteenth-century appearance of the space. (Bush)

Union District in the South Carolina Legislature from 1840 to 1844, and served in the South Carolina Senate from 1844 until 1856. Between 1848 and 1850 he served as both a senator and as lieutenant governor.

When Gist, former state senator and leader of the secessionist movement, was elected as the state's chief executive for a two-year term beginning in 1858, the mansion at *Rose Hill Plantation* served as South Carolina's governor's mansion. Gist was the last governor to undertake the duties of his office from a private residence. During the months leading up to the Civil War his plantation was the scene of much activity, including a ball held on September 17, 1860, attended by political leaders and their wives from all over the state. Much discussion was held at that event about secession.[7]

One of Gist's last acts as governor was to issue a call for the Secession Convention. Gist represented the Union District at the convention and was one of the first signers of the South Carolina Ordinance of Secession. On December 20, 1860, five days after Gist's term as governor had expired, South Carolina seceded from the Union, an act

that ultimately led to the beginning of the Civil War. Because of Gist's role in calling for the convention, he has been labeled the "secession governor" by historians.

During the war, *Rose Hill Plantation* was raided by Union troops, but miraculously it was not destroyed. Many tales exist of how the Gists hid many of the family's valuable possessions during the conflict and how slaves and other farmworkers corralled livestock in nearby woods to keep them from being stolen by marauding troops.

Gist died in the mansion in 1874 and was buried in the family's cemetery on the property. Ownership of the plantation then transferred solely to his widow, Mary Elizabeth Rice Gist. Upon her death in 1889, the property was inherited by three grandchildren who owned the estate for much of the next forty years, during which time they rented the plantation to tenants and sharecroppers.

Following Franks's purchase of the home in the 1940s, it was opened to the public for tours on a regular basis. Thousands of locals and tourists flocked to *Rose Hill* each year to see the mansion and to walk through its restored formal gardens. In 1960, Franks sold the home and forty acres to the State of South Carolina, and it was renamed the *Rose Hill* Plantation State Historic Park. The opening of the park included a ceremony at the mansion attended by more than one thousand eager visitors.[8]

The second-floor ballroom is the largest room in the mansion. On occasion this room was divided by a movable partition and used as two bedrooms. (Bush)

The interior doors, mantels, and baseboards have been recently restored to their pre–Civil War finishes and colors. (Bush)

On December 20, 1960, exactly one hundred years to the hour since the signing of the Ordinance of Secession, the dedication ceremony of the new state park was held with scores of local, state, and regional dignitaries in attendance. A Civil War cannon boomed a twenty-one-gun salute from the south lawn, and a major collection of Confederate relics was displayed in both the mansion's drawing room and ballroom.

"It was a very exciting day," recalls Kelly, who attended the dedication ceremony on that sunny afternoon dressed in period attire along with hundreds of other Union County residents. "*Rose Hill Plantation* is a great old house. Her story is even more amazing since she was nearly lost and has now been restored and opened to the public for more than 70 years."[9]

Today, *Rose Hill Plantation* still enchants visitors, and efforts continue to restore and preserve the mansion and its gardens. Beginning in 2012 and continuing to the present, Governor Gist's home has become the focus of more scholarly restoration thanks in part to a small team of graduate students, volunteering their time and expertise, as well as other preservationists and artists, including Grace Washam and Brendan Abernethy. Those individuals have made remarkable discoveries hidden beneath the bland palette of white and pastel paints slathered on the walls during earlier refurbishments.[10]

Careful analysis has revealed that the walls on either side of the front door were originally rust red, and the fanlight above the door had gilded details. The molding around the doors into the drawing room and dining room was black, while the chair rails in the entrance hall were a dark Venetian green. In the main parlor, where respected guests to the plantation would have been introduced to members of the Gist family, the original color of the room—a vibrant Prussian blue—was discovered underneath nine coats of white paint. Throughout the home, vestiges of faux marbling have been discovered on mantels and baseboards. Much of that detail is currently being restored with the help of trained preservationists and volunteers.

"This is a way of looking back in time," says Trampas Alderman, park manager. "A home like the mansion at *Rose Hill Plantation* would have been a showplace for the Gist family. And the restoration and preservation work performed here will allow future generations to witness what life was like for a wealthy family living in the upcountry of South Carolina before the Civil War. This plantation is an amazing historic site with an incredible story."[11]

WOODBURN PLANTATION
The Pride of Pendleton

◉ Pendleton, South Carolina

Few antebellum homes in the Carolinas are endowed with as grand a veranda as the one seen at *Woodburn Plantation*, near Pendleton, South Carolina. The deep, two-tiered porch stretches across the entire façade and wraps around the east and west sides of the home. Stout wooden columns support the porch, which is accessed from ground level by two wide staircases with wrought-iron railings.

It was the mansion's great veranda and roof that needed immediate attention when a small group of historically minded citizens gathered outside the house in the deep winter of 1960 to discuss saving the structure from ruin. Rainwater had been pouring into the dwelling's interior for years, and vagrants had camped out in its spacious rooms breaking and stealing remaining pieces of furniture and original millwork.

The home, perched on a promontory with a view of the Blue Ridge Mountains in the distance, had been the social hub of the plantation community around Pendleton in its heyday. Great parties and balls were once held in rooms that later lost their polish when they fell victim to age and neglect. Making sure that the mansion was preserved and restored for future generations became the work of numerous volunteers who rescued the property from near ruin at a time when many old homes were being abandoned all over the South.

The mansion at *Woodburn* was built in the 1830s as one family's refuge from the heat and humidity of the Carolina coast, and as a safe haven from lowcountry diseases and maladies such as malaria and yellow fever. The first owner of the plantation was Charles Cotesworth Pinckney, son of Andrew Pinckney, a successful planter who served as an early governor of South Carolina. Charles Cotesworth Pinckney was a graduate of Harvard College and became lieutenant governor of South Carolina in 1833. Pinckney was a devout Christian, and he devoted much of his adult life to converting his slaves to Christianity. He was also a leader in a movement to create an organized system of religious instruction for slaves.[1]

Beyond his successful political career, however, it is said that Pinckney greatly enjoyed his role as a planter and took great pride in riding horseback over his properties and discussing crop production and the raising of livestock with his neighbors. It was common for Pinckney to spend all day on his horse. He visited local farms and plantations, stopping only to drink from a stream or river, or to visit at a humble cabin or a more refined home of his planter friends for a meal of cornbread and rabbit stew, or roast turkey and wine.[2]

Woodburn reflects the Pinckney family's stature and influence. It is a grand home built on a grand scale. The home sits on a full-height basement floor accessed from the rear of the structure. With its large rooms and fourteen-foot-high ceilings on both of the principal floors, as well as its fashionable Greek Revival millwork, the mansion is truly symbolic of the wealth attained by many families in the Old South.

The interior of the home features multipaned French doors that open directly onto the veranda from the pair of drawing rooms facing the front of the house. Exterior trim includes deeply fluted door and window moldings and Greek key designs. The interior showcases similar trim with corner blocks emblazoned with federal stars. The drawing rooms, and the dining room, which overlooks a single-story rear porch, each contain marble mantels originally brought from Charleston. Two of the bedrooms on the third floor open onto the veranda through windows modified to open as doors.

The Reverend Dr. John B. Adger, a son of wealthy Charleston parents, enlarged *Woodburn* in the 1850s. During the Civil War, the mansion housed many guests who fled from Charleston before its occupation by Union troops. In 1881, the plantation passed to Maj. Augustine Smythe, a nephew of Reverend Adger, who turned the property into a stock farm renowned for its fine horses and prize cattle. In addition to his agricultural pursuits, Smythe was for a number of years a trustee of Clemson College (university). One of Major Smythe's children, Susan Smythe Bennett, forever captured her feelings for the plantation by writing in her diary, "I think I loved *Woodburn* more than any other place I have lived. It is beguiling and beautiful."[3]

Members of the Adger family lived on the plantation longer than any other occupants. Although the Adgers sold the property in 1908, their descendants have been involved in many important ways with the home's restoration and interpretation as a historic house museum. They have donated numerous items to the Pendleton Historic Foundation for use in the mansion, such as furniture, glassware, and portraits. Those items have been invaluable to telling the plantation's story.

After the turn of the twentieth century, the home saw many different owners and occupants, each who attempted to farm the land and maintain the collection of buildings on the property. But the Great Depression and the declining viability of agriculture at the time made farming difficult. By the end of World War II, the mansion was in a serious state of decline. Portions of the great porch had begun to collapse and the roof leaked badly. It was during that era that the home sat vacant and deterioration quickly advanced.

In the 1950s, the US Government acquired the plantation property and donated it to Clemson University. In 1966, Clemson deeded *Woodburn* to the Pendleton Historic Foundation, the nonprofit, grassroots organization that was established to save the structure and bring it back from ruin. The restorers of *Woodburn* stated in the foundation's charter that the purpose of the organization was to "preserve, restore, and display

The mansion at Woodburn Plantation, near Pendleton, South Carolina, boasts an impressive two-story veranda that spans the entire length of the front façade and extends around both the east and west sides of the home. (Bush)

The mansion fell into an advanced state of disrepair during the early to mid-twentieth century. The structure was snatched from near ruin in the 1960s when it was acquired by the Pendleton Historic Foundation, which launched a full-scale restoration of the dwelling. (Library of Congress)

Large, multipaned glass doors open from the home's double parlors onto the front veranda. The rooms are furnished with several pieces once belonging to the Pinckney family. (Bush)

again some of our cultural heritage; to recapture the spirit of the great people, of fine living and a lovely home, to the end that we and those who come after us may experience again the virtues and greatness of those who lived before us."[4]

"Taking proper care of a home like *Woodburn* is a major task," says Pendleton Historic Foundation president Carol Burdette. "We depend on our volunteers and local citizens who understand and appreciate what this house means to our local history and to the greater story of South Carolina to keep the home in good repair and to keep the doors open to the public."

While many house museums are presented with an assemblage of antique furniture of many different periods donated by historically minded citizens, a concerted effort has been made at *Woodburn* to present the home as it would have looked during the last decade before the Civil War, and to use as many original pieces belonging to the Pinckney and Adger families as possible. Paint colors, wallpapers, rugs, and other decorative elements used in the house today were common to the 1850s, and much of what is seen at *Woodburn* is an authentic replication of what was actually used in the mansion during that era.

A pair of matching, nineteenth-century marble mantels was acquired by the Pendleton Historic Foundation in the late 1960s from an abandoned neighboring plantation to replace ones that had been stolen from Woodburn Plantation during the many years that it sat uninhabited. They are used today in the dwelling's double parlors. (Bush)

"A great deal of work has been done here at *Woodburn* to insure that we are being as authentic as possible with our interpretation of decorative arts of the period and how the entire plantation is presented to the public," comments Dr. Tim Drake, board member of the Pendleton Historic Foundation. "We take great pride in growing and enhancing the educational component of *Woodburn* at every opportunity. We want our guests to go away from this place with a genuine appreciation for what they have seen on their visit."[5]

In addition to the lives of the earliest owners at *Woodburn Plantation*, great emphasis is also placed on recognizing the role of African American slaves on the estate and their contributions to the construction of the home. Special attention is also given to tenant families who worked the property in the decades of the late nineteenth and early twentieth centuries.

One individual of a tenant family at *Woodburn Plantation* made great strides toward improved health and civil rights for African Americans. Jane Edna Hunter, who assisted in establishing the nationally recognized Phyllis Wheatley Society, was born in a tenant

Heavy rosewood and walnut tester and canopy beds are used to furnish the principal bedrooms at Woodburn Plantation. This bed belonged to the Reverend Dr. John B. Adger, who acquired Woodburn in the 1850s. (Bush)

house on the *Woodburn Plantation* in 1882. Hunter studied nursing in South Carolina and Virginia before moving to Cleveland, Ohio, in 1905, to help young African American women who migrated to the North to find employment. A replica of the cabin in which Hunter was born has today been erected on the plantation property.

"We are very proud of the history of this house and all of the people who lived on the plantation," says Jackie Reynolds, past president of the Pendleton Historic Foundation. "So much has been preserved here, but there is still so much work to do. We all know at the Pendleton Historic Foundation that taking care of this property is something that can never end. It is too important to ever let slip away. It must be preserved for all time."[6]

Woodburn was placed on the National Register of Historic Places on May 6, 1971. In 2008, the property was presented an Award of Merit from the Confederation of South Carolina Local Historical Societies, and in 2009 was presented with the Heritage Tourism Advancement Award from the South Carolina Heritage Corridor (SCHC) for being one of Upstate South Carolina's leading historical sites open to the public.

KENTUCKY

Despite the obvious need for
external repairs, Ward Hall is no
less impressive today than it was
in 1857. (Kitchens)

WARD HALL PLANTATION

One of America's Iconic Treasures

📍 Georgetown, Kentucky

Ward Hall is the unchallenged queen of Greek Revival architecture in Kentucky. Architectural historians regularly refer to it as "Kentucky's preeminent *antebellum* Greek Revival residence," "one of the finest examples of its kind in the United States," "the grandest Greek Revival home ever built in Kentucky," and "a masterpiece of plantation design."[1] It is, indeed, considered one of the most important structures of its kind in the United States, along with other iconic antebellum residences such as *Millford* in South Carolina, *Stanton Hall* in Mississippi, *Berry Hill* in Virginia, and *Rattle and Snap* in Tennessee.[2] As invaluable as the home is to Kentucky's architectural history, for the better part of thirty years, it has needed significant repair and restoration. Since 2004 motivated individuals have banded together in an effort to rescue the archetypal residence.

To build such an imposing residence, it took the ambition and wealth of Junius Ward to make it a reality. Ward came from an already rich and well-connected family. His mother, Sarah Johnson Ward, was the niece of Richard M. Johnson, who served as the vice president of the United States under President Martin Van Buren from 1837 to 1841. Junius's father, William, became the Choctaw Nation Indian agent in the newly ceded lands in Mississippi from 1821 until 1833. His family was among a closely connected group of Kentuckians who went to the Mississippi Delta to purchase the exceptionally fertile land recently opened up to white settlers and then to establish extensive plantations there.

One of the first Kentuckians to reach the Delta in the mid-1820s was Junius Ward. Ward left for Mississippi just after he married Matilda Viley in 1824. He then acquired a large amount of land in Washington County, Mississippi, and operated a cotton plantation on his new property, which he named *Kentucky Bend*. The profits from his plantation, along with his other business interests which included hemp production and mercantile and shipping interests, made Ward a very wealthy man. In 1829 Ward built the Erwin house at Lake Washington, Mississippi, to use as his Mississippi

Ward Hall's massive double parlors are separated by huge sliding pocket doors and heavily decorated with wood and plaster trims. (Kitchens)

residence. This structure still stands. However, in the 1840s, Ward built another, much larger house, at Princeton Landing, Mississippi. Although his friends advised him to avoid building a house on the site he chose, he ignored their advice and built a forty-room mansion that was one of the finest mansions in the area. Then in 1858 the Mississippi River flooded and his Princeton Landing home was washed into the river along with most of the town of Princeton.[3]

Ward always had a love of horse racing. In 1853, he partnered with two other Kentuckians to purchase the horse, *Lexington*. *Lexington* was considered by many to be the best race horse of his time, having won six of seven major races. The horse had to be retired just a few years later because of poor eyesight, but he was still a good studhorse. In 1858 Ward's partnership sold *Lexington* for $15,000, which at that time was the highest price paid for an American-bred horse. In later years, *Lexington* was among the first class of horses inducted to the Racing Hall of Fame.[4]

Junius and Matilda Ward lived in Mississippi in the 1850s. However, they were in the habit of returning to Kentucky each summer to enjoy the cooler climes of their native state. The couple decided to build a suitable home in Kentucky as a retreat at which they would live from May through October. Ward paid $50,000 in gold to build what many believe is one of the most impressive mid-nineteenth-century residences in America.

Ward Hall's ceiling medallions are not only unusually beautiful, but unlike other antebellum medallions, they are also highlighted with colors. (Kitchens)

Although no documentary evidence remains to confirm the architect who designed the structure, many believe that famed Lexington, Kentucky, architect Maj. Thomas Lewinski may be responsible for its design. Lewinski had retired as an architect several years before *Ward Hall* was built. However, Ward's Kentucky mansion bears many striking similarities to the David A. Sayre house, which was later known as *Bell Place*, in Lexington. *Bell Place* predates *Ward Hall*, but it is known to have been designed by Lewinski.[5] If Lewinski was responsible for the design of *Ward Hall*, he borrowed heavily from Minard LaFever's pattern books for the home's many impressive architectural details. Ward's four-story, 12,000-square-feet mansion was completed in 1857.

The central hall in Ward's mansion stretches sixty-five feet front to back and is ornamented with heavy, classical door surrounds of walnut, and multicolored ceiling medallions and cornice moldings. Three large rooms are on the left side of the hall comprising double parlors and a large dining room. Each of these rooms was designed for public entertainment, possessing the same decorative door surrounds, cornice moldings, and colorful ceiling medallions as the central hall. Extending down the right side of the hallway are three slightly smaller rooms reserved for family relaxation and a stair hall containing a gracefully spiraling staircase rising three stories in a continuous ellipses. The family rooms also have walnut door and window surrounds and decorative plaster moldings, but they are slightly less elaborate than those found in the public entertaining rooms. The second floor of the mansion contains five large bedrooms. One of these bedrooms was a "traveler's room" in which travelers were given lodging, but at night the traveler was locked into the room with no means of escape until the door was unlocked in the morning. Additional rooms serving a variety of purposes are found on the third floor and in the basement.

Although *Ward Hall* is in need of significant restoration on the exterior, many of its interior features are in remarkably good condition. Some of the plaster medallions and moldings retain their multicolored appearance obtained in a process known as

distempering. The original sterling silver doorknobs and hardware remain in the main rooms while original cast-iron knobs remain on doors in the basement. Carved wooden door and window trims remain in a beautiful state of preservation.

War and Reconstruction in the 1860s devastated Ward financially. He fell into bankruptcy and was forced to sell his enormous Kentucky summer house in 1867. For the next century *Ward Hall* would pass through the hands of no fewer than eleven owners, most of whom could ill afford to properly maintain such a large home. Over the decades, the house fell into disrepair.

The last family to own *Ward Hall* had eight different family members who shared ownership. Unfortunately, not all of the family members could agree on what to do with the mansion. As a result of the conflict, the house suffered from a lack of proper management. With the house languishing and the suburbs of Lexington expanding toward nearby Georgetown, *Ward Hall* and the property on which it stands became the target for developers who planned to demolish the mansion and build new homes in a subdivision that would cover the property.[6] Fortunately, the family sold the mansion instead to the Ward Hall Preservation Foundation.

Perhaps the best hope for the rescue of *Ward Hall* is David Stuart and the Ward Hall Preservation Foundation. The nonprofit foundation acquired *Ward Hall* and fifty surrounding acres in 2004 as an organization that is "dedicated to the preservation and promotion of the mansion and its grounds as an educational center, to illuminate

Ward Hall's dining room is not the largest found in antebellum mansions, but it is exceptionally appointed with expensive trims and marble mantel. (Kitchens)

The staircase at Ward Hall rises three stories in a continuous spiral and is as much art as functional. (Kitchens)

important aspects of the history and culture of Kentucky and, to some extent, the antebellum South."[7] Since acquiring the historic house the foundation has secured the roof and made gutter repairs. These repairs have stayed the water incursion problems that had been plaguing some of its interior plaster walls and decorative details. The foundation has also established a three-phase restoration plan. Phase one will not only ensure that the roof is in good repair, but it will also repair and restore the brick chimney stacks, parapet walls, and entablature. The projected costs of phase one alone is over

$800,000. Phase two will restore the front portico and continue work on the gutters. Phase three will restore the rear portico and the brick paving around the perimeter of the home.

The foundation raises funds for restoration efforts by opening the house for tours on weekends and for special events. They also actively seek funding through grants, endowments, and donations. The organization welcomes volunteer assistance from craftsmen and volunteer groups to perform some of the ongoing and necessary cosmetic repairs and maintenance that are constantly required of such a large structure.

David Stuart and the foundation have grand plans for *Ward Hall*. Once the home's roof and exterior are fully restored, the interior will undergo a similarly loving restoration. Long-term plans for the property are to reconstruct the outbuilding that once serviced the mansion and its occupants. In the meantime, Stuart has furnished the mansion with high-quality period antiques appropriate to such a fine home. Visitors, whether in groups or as individuals, are welcomed into the home, which provides them with a glimpse into how Kentucky's elite once lived and entertained. With each new group visiting *Ward Hall*, Stuart hopes to bring additional attention to this historic home and the high costs of maintaining it as an unusually fine example of mid-nineteenth-century architecture.

The Ward Hall Preservation
Foundation has a plan to fully
restore Ward Hall's exterior.
(Kitchens)

Waveland is a Kentucky State Historic Site near Lexington and is one of the most beautiful Greek Revival mansions in the state. (Kitchens)

WAVELAND

Pinnacle of a Family's Westward Migration

♥ Fayette County, Kentucky

F ayette County, Kentucky's *Waveland,* as it currently exists, has its genesis in well-known families from North Carolina. Although Joseph Bryan built today's *Waveland* mansion in the mid-1840s, it was his father, Daniel Bryan, who began the family's connection with *Waveland.*

Daniel Bryan came from a prominent family living at Bryan Settlement in North Carolina. Daniel was the nephew of Daniel Boone, whose family also lived in the Bryan Settlement vicinity. In 1779, Bryan helped his father move nearly the entire family from their home in North Carolina to Kentucky to a settlement known as Bryan's Station, where the city of Lexington now stands. Daniel Boone and Bryan's father led the emigrating group on the journey through the Appalachian Mountains since they were already acquainted with the difficult and dangerous route. This expedition, however, was doomed when they encountered a band of hostile Indians who attacked the group. Daniel Bryan's father and one of his brothers were shot and killed. The attack was too much for Bryan's mother, who demanded to return to their home in Rowan County, North Carolina. So the entire group reversed course and made their way back to Bryan Settlement.

Daniel Bryan made as many as eleven trips to Kentucky over the next seven years. Finally, in 1786 he permanently moved his family to central Kentucky. His father, William, had been granted one thousand acres south of Bryan's Station, Kentucky, for his service in the Revolutionary War. The acreage spread across rolling hills near what would later become Lexington, Kentucky. Family lore maintains that Bryan retained his uncle, Daniel Boone, to survey this property. Once settled on his new acreage in 1790, Bryan built a substantial stone house for his family residence. By 1817 he was referring to the place as "Waveland." How Bryan arrived at this name is uncertain. However, the most commonly accepted explanation of the name seems to be that it was derived from the movement of the wind over vast fields of grain which made the crops undulate as waves in the ocean.

Daniel Bryan had quite a vision for his *Waveland* property. Around 1831 a town using the name Waveland had formed on the Bryan property where he built a gun manufacturing shop, gristmill, paper mill, distillery, and blacksmith shop employing twenty-five blacksmiths. He also built a Baptist church and founded a girls' school there.[1] His gun manufacturing operation must have been substantial as Bryan was retained to manufacture guns and gun powder for the United States Government during the War of 1812. He also seems to have had skill as a silversmith, for he crafted silver buttons for his uncle Daniel Boone's coat when Boone was elected to the Virginia General Assembly.[2]

By 1844 Daniel Bryan had grown old and began to turn over the farm and the family businesses to his son, Joseph Bryan. From a young age, Joseph Bryan had shown great promise as a farmer and businessman. Before he was twenty-three years old, Joseph had begun purchasing land to expand the family's landholdings. So Daniel suggested to Joseph that he should undertake construction of a new home more befitting the family's social position and better able to serve the family's needs. By this time, Joseph had been married to Margaret Cartmell Bryan for over twenty years and the couple had already started growing their family. Joseph and Margaret Bryan had eleven children in all.

Joseph dutifully began construction on a new house within a short distance from Daniel's original stone house. He hired one of Lexington's premier builder/architects, John McMurtry, to design and build the new home. McMurtry left his family farm at

Waveland's interior has been decorated with wallpapers, carpets, and furniture that would have been familiar to the Bryans. (Kitchens)

The dining room at Waveland is contained in the ell extending from the back of the mansion. (Kitchens)

a young age and went to Lexington where he apprenticed with carpenters and masons. In the 1840s, McMurtry experienced his heyday for designing grand residences in central Kentucky. In addition to *Waveland*, McMurtry is known to have designed, and probably built, remarkable mansions such as *Elley Villa*, the Thomas January house, *Loudon House*, *Botherum*, and the Watkins house in Lexington.[3] He also is responsible for the Benjamin McCann house, which is almost identical to *Waveland*, and located a short distance from Bryan's new mansion.[4]

Their new home was one of the most beautifully proportioned Greek Revival structures in Kentucky. McMurtry built for them a two-story home constructed nearly entirely of brick with materials harvested either on Bryan's farm or very closeby. The smooth-faced cut stone used in the foundation is Kentucky white marble quarried just twenty miles from *Waveland*. The thousands of bricks used to build the house were made from clay found at *Waveland* and fired in kilns built on the property. Nearly all of the lumber and wood trims for the home were from oak, ash, walnut, and cherry trees cut on the property. Even the wrought iron needed to build the home was manufactured at Waveland village's blacksmiths shop.[5] Joseph's father died while the new mansion was under construction, thus he never saw it in its completed form. Once the new mansion was finished, the stone dwelling Daniel built fifty years before was torn down.

After four years of construction, Bryan's new mansion at *Waveland* was completed and the family wasted no time in moving into it. But Bryan still had a one-thousand-acre farm to run. His main cash crop was hemp, which was used for products vital to a young American Republic in the nineteenth century such as canvas, sailcloth, and cordage for rigging. However, he supplemented his earnings by also growing corn, oats, and wheat. Bryan had significant assets in livestock, including large herds of cattle, pigs, and sheep. He also had a passion for raising fine horses.[6] The farm at *Waveland* was not a labor-intensive operation, so Bryan was never required to own many slaves. In 1850 there were just twelve slaves at *Waveland*, some of whom provided services to the family in the mansion and the rest worked in the grain and hemp fields over the farm. Bryan was never known to own more than eighteen slaves at a time.

When the War between the States erupted in 1861, Kentucky's allegiances were split between Unionist and Confederate sympathizers. Both the Union and the Confederacy claimed Kentucky. Joseph Bryan's allegiance, however, was unambiguous. Although he did not enter service in the Confederate army or cavalry, he equipped an entire troop of Confederate cavalry with blooded horse stock. These horses probably went to Gen. John Hunt Morgan's troops. Unfortunately, Union soldiers quickly learned of his horse donation and set out to detain him. Joseph escaped to Canada to avoid arrest.[7] In an effort to get a little closer to home, Bryan left Canada and took up sanctuary with some of the Boone family in Missouri until the war ended. He was never apprehended by Union officials.

The war wreaked havoc on Bryan's finances, leaving him with little cash or assets, other than his land. But, the Bryans survived both the war and Reconstruction with *Waveland* still in their possession.

In 1874 Bryan passed *Waveland* on to his children while he and his wife moved to Lexington. The mansion at *Waveland* was turned over to Bryan's son, Joseph Henry Bryan. Young Joseph and his family made it their home for nearly two decades. However, Joseph Jr. had a terrible habit of gambling, which was made worse by his abiding love of race horses. He built two race courses at *Waveland*, one of which once occupied the grounds directly in front of and across the road from the mansion. Horse races were notorious settings for the gambling in which some gentlemen engaged, so social etiquette required that women avoid attending the races. But with the race course just across the road from the mansion, the women seized upon the opportunity to watch the races at *Waveland* from the mansion's upstairs windows and balcony. They remained a safe and appropriate distance from the wagering, but were able to enjoy the events nonetheless.

Unfortunately, the appeal of raising and racing his own horses out-paced Joseph Jr.'s ability to pay for it. His compulsive gambling resulted in financial devastation for

Waveland is an L-shaped mansion with long verandas extending down most of the rear ell. (Kitchens)

As seen from the rear of the home, the rear ell is actually larger than the main block of Waveland. (Kitchens)

the Bryans. As a consequence, in 1894, he was forced to sell the mansion and its acreage at auction. While the auction raged around him, Joseph Henry Bryan sat in his rocking chair on *Waveland*'s porch and sipped on a glass of brandy while all that his family had worked for was sold to the highest bidder. All the while, Bryan's pet mockingbird stood perched on his shoulder, perhaps mocking the sweet songs of other, more fortunate birds. Mrs. Sallie A. Scott purchased *Waveland* and around two hundred surrounding acres.[8]

Just five years after purchasing *Waveland*, Mrs. Scott sold it to James A. Hulett and his family, who lived in the mansion for the next fifty-seven years. By the time the Hulett family sold *Waveland* in 1956 to the University of Kentucky, the home was in dire need of repair. Some of the outbuildings had rotted so badly that a few of them had to be demolished. The main house at *Waveland* still stood in reasonably good condition, but also needed restoration.

The University of Kentucky purchased the *Waveland* mansion and over three hundred surrounding acres. The university established an agricultural research farm there and turned the house over to Hambleton Tapp, who established the Kentucky Life Museum in the residence in 1958. The university turned over the residence and twenty-five acres around the house to the Kentucky State Park System in 1971.[9] Since that time the park system has opened the house as a museum in the Waveland State Historic Site established to interpret life in an antebellum manor house in central Kentucky. The home is open for tours five days per week for nine months of the year.

WHITE HALL

Founded on Treachery, Expanded on Compassion

♀ Madison County, Kentucky

The story of a great house is nearly always the story of a great man or woman. It almost always involves someone of substantial wealth, large ambition, and a large ego. But, it is not always about someone with laudable character or enviable leadership. *White Hall*'s beginnings are inextricably tied to just this sort of dastardly personage, but its eventual expansion offers a redemptive heir that rolls back the dark clouds of its earliest beginnings.

White Hall, though not known by that name in its earliest iteration, is firmly tied to the person most responsible for the wealth that created it—Green Clay. Clay was born in Powhattan County, Virginia, in 1757. While still a very young man, the somewhat disagreeable Clay had a tiff with his father that resulted in Clay leaving Virginia and relocating to what would soon become Madison County, Kentucky. This made Clay one of the early settlers to the area and, along with his innate ambition, placed him in a prime position to become a leader in the newly settled region. By the mid-1790s, Clay had become a magistrate judge. It was a post he would use for personal gain time and time again.

At that time, a magistrate judge was responsible for appointing inspectors and other government positions of importance. Magistrates were empowered to assign the going rates or fees for taverns, ferries, and turnpikes in their region. A magistrate also had the power to sanction precisely where toll roads would be built. Clay used the power with which he had been entrusted to ensure that it had the maximum personal benefit to him. He is known to have placed toll roads on land he owned and to decide upon "fair" tolls to his own advantage. In appointing local leaders, he made sure that they either were corruptible or beholding to Clay's wishes. Since Clay owned taverns and ferries, he used his position to make sure that his profits were maximized.[1]

Clay had an insatiable hunger for land. He adopted the dubious, if not illegal, practice of carving his initials into landmarks such as rocks and trees. Then, when a surveyor was sent to survey the property for a new landowner, it would appear to

This side view of White Hall shows the original house, Clermont, which was built onto to form the new mansion in the 1860s. (HABS)

the surveyor that Clay already owned or had staked a claim to that parcel of land. He had not. But, the markings, coupled with Clay's propensity to sue at the drop of a hat, provided him with the argument that he owned the property. Because of Clay's tenacity and position on the bench, many rightful property holders gave up claims to their land. So infamous was Clay in his pursuit of land and dirty dealings that at least one land grant issuer instructed his subordinate "to go ahead and approve Green's land grants no matter how illegal they appeared because Green would just end up filing a grievance in the court of appeals and acquiring the land anyway."[2] Clay once went so far as to sue "two infant girls" whose father owed Clay a small debt before the young father died. Clay wanted the land this man possessed and claimed a right to it in payment for the debt. Unfortunately, Clay was successful in court in dispossessing these children of their acreage, despite the fact that the debt their father owed was quite minor.[3] Through all of these tactics, Clay became the largest landowner in all of Kentucky and an enormously wealthy man.

Opposites apparently attract. Despite the despicable lengths to which Clay would go to increase his landholdings and wealth, he married Sally Lewis, a particularly pious woman. The seemingly mismatched couple had seven children.[4] Sally always maintained a safe distance between herself and her husband's business dealings.

In 1798 Green Clay purchased the land on which *White Hall* stands today from Rev. John Tanner. Immediately, Clay began construction on a new brick house from bricks made and fired on the property. The resulting home was a large two-story, Georgian-styled home.[5] However, within just a few years, he made a modest-sized addition to the house, connecting it to the side of the earlier edifice. The new two-story addition was completed sometime before 1810 and provided a single large room both upstairs and down. At that time, he also improved the home's appearance with

In the 1960s White Hall was boarded up in an effort to prevent further abuse to the mansion from vandals, vagrants, and the curious. (HABS)

the addition of a single-storied portico over its front entrance. The pedimented portico was supported by attractive Corinthian columns that gave the entire home a more regal appearance. He called his estate *Clermont*.[6]

He would enjoy *Clermont* for about eighteen years before he died in 1828 after developing skin cancer on his face. His youngest son, Cassius Clay, dutifully nursed his father during his last days. As a result, Green Clay's last will bequeathed his Madison County estate, consisting of two thousand acres and the family home, to Cassius. In one last act of egomania, Green Clay's will required that paintings of he and his wife remain hanging in the family home in perpetuity. The paintings remain at *White Hall* today. It is interesting to note that Green's wife, Sallie, wanted nothing to do with his property or will. In December 1828 she signed a document giving up any right to her husband's estate. A few years later, she married a minister and the couple moved to Frankfort, Kentucky.[7]

Cassius Clay was more his mother's son than his father's son. He was careful with his money and, unlike his father, was not known for double-dealing. Also unlike his father, Cassius deeply believed in freeing slaves. He was not an abolitionist, who believed in the sudden and immediate end of slavery, but he was an emancipationist, who believed in a gradual and measured end to slavery. He preferred emancipationism because it allowed the slaveholder some time to absorb the huge financial loss from being dispossessed of his slaves and time to get used to a new labor system, and it allowed the enslaved person time to prepare for freedom and the economic realities of personal responsibility.

Cassius lived his beliefs. He freed the slaves he inherited, except for a handful he was required to retain by law because they had been put into a trust for his children in Green Clay's will. On Cassius's controversial view of slavery, he wrote, "I never received

One of White Hall's staircases as it appeared in the mid- to late 1960s. (HABS)

a dollar from a slave in my life. On the contrary, I liberated all the slaves I inherited from my father and thirteen others whom I bought to bring families together, or liberated at once . . . The buying and liberating of these slaves, half of whom never entered my service, cost me about ten thousand dollars."[8]

Cassius's position on slavery was uncommon for a slave owner with significant planting interests. His outspokenness on the issue brought him to the attention of US president Abraham Lincoln, who later appointed Clay as the US minister to Russia during the American Civil War. While in Russia, Clay witnessed Tzar Alexander II issue the Emancipation reform of 1861 in which the tzar abolished serfdom. After returning briefly to America in 1862, Clay made his way back to Russia as the American ambassador in 1863, serving in that capacity until 1869. He was instrumental in negotiating America's purchase of Alaska from Russia during this term.[9]

Clay's controversial views on emancipation of slaves put him at odds with most citizens in his native state. Throughout Clay's political career, some who opposed Clay threatened physical violence. But Clay never backed down from a fight and could not be intimidated. In 1843 a hired assassin, Sam Brown, shot Clay in the chest at point-blank range. After being shot, Clay defended himself using his trusty Bowie knife to

slash and cut the assassin, inflicting multiple wounds and then throwing him over an embankment. Again in 1849 Clay was making a speech in favor of emancipation when he was attacked by six Turner brothers, who beat him, cut him with their knives, and tried to shoot him. However, Clay pulled his Bowie knife once again and fought off all six brothers. In the fight he killed one of them.[10]

There were many other instances when Clay was forced to defend himself from violent attacks. His always successful efforts to defend himself won for Clay the title, "The Lion of White Hall." When Clay was asked about his reputation as a fighter, he responded, "My reputation as a 'fighting man,' as the phrase goes, I never gloried in . . . I have never acted on the offensive; but have confined myself by will and to act to the defensive."[11]

In 1863 while on assignment in Russia, Cassius made plans to enlarge his Kentucky residence. He retained famed architect Maj. Thomas Lewinski to design the addition, and well-known architect and builder John McMurtry to execute its construction.[12] The addition would clearly reflect the Italianate style, but it would incorporate the older, Georgian house into its design. The foundation for the addition was begun in April 1863, but with the war at a fevered pitch around them, the foundations were not

yet finished a year later. While the new house was taking shape, the family lived in the old "Clermont" house as construction noisily continued around them. It was not until 1866 that enough of the new house was completed for the family to occupy part of it. However, even then, the family had to sleep on the third floor in rooms where the windows had not yet been installed. Since it was mid-October in Kentucky at that time, the ladies had to endure some terrifically cold nights.[13]

Clay's massive addition was not completed until the early 1870s. The new home boasted of forty-four rooms, as compared with the seven rooms of the old house. Clay named the new structure *White Hall*, though it is not known precisely how he arrived at that name. Guests entering the mansion's new entrance were greeted with sixteen-feet-high ceilings and a massive curving staircase. First-floor rooms were decorated with fine furnishings and decorative features such as Corinthian columns, plaster friezes, and elaborate ceiling medallions. Perhaps the most striking features of the new home were not seen by guests. Clay had the most modern of conveniences installed, including a central heating system much as we know them today with a furnace in the basement forcing hot air into rooms through vents. Clay still built fireplaces into the new section of the house, but they were for visual appeal only and were not operational. *White Hall* also had indoor plumbing and bathroom facilities. A huge cistern in the attic supplied gravity-fed water to a grouping of three "closets" serving three different bathroom functions. One closet held a tub with a shower. Another closet held a flushing toilet. The third closet's use is somewhat uncertain, but it is believed it held a water flushing system for disposal of chamber pot contents.

Although the mansion was huge, it would never hold a large family. Clay's wife, Mary Jane, left him and the house in 1872. He then filed for a divorce in 1878. For many years, only Cassius and his adoptive son, Launey, occupied the house along with a handful of servants. Cassius dated a number of women over the years, but he only asked one, a young girl who was the sister of one of his tenant farmers, to marry him. The two dated for a while until the eighty-four-year-old Cassius proposed to the then fourteen-year-old Dora Richardson. She accepted his proposal and the pair were married in 1894. Dora would remain married to Cassius for only four years, but spent more than two of those years separated from him. Oddly, after she obtained a divorce from Cassius, she returned to *White Hall* with her new husband a few years after she left it. Dora worked as Cassius's housekeeper and her new husband was a maintenance man on the property. In an unexpected twist, Dora and her husband named their first child Cassius.[14]

White Hall was put on the auction block just after Cassius Clay died in 1903. For the next sixty years, the house was periodically occupied by tenants who resided mainly in the *Clermont* part of the house. Vandals, partiers, and vagrants used the grand halls of the 1860s addition as their playground. The interior suffered from abuse by trespassers who thoughtlessly marred it with graffiti and wanton destruction. By the 1960s the upstairs floors were rotted and unsafe to walk on. Mantels had been stolen and part of the bannister of the grand staircase had been destroyed.

In 1965 a group of local concerned citizens engaged in an attempt to save the house. By 1971 their efforts led to more widespread interest in saving the mansion from two Kentucky governors and the appropriation of funds from the Kentucky state government to accomplish the work. In September 1971 the home was opened for tours as the White Hall State Shrine. In the mid-1980s the name of the park was changed to the White Hall State Historic Site and it continues to be operated as a state park today.[15] The 10,000-square-foot mansion is opened for tours in which guests can see nearly all of the home's three floors. The dwelling has been carefully restored and filled with period-appropriate furnishings, including many items that are original to the mansion and/or the Clay family.

TENNESSEE

Fairvue plantation's big house is still imposing even though its bucolic setting has been destroyed by development on all sides of the mansion. (Kitchens)

FAIRVUE PLANTATION
Country House Extraordinaire

📍 Sumner County, Tennessee

I n the 1830s plantation manors and country estates dotted the central Tennessee countryside. In the early years of European settlement in the area, log cabins, sometimes substantial in size, were the norm. Slowly, homes of the prosperous became more refined, some as large frame structures and others of brick. However, it was Isaac Franklin's enormous mansion built at *Fairvue* that broke the mold for country houses and ushered in a thirty-year period of building exceptional architectural estates and plantation houses in the area. But even thirty years later, few would favorably compare with *Fairvue*.

Isaac Franklin was born in 1789 as the son of a Revolutionary soldier who was awarded a military land grant for his patriotic service. Isaac was born on *Pilot Knob* plantation in Sumner County in what would soon be the state of Tennessee. As a young man working for his brother on a flatboat that ran from Gallatin, Tennessee, to New Orleans, Louisiana, Isaac became convinced that he should enter the slave trade. He entered into a partnership with his nephew, John Armfield, and the partnership soon became the largest slave-trading enterprise in the South: Armfield & Franklin.[1] The business made Franklin a very wealthy man, but because slave traders were ostracized in polite society, Franklin left the business in 1835. Franklin set his sights, instead, on becoming a planter. He had seen the success of cotton production in other states and was one of the first to recognize the potential for the success of cotton in Middle Tennessee.

In 1831, he purchased two thousand acres near Gallatin. By this time, he was already a millionaire living the life of the wealthy of his day, spending summers in the North and winters in Natchez, Mississippi.[2] Then in 1832, Franklin, though still a bachelor, started construction on a brick mansion that dwarfed other large dwellings of the period. When finished, Franklin's *Fairvue* mansion was considered to be the finest mansion in Tennessee. In addition to the refined brick manor house, Franklin built an entire village of brick structures for outbuildings including twelve servants' houses, overseer's

Even after 140 years, the central hall at Fairvue was still impressive when this photograph was taken in 1971. (HABS)

quarters, well house, ice house, blacksmith shop, barns, carriage house, stables, carpenter shop, mill, kitchen, and other buildings required for the proper functioning of a self-sufficient plantation. Lawsuit filings involving an attempt to break Franklin's last will provide a description of the estate: "The grounds around were planted with choice trees and laid out in the best manner; here he had greenhouses, flower gardens, sumptuous furniture, several fine carriages, choice wines of all kinds, a stable of race horses, a large quantity of blooded stock, and a number of picked servants, more than sufficient even for such an establishment."[3]

The exterior of Franklin's completed mansion looks substantially the same today as it did in 1832. It is of Georgian design featuring identical two-tiered pedimented porticos on both the front and the rear entrance. Each portico is graced with large entryways on the first and second floors surmounted by elliptical fanlight transoms with flanking glass sidelights. Echoing the classical Ionic columns on the portico are disengaged Ionic columns on either side of the doorway supporting carved cornices framing the entry. Other than the stone lintels above the windows, the exterior bears no other striking architectural features except its careful attention to scale and proportion, which makes it one of the most beautiful mansions in the South.

The floor plan of Franklin's mansion is in keeping with most other homes of the time. It has a wide central hall extending from the front door to the back door. On one

The double parlors at Fairvue once entertained the elite and powerful of Tennessee. (HABS)

side of the first-floor hallway are double parlors divided by huge sliding doors, and on the other side there is a music room and dining room.

Fairvue was not the only income-producing property Franklin owned. He also had a half interest along with a partner in extensive acreage in Louisiana, including eight thousand acres in West Feliciana Parish, over two hundred slaves, and valuable animal stock. His plantations in Louisiana operated under the names *Bellevue*, *Killarney*, *Locklomond*, and *Angola*. Franklin also acquired vast acreage in Texas, which totaled nearly fifty thousand acres. Business interests outside of planting, such as bank shares, a turnpike company, and interests in a Nashville race course, supplemented his already substantial assets.[4]

With this background in mind, perhaps it is no surprise that a pretty, twenty-two-year-old girl, Adelicia Hayes, would meet Franklin at *Fairvue* while attending a party and win his heart. Although Franklin was fifty years old at the time, he fell for the head-strong young woman and the couple married in July 1839. Adelicia also came from a prominent family. She was gracious, but sometime brash. As a great fan of horse racing, Franklin must have admired that his young wife was also a skilled horsewoman. In marrying Franklin, Adelicia had married into one of the greatest fortunes in Tennessee, but Franklin also realized a benefit from the union. He married into a

well-respected and socially important family who could help him shed his reputation as a slave trader and transition into society as a respected planter.

During the couple's brief seven-year marriage, they had four children, but only one survived past the age of ten. Franklin died in 1846 while at his *Bellevue* plantation in Louisiana. His body was preserved in alcohol and shipped back to Tennessee so that he could be buried at *Fairvue*.

Franklin's will made Adelicia a very wealthy woman. He gave her *Fairvue*, its revenues, and all of its furniture and provisions along with the right to live there for as long as she was a widow. However, if she remarried, she would forfeit *Fairvue*, and instead, would receive either $100,000 in a lump sum or $6,000 per year for her life, but would have no claim to any of his other properties. Franklin also left a substantial portion of his estate for the establishment of a school at *Fairvue*.

Initially, the young widow gave up her interest in *Fairvue* plantation by selling her life estate interest in the estate to Franklin's brother. She then took the $100,000 lump sum to which she was entitled under the will. Exercising this option allowed Adelicia to remarry if she wished.

However, Adelicia then challenged the terms of Franklin's will in both Louisiana and Tennessee, resulting in protracted, expensive litigation. But, in 1852 she found conclusive success in the court system. Franklin's will was declared void and the entire estate descended to his heirs, Adelicia and Emma, her last surviving child from her marriage to Franklin. She had become perhaps the wealthiest woman in America. It was then that her attentions turned squarely on building a new home, *Belmont*. However, Adelicia's interest in *Fairvue* had not been quelled. Just after the War between the States, she

The wing extending off of Fairvue's right side was constructed as early as 1839 and housed rooms for servants to use and guest bedrooms for visitors to the estate. (Kitchens)

One can almost glimpse the Fairvue of old when seeing its rear portico still appearing in its garden setting. (Kitchens)

purchased *Fairvue* from John Armfield, who had been an executor of the estate of Isaac Franklin. It was once again her home and domain.

For about three years after Franklin's death, she had remained at *Fairvue* as a widow. But, in 1849 she met Joseph Acklen and the couple was married later that year. The brash, young Adelicia signed a marriage contract with Acklen guaranteeing that certain properties she owned would remain under her sole control, thereby preventing Acklen from assuming control of them. Not long after marrying Acklen, Adelicia began construction on another of the state's most imposing mansions, *Belmont*. Built in Nashville, *Belmont* was to be her summer home, while during the remainder of the year the Acklens would reside at a house Adelicia had purchased in Nashville or her Louisiana properties.

Once Adelicia reacquired *Fairvue* just after the war, it remained an Acklen property until she sold it in 1882 to Charles Reed from New York. Reed's ambition was to own a farm for the breeding of race horse stock. *Fairvue* would be his primary breeding and racing farm. He undertook improvements to the property, chiefly related to the improvement of facilities for the care of horses. He built a huge stone barn with stalls trimmed in oak crafted by expert cabinetmakers. Reed entertained guests at *Fairvue* on a lavish scale. He had a special set of china dinnerware made featuring his own portrait in the center of each dish, and another set of china with paintings of his favored horses, including statistics of their records and the jockeys who raced them. Although he experienced some success with his breeding farm, producing foals that sold for exorbitant prices and some who won large purses, his revenues could not keep pace with his spending. Reed was forced to sell the farm at *Fairvue*. The estate then passed through the hands of a variety of owners. By the 1930s *Fairvue* was showing signs of neglect.

Some of its sturdy brick walls were cracking, moss grew on its columned portico, and some of its imported marble mantels had been removed.[5] *Fairvue*'s glory had faded, but all hope was not lost. A new owner cared for *Fairvue* and preserved the mansion for several more decades.

Fairvue experienced another close call in the late 1990s and early 2000s when the estate was offered for sale once again. A number of potential buyers looked at the property, including at least one of country music's iconic stars, but the home's future remained in doubt. When news came that a property developer had purchased the site, many feared the home would be bulldozed to make way for a modern subdivision. Fortunately, the *Fairvue* mansion was preserved, but its setting was forever destroyed. *Fairvue* today sits amid a large subdivision of large, very attractive homes. Rather than rolling fields spreading below the mansion, a golf course now provides the semblance of once broad lawns. Most of the brick outbuildings that remained on the estate were saved. The brick slave houses, overseer's house, and blacksmith shop were preserved and incorporated into a country club clubhouse and parking facility. A row of impressive brick stables that were built after the Acklen ownership were also saved and now line one side of a fairway along the golf course. The *Fairvue* mansion is now a private residence standing among streets of other large, though not nearly as impressive, modern homes.

Fairvue, thankfully, stands. However, those driving to the house today will never again be able to envision the bucolic scene that the mansion once centered. Rolling fields, deep forests, long lanes lined by trees, and a tranquil setting were once taken for granted by the occupants and visitors to *Fairvue*. Never again will this estate be seen in that light.

CARNTON PLANTATION
Everlasting Memorial to Confederate Dead

♀ Franklin, Tennessee

The "carns" in County Antrim, Ireland, are a heap of stones serving as a memorial to graves of the dead. The carns were well known to the McGavock family for it was at Carntown, County Antrim, Ireland, that Randal McGavock's father was born. Perhaps it is not surprising that in 1824 when Randal McGavock built a mansion on his plantation near Franklin, Tennessee, he would name it for Carntown, Ireland. But McGavock could not have known then how his *Carnton* plantation would be forced to live into its name.

Randal McGavock and his wife, Sarah, lived in Nashville in the early 1820s. They purchased a fourteen-hundred-acre tract of land about thirty miles south, near Franklin, and began construction of a large Federal-style residence on a beautiful hill providing them with views over much of their estate. The McGavocks, a prominent family in central Tennessee, were friends with many political leaders, including President Andrew Jackson and future president James K. Polk, both of whom were frequent visitors at *Carnton*.[1] In fact, Andrew Jackson gave the McGavocks a cherished rocking chair, which remains in the mansion today.

After Randal McGavock died in 1843, Sarah continued to operate the farm at *Carnton*. McGavock left the plantation house and about half of the land to his son, John McGavock; the other half of his land to son, James; and a life estate to his wife, Sarah. Under John's direction *Carnton* expanded and the farm became one of Middle Tennessee's showplaces. John modified the appearance of the house in 1847 by adding a Greek Revival portico to the front and enlarging the front yard. The next year he added to the size of the family by marrying Carrie Elizabeth Winder, the daughter of a Louisiana planter with a large sugar plantation. The couple bore five children, but only two survived to adulthood—a daughter named Hattie and a son named Winder.[2] Despite their losses, John and Carrie McGavock made *Carnton* a home reflecting their tastes and style. Set amid lush fields and extravagant gardens, the McGavocks' home was the picture of southern rural beauty.

However, the dark cloud of war soon overshadowed this setting. On November 30, 1864, the Battle of Franklin was fought on and around their bucolic farm. Just prior to the battle, Confederate general John Bell Hood made the decision to attack federal positions that had been fortified just south of Franklin. At midday famed Confederate general Nathan Bedford Forrest visited *Carnton* to conduct reconnaissance of the area. Carrie McGavock later recalled that "Forrest strode through her halls and up the stairway to a gallery above, seemingly unconscious of her presence, so absorbed was he in the great tragedy enacted around them." Forrest used the upper balcony on the rear of the house to gain a better view of the federal fortifications just beyond.

Late in the afternoon of the same day, the battle commenced with about 20,000 Confederates assaulting the federal lines. The Confederate right flank, commanded by Maj. Gen. William W. Loring, formed a battle line just south of *Carnton*. Loring's advancing Confederates flooded the McGavocks' fields, yard, and home, as Carrie McGavock stood near the front gate and watched in dread. Once the fighting commenced, casualties quickly piled up near the house. Carrie willingly opened her home as a field hospital to care for rapidly multiplying wounded and dying men. Thomas Markham, a Confederate chaplain, describes the generosity of the McGavocks that day: "[a]ll that was theirs in that great house was ours . . . They opened their hearts and their home." Loring's division of thirty-five hundred men suffered losses that afternoon of nine hundred men. For more than twenty-four hours a constant flow of wounded

soldiers streamed to the house, while cannons roared and bullets filled the air. Contemporary accounts of the scene at *Carnton* describe how every room and every space was filled with bodies of the injured, including even the corner under the stairs. Just one room in the mansion was reserved for the entire McGavock family to live in and share.

Even the long back porch and the yard were filled with injured, dead, and dying men. Inside the mansion, surgeons and nurses worked around the clock to treat the wounded while Carrie McGavock and others in her family worked tirelessly to treat suffering men. Col. W. D. Gale recounts the scene in the McGavock home in a letter to his wife written on January 14, 1865: "During all this time the surgeons plied their dreadful work amid the sighs and [screams] and death rattle. Yet, amid it all, this noble woman, the very impersonation of divine sympathy and tender pity, was active and constant at work. During the night neither she nor any of the household slept, but dispensed tea and coffee and such stimulants as she had, and that, too, with her own hands."[3] The next day, among the hundreds of other casualties, the bodies of five dead Confederate generals, including John Adams, Hiram Granbury, Otho Stahl, Patrick Cleburne, and States Rights Gist, lay on the back porch.

Injured Confederate soldiers remained in the house for weeks after the battle. Even after the Confederate army retreated from Nashville in mid-December, *Carnton* still housed at least twenty-nine critically injured soldiers. Carrie McGavock and her friend, an older black woman, managed all of the cooking, washing, and cleaning for

The floors of the upstairs bedrooms are still stained with the blood of soldiers who were brought to Carnton for treatment during the Battle of Franklin. (Kitchens)

themselves and the wounded men. The memories of this terrible time stuck with the McGavocks for decades. Hattie McGavock recounts, "I can still sense the odor of smoke and blood. . . . I can still see the swarms of soldiers coming with their dead comrades and lying them down by the hundreds under our spacious shade trees and all about the grounds. I was only nine years old then, but it is all as vivid and real as if it happened only yesterday."[4] Still clear in the nostrils of her memory was "The smell. I'm not sure it really ever went away."

As the number of dead soldiers, both Union and Confederate, on the McGavocks' extensive grounds rose, they were buried in place, sometimes in mass graves. After the Battle of Nashville, Union soldiers returned to Franklin and removed the Union dead at *Carnton* to reinter them at Murphreesboro, Tennessee. The burial plots of

thousands of Confederate soldiers, however, still lay strewn all over *Carnton*'s fields for two years after the war. The McGavock family decided that a more respectful interment for these honored Confederates who had sacrificed everything for their country was necessary. They organized an extensive and grim task of exhuming and then reinterring twenty-five hundred soldiers onto a two-acre site adjoining their family cemetery, which they set aside for that purpose, within sight of their home. When the last of the Confederate dead were reinterred, the McGavocks had created one of the largest private military cemeteries in America. Just as its name foretold, *Carnton* had become a place where stacks of stones stood as a memorial to honor the fallen.

For decades after the war, the McGavock family continuously cared for the graves, worked to identify as many of the fallen as possible, and opened the cemetery to the families of those who had fallen. For thirty-nine years, Carrie McGavock worked tirelessly to tend to the graves of thousands of soldiers, until she too was laid to rest among her family and the men she so relentlessly honored.

Carnton was sold out of the McGavock family in 1911. As the twentieth century progressed, so did the movement of residential development of Franklin. *Carnton* became terribly dilapidated, even reaching the point to where its survival was in doubt. Fortunately, a group of motivated people who recognized the site's unique historical

The McGavock family buried thousands of the Confederate dead in a cemetery just behind their home, which is visible in the background of this image. (Kitchens)

In the 1980s the work to restore Carnton's exterior was well underway. (Image courtesy of The Battle of Franklin Trust, Franklin, TN)

In spite of the tragic events that happened in and around Carnton in 1864, the home is undeniably stunning as one of Tennessee's most important historic museum houses. (Kitchens)

importance banded together to save it. The Carnton Association was organized in 1977 to raise money to preserve the house and cemetery. Dr. and Mrs. W. D. Sugg, who had owned the house since the 1950s but had never lived in it, donated the house and ten acres to the association in 1978. Identifying the most compelling reason to save *Carnton*, it was said, "Let other houses be saved because of the mighty who lived there. This is the story of *Carnton*—a story of defeat and suffering and the triumph born out of it all. This is where the Old South died."

By the mid-1980s the organization was able to undertake restoration of the home's interior with the goal of returning it to its original grandeur. *Carnton*'s interior today is resplendent, reflecting a style and appearance that would have been comfortably familiar to the McGavocks. Evidence of the horrifying days of pain and suffering in December 1864 remains in some of the upstairs bedrooms as large bloodstains permanently mar wood floors. Within sight of the mansion remains the McGavock family cemetery with the graves of Confederate victims of war. Plaques recounting and interpreting the horrible scene during the Battle of Franklin now attempt to bring context to the house and cemetery. Today, *Carnton* is opened to the public for guided mansion tours and self-guided tours of the grounds and cemetery. The historic site is now operated by the Historic Carnton Plantation Association, whose ongoing goal is to preserve the house and its history.

Clouston Hall is lovingly
maintained by Kelly Harwood,
who enjoys sharing the home's
history. (Kitchens)

CLOUSTON HALL

Enduring Home for Entertainment and Art

♀ Franklin, Tennessee

Whether built in the nineteenth or twenty-first century, the vast majority of dwellings are built primarily as a place to live with secondary functionality as a place to entertain one's guests. However, *Clouston Hall*'s construction appears to have been one of the rare exceptions where its primary function was to entertain guests with secondary functionality of serving as a home. During its nearly two-hundred-year existence, it has admirably endured as a welcoming hall for lavish entertainment and a pallet for artistic expression.

Edward G. Clouston, a prominent merchant in the area, hired builder Joseph Reiff to design a new home he would build a few blocks from downtown Franklin. Reiff is the same builder who in 1834 rebuilt Andrew Jackson's *Hermitage* outside of Nashville after it was severely damaged by a fire. Reiff's design for the reconstructed *Hermitage* is the *Hermitage* we recognize today.[1] Reiff applied his obvious skill in high-style residential design to build for Clouston an exceptional Federal-style house with many notably unique details. Reiff may also be responsible for the design of Franklin's historic Carter House, which bears many similar features to *Clouston Hall*, including a strikingly similar façade. The Carter House was erected at about the same time as *Clouston Hall*.

Clouston Hall's construction date is uncertain. Most sources place the building date at 1821, while others insist that it was not built until 1828. Regardless of the precise construction date, what is known is that Clouston built his new townhome as an edifice sufficient to entertain his many social, business, and political guests. The home would also serve as a place for Clouston and his family, who apparently made their permanent residence elsewhere, to stay when they visited Franklin. However, the house was most frequently used during its early years as a party house and political gathering place. Clouston hobnobbed with many of Tennessee's political elite, for included among the notable visitors to *Clouston Hall* are three United States presidents: Andrew Jackson, James K. Polk, and Andrew Johnson.[2] Jackson and Polk are believed to have been entertained in the home on multiple occasions.

Clouston Hall as it appeared in years past. (Image courtesy of Rick Warren at The Heritage Foundation of Franklin, TN)

Clouston's home is a masterpiece of early American architecture. The all-brick structure is a story-and-a-half pile resting upon a granite foundation. Its four primary rooms on the main level are divided by a very wide central hall. With sumptuous entertaining in mind, the home's four downstairs rooms consist of large double parlors on the left of the hall and a large dining room and library on the right. The upstairs contains two more large rooms, originally used as the bedchambers, and a hall. In all, the home is deceptively large, encompassing 3,340 square feet.

The entrance and windows of the façade are the building's most notable features with an elliptical fanlight over double-leafed doors. Flanking the doorway are finely detailed sidelights framed by partially disengaged, fluted columns. Front windows are tripartite in form with wood-carved columns separating the central windows from the sidelight windows. Window encasements are surmounted by shallow pediments that bespeak of classical refinement.

The unusually fine architectural details were not exhausted on the exterior. Dividing the double parlors are four-leaf folding doors surrounded by classical Federal-styled wood trim that includes a deep-carved cornice supported by partially disengaged columns. Cornice moldings, carved mantels, door surrounds, and the arched opening separating the front hall from the back hall all bear the detail and proportion one would expect in a Federal home, including carved sunbursts and reeded pilasters. Whether in the front yard, the hallway, the parlors, or the dining room, Clouston's guests would have had no doubt that they were in one of the most beautiful homes in central Tennessee.

Perhaps the lavish entertaining and lifestyle of Clouston outlasted his ability to pay for it. In 1840 the home was offered in a sheriff's sale, and in 1842 Clouston was forced to forfeit the home and its surrounding property to the bank. The home was sold again in 1854 to Oscar Reams, a Franklin merchant, for just $2,250. However, just six years later the home was placed on the market again, along with its servants' houses, detached kitchen, stables, sheds, and adjoining lot filled with fruit trees and gardens.

Paneled, folding doors separate the front parlor from the rear parlor and display fine Federal wood trims and moldings. (Kitchens)

Apparently the house did not sell, for Reams still owned the home in 1864 when Franklin became the backdrop for the carnage of the Battle of Franklin. *Clouston Hall* was used as a field station for Confederate soldiers and then an infirmary after the battle. Fascinating lore surrounds the home as a place where a lady known as Miss Ninnie attempted to shoot at Union soldiers from an upstairs window. Miss Ninnie got one shot off, but as she pulled the trigger to deliver a second round, the gun backfired, amputating her thumb. She was known thereafter for always wearing a glove on the affected hand to hide the wound.[3]

Though surrounded by the lingering destruction of battle and war, romance was not stifled. The journal of C. D. Hammer of the 124th Ohio Volunteer Infantry, published in 1914, recounts the "near-romance" he had with Sallie Reams, a belle of *Clouston Hall*. He had taken ill during the Battle of Franklin and was recuperating in a house just

Today, Kelly Harwood utilizes this venerable home as an art and antique studio. (Kitchens)

south of Franklin. During his recovery, he met sixteen-year-old Sallie Reams and the two developed a friendship, though it seems that this northern invader was smitten by the charms of a southern belle. For reasons that will never been discovered, Hammer's "near romance" with Sallie would not grow into anything more.

Oscar Reams's heirs were finally able to sell the house several years after the war to Henry P. and Sarah Jane Marshall. For sixty years after the Marshalls purchased it in 1869, *Clouston Hall* passed through a succession of owners. In 1942 the historic home was purchased by the Briggs family, who made it their home for the next twenty years. However, late in their occupancy of the house, it became dilapidated.

Clouston Hall became endangered in 1964 as Sinclair Oil Company wanted to purchase the property so that it could demolish the historic home and build a service station on the lot. Fortunately, the house was saved by artist Bunn Gray, who convinced the owners to sell it to him instead. In November 1964, Gray purchased the home for just $13,000.[4] For the next thirty-eight years he lived in *Clouston Hall* and used it as a backdrop to display his artwork. Bunn was an artist of some renown, with his art displayed in the galleries and collections of Elizabeth Taylor, Neil Simon, and Marsha Mason.[5] At Gray's death in 2002, the house was inherited by Franklin contractor Rusty Womack.

When Womack took possession of *Clouston Hall*, it was in near ruinous condition. Some feared the house would be condemned as uninhabitable. However, Womack undertook an extensive restoration to save the house and to return it as nearly as

The Federal-style stair hall at Clouston Hall when it was still being used as a residence. (Image courtesy of Rick Warren at The Heritage Foundation of Franklin, TN)

possible to its original condition. For this restoration, Womack intended to add some modern conveniences. In 2004 Womack began leasing the home to business tenants. The home that Gray had purchased for $13,000 in 1964 was estimated to be worth $1,675,000 when it was placed for sale again in 2009.

Clouston Hall remains in the hands of owners who are vitally interested in its preservation. In 2010 Ira Shivitz and Kelly Harwood purchased it, and Harwood opened it as Gallery 202.[6] Gallery 202 is an art gallery featuring fine southern antiques and fine art that is predominantly the creation of local artists. Harwood regularly opens the house for impromptu tours. He is cognizant of the historic value of the home his gallery now occupies and embraces the interest shown by those who want to learn its history and witness its exceptional architectural features. *Clouston Hall* remains a home whose purpose is to entertain visitors and display art.

Up-close view of the Belmont
mansion's façade showing
the many architectural details
displayed on the structure.
(Kitchens)

BELMONT

Villa for a Remarkable Woman

♦ Nashville, Tennessee

To some, a house is just a place to live. It matters little how the structure looks or how it is decorated as long as it is neat, clean, and functional. To others, however, the wood, brick, and mortar in which they make their home is an extension of their personality and a reflection of their view of themselves. But, for a rare few, their home is far more. It is a glimpse into their heart and mind. Indeed, for some, the abode in which they live so clearly displays their mindset and thoughts that the pile becomes as an animation of the owner's biography and all that he or she holds dear. For example, can anyone imagine any person living in *Monticello* but Thomas Jefferson, or in *Mount Vernon* but George Washington, or in *Hermitage* but Andrew Jackson? Are not these dwellings as much a biography of their owner and builder as any study or written dissertation about them? Just as *Monticello* is a standing biography of Jefferson, so too is *Belmont* in Nashville a telling and informative study into the life, heart, and mind of its builder and owner, Adelicia Hayes Franklin Acklen.

Adelicia's ascension into enormous wealth and her home at *Fairvue* plantation in Sumner County, Tennessee, has already been chronicled.[1] After her first husband, Isaac Franklin, died in 1846, she was still a young woman and, now, a very wealthy widow. So, it should come as no surprise that her widowhood would not last long. In 1849 she met Joseph Alexander Smith Acklen, a Mexican War hero and former United States attorney in Alabama.[2] Perhaps adding to Adelicia's attraction to Acklen is the fact that he was her own age. That same year, Adelicia and Joseph were married with James K. Polk, the former president of the United States, attending. Before President Polk died just a month later, he wrote of Adelicia's wedding, describing the event as being one held on "a magnificent scale."

Joseph Acklen undertook the management of Adelicia's plantations in Louisiana, and he was dedicated to the work. For eight months of the year, he lived on their Louisiana plantations, but he spent the hot summers in the cooler climes of Nashville with Adelicia.

This view of Belmont from 1863 shows the extensive gardens stretching in front of the mansion as well as the full length of the mansion's wings. (Image courtesy of Belmont Mansion Association, Nashville)

As a couple, Adelicia and Joseph were enormously successful. The couple held $2,000,000 in real estate holdings and $1,000,000 in personal property, including one thousand slaves. Their plantations produced the astounding output of 5,000 to 6,000 bales of cotton each year. As quickly as their wealth expanded, so did their family. Between 1850 and 1859, Adelicia and Joseph bore six children. The twins both died in 1855 just seventeen days apart while still toddlers, but the rest of the children survived to maturity. Adelicia's last surviving child from her marriage to Isaac Franklin also died in 1855 from diphtheria when only eleven years old.[3]

Just a short time after her marriage to Acklen, Adelicia began construction on the *Belmont* mansion near Nashville. The *Belmont* property was nestled among other country estates owned by Adelicia's family. On adjoining properties were *Rokeby*, at the time owned by Adelicia's father; *Ensworth*, owned by Adelicia's brother and his wife; and *Hillside*, owned by another of Adelicia's sisters and her husband. But, *Belmont* would dwarf these other estates. By 1853, the first iteration of *Belmont*, primarily the

The grand salon was added to Belmont in 1859 when Adelicia had the rear porch enclosed and enlarged to form this enormous room in which her many guests could be properly entertained. (Kitchens)

main block of the house we see today, was completed and the Acklen family moved in. However, Adelicia constantly found ways to enlarge and improve her home. In 1857 the east and west wings were added to the mansion and the home was stuccoed in a shade of pink to resemble exotic cut stone.

Again, in 1859 Adelicia undertook improvements to *Belmont*. She retained renowned architect Adolphus Heiman to enclose the back porch and make it a large space for entertaining that Adelicia called the Grand Salon. By 1860 the house took on the form in which it is seen today, except that the east and west wings at that time were much longer. The final iteration of *Belmont* would make it appear more as an Italian villa using Corinthian columns, Venetian glass in transoms and sidelights, consoles under windowsills, and cornices and pediments over doorways. Adding to the grandiosity of the home's appearance is the placement of six statues on blocks along the parapet running across the edge of the roof. Only four of these statues remain in place today. Softening the solid mass of the exterior are ornate cast-iron balconies extending across the entire front of the east and west wings. Like a crown over the entire regal structure sits an octagonal cupola. In 1860, *Belmont* had grown to thirty-six rooms.

The grounds in front of and around *Belmont* were as impressive as the mansion. The mansion sits at the crest of a hill. Descending down the slope in front of the dwelling were extensive gardens laid out in three circles down to a 200-feet-long greenhouse and a 105-feet-tall brick water tower. Springs supplied water, which was pumped into

the tower and then gravity pulled the water down with enough force to power various water fountains in the gardens and supply running water to the house. Other imposing features of the grounds were massive gates at the entrance of the estate, a rococo carriage house, stables, a large marble water fountain surrounded by four marble statues from Italy depicting the four continents, gazebos covered with jasmine and roses, a deer park, a zoo with ornamental cages, an artificial lake stocked with alligators, and a two-story, octagonal bathhouse. Adelicia also built separate outbuildings including an art gallery in the form of a Greek temple, a bowling alley, and two additional greenhouses.[4] Life-sized Italian statuary of mythical beings served as ornamentation through the acres of gardens.

Adelicia's *Belmont* was more akin to one of England's great estates. Describing a visit she made to *Belmont* in 1860, Mother Frances Walsh, a Dominican sister who had recently opened an academy for girls named St. Cecilia, describes her early summer experience there:

> A most gracious welcome was accorded the visitors who were made to feel at home in the spacious reception hall, the surroundings suggestive of Oriental luxury. . . . On leave taking a scene of sylvan loveliness greeted the view; such a dazzling array of art and nature, commingling so as to beautify each other, was arranged as by the hand of a master artist. Here and there were statuary, marble and bronze, placed in groups and singly. Fountains, costly vases and flowers of the richest hues intermingled in endless profusion. There were

Faithful reproduction of Belmont originally painted in 1860 and serving as perhaps the most accurate depiction of the Belmont mansion and gardens. (Image courtesy of Belmont Mansion Association, Nashville)

Belmont's large dining room at which many formal dinners were served. (Kitchens)

summer houses and grottos of all devices, some so dainty that they might be fitting haunts of wood-nymphs or water spirits.[5]

As if all of this grandeur were not enough, Adelicia had plans for an even more magnificent display on one of her Louisiana plantations. She had already begun acquiring materials to build a "palace" in Louisiana where she lived part of each year. Her Louisiana palace was designed to contain fifty rooms in addition to bathrooms and closets. It was to stand along the Mississippi River and would be a castellated Gothic mansion expected to cost $150,000 to build and another $125,000 to furnish. The center block of the mansion would be 220 feet deep and topped by a tower. Extending on each side would be 105-feet-long wings. Such a mansion would have been unlike any other residence in America, but it was never begun.

Not long after Mother Walsh visited *Belmont*, it experienced its first threat of destruction. Toward the end of the War between the States, the devastation of war found its way to Nashville. Federal forces, defending their hold on Nashville from Confederates approaching from the south, erected defenses that crossed the *Belmont* estate. It had become the front lines. Union officers made *Belmont* their headquarters and its lavish rooms were used as offices. One Union soldier describes the destruction they visited on the once stunning grounds of *Belmont*, writing, "I am satisfied that never before was army headquarters so ornamented with such paintings and marbles. We, on the outside, were equally well off, for the spacious grounds were surrounded by

The Adelicia Acklen bedroom is stunning with its reproduction of the original Defour scenic wallpaper manufactured in France. (Kitchens)

nicely built stone walls that were worked into chimneys noiselessly as was the building of Solomon's Temple . . . The ornamental trees did not make first rate firewood on account of being green, but we had not time for them to dry, and had to get along with them as best we could."[6] The threats to Adelicia's home were real. One Union officer boasted of how easily the *Belmont* mansion would burn.

Confederate forces were advancing on Nashville and Union commanders determined to push them back made *Belmont* a center for the battle. A journalist observing the battle that ensued reported, "while I watched the battle of Nashville, I was certain that the Acklen house would be demolished by the bursting shells. It stood nearly right between the lines of the contending forces and I could have almost sworn I saw bombs bursting directly over the house."[7] However, the house survived the battle with surprisingly little damage.

Belmont survived the war and by 1867 Adelicia was using *Belmont* to lavishly entertain guests once again. Visitors to the estate included inventor Alexander Graham Bell, evangelist Dwight L. Moody, the Mexican emperor's grandson Augustin Iturbide, as well as scores of actors, poets, and authors. Adelicia sold her beloved *Belmont* in 1887 along with seventy-eight surrounding acres.

Between 1888 and 1951 the *Belmont* mansion was used by a succession of schools as classroom, dormitory, and entertaining space. In the 1960s the Tennessee Baptist Convention established Belmont College as a four-year coeducational college. But Belmont College had limited revenue and could not afford to maintain the mansion properly.

Beautiful Belmont Mansion as it appears today on the campus of Belmont University. (Image courtesy of Belmont Mansion Association, Nashville)

The historic home became dilapidated to such an extent that its entire second floor had to be closed off for fear that the floors would buckle.

In 1971, history professor Dr. Albert W. Wardin Jr. formed a committee to consider ways to renovate the house. The Historic Belmont Association was established the next year and ten years later, the organization became the Belmont Mansion Foundation, which was founded to rescue the mansion and restore it to its former glory. In 1976 enough progress had been made in restoring the mansion to open it for regular tours. Since 1986 serious and regular renovations have been made to Adelicia's home, and it is slowly being returned to its 1860 appearance. Paint and wallpaper analysis have revealed original finishes in the mansion while diligent efforts have been undertaken to reacquire some of the furniture and art that Adelicia once knew in the home.

Belmont is opened daily for tours. Although one visiting today is not able to glimpse the lavish grounds the estate once possessed, she can gain a reasonable understanding of the home so loved by the very wealthy in early America. Visitors can enjoy the residence of perhaps the most fascinating, independent, and brash woman in early Tennessee; a woman who cast aside the customs of her time to build an empire.

The Hermitage mansion today
is one of the most visited
house museums in Tennessee.
(Kitchens)

THE HERMITAGE PLANTATION
Presidential Retreat

♥ Donelson, Tennessee

Books by the dozens have been written about Andrew Jackson. He was one of the most compelling leaders of the United States while it was still a young Republic. He endured hosts of struggles in war, love, and politics. Practically nothing about his life was easy. Perhaps he was lucky here and there, but he was also an entirely self-made man with a remarkable self-confidence that bolstered an even more remarkable bravery. What he loved, he loved with all of his heart. Perhaps the two things he loved the most were his wife and his home at *The Hermitage*.

Jackson lived most of his early life in South Carolina and North Carolina. In 1787 he was admitted to the bar as a lawyer, and the next year he was appointed as a public prosecutor in North Carolina's Western District—an area that later became the state of Tennessee. He moved to the tiny town of Nashville. It was there that he fell in love with Rachel Donelson, who was mired in a terrible marriage. Rachel filed for divorce and once Andrew and Rachel thought the divorce was finalized, they married. However, they later found out that her divorce had not yet been officially decreed, so the couple legally married "again" in 1784 after confirmation that the Donelson divorce was legally final.

In 1804 Andrew and Rachel Jackson purchased a modest farm known as *The Hermitage*. Jackson resigned as a superior court judge to become a farmer on his new property. His time as a farmer did not last long. He spent significant time away with the militia fighting first the Creek Indian nation and then the British in the War of 1812. Jackson returned to *The Hermitage* again in 1815 with a national reputation as an Indian fighter and the hero of the Battle of New Orleans. The acclaim that came with his military successes took him from home several more times in the next few years. By 1819, after spending time as the first governor of the new Florida Territory, Jackson grew weary of public life and wanted to return home. He retired as governor and immediately returned to his log cabin at *The Hermitage* in Tennessee.

Once back home, Jackson began to make improvements. His farm had expanded to nearly one thousand acres. In 1819 Jackson undertook construction of a brick home

This image of The Hermitage was taken in the 1880s when the house was beginning to suffer from neglect. (Kitchens)

that would be more suitable to his wife, Rachel, and more befitting of his nationally prominent position as war hero and political leader. The new brick home was a "simple" Federal-style home. It would also have a formal parterre garden for Rachel to enjoy. The garden and the home were very similar in design and style to those that Jackson had seen farther east as homes that the country's Founding Fathers favored. Jackson's new two-story brick residence was completed by 1821. The log home that the Jacksons had lived in for the past seventeen years was put to other uses just behind the new mansion.[1] Indeed, the log home remains on the property today.

Shortly after Jackson's new home was completed, he was once again spending most of his time out of the state. He had been elected as a United States senator from Tennessee in 1823. Then his name was thrust into the national spotlight in 1824 as a candidate for president of the United States. Although Andrew Jackson won the national popular vote, he failed to win a majority of the votes in the electoral college. The election was sent to the House of Representatives for a final selection, and John Quincy Adams became president. Immediately, Jackson's many supporters began work to elect Jackson as president in the next election cycle.

During the presidential election in 1828, Jackson ran a Populist campaign. His chief opponent was once again John Quincy Adams, who was now the incumbent, and the campaign that ensued reached an all-time low for mudslinging. Jackson's opponent raised scurrilous allegations about Rachel Jackson's reputation. The strain and

The French wallpaper originally installed at The Hermitage was the delight of Rachel Jackson and appears today precisely as it did in the 1840s. (Image courtesy of Andrew Jackson's Hermitage, Nashville, TN)

embarrassment brought on by the election process was too much for Rachel. Just a month after Andrew Jackson was elected president, Rachel died suddenly at *The Hermitage*. Jackson was nearly broken by the loss. She was laid to rest in the garden just outside the mansion that she loved so much.[2]

Jackson was a very popular president. He won election for a second term in 1832. However, at *The Hermitage* all was not well. His adopted son, Andrew Jackson Jr., was running the plantation and had increased its size to twelve hundred acres. But, he was not up to the task of properly managing the plantation, which resulted in heavy financial losses. To make matters worse, while the mansion was undergoing a renovation that had begun in 1831, the home caught fire and burned in 1834. The fire destroyed most of the interior of the home, but its sturdy brick walls and foundation remained in usable condition. President Jackson decided to remodel the mansion into a more impressive Greek Revival–style residence. By 1836, the renovation was completed, and Jackson had a home that seemed more suitable to a sitting president.

Jackson retired to *The Hermitage* for the final time when he left the presidency in 1837. He was then seventy years old. However, he was deep in debt due to the high costs

of remodeling the mansion and his son's mismanagement of plantation operations. The former president was forced to sell off acreage he held in Alabama and Tennessee to pay some of the debts. He was, however, able to return *The Hermitage* to profitability.

As a former president, Jackson was called upon frequently by friends and political figures seeking his advice or approval. *The Hermitage* was constantly hosting visitors. Despite all the activity, Jackson found time every day to visit Rachel's grave. Finally, on June 8, 1845, Andrew Jackson died at his beloved home at the age of seventy-eight. Two days later, thousands gathered in front of his mansion to hear a moving eulogy. Jackson was buried next to Rachel in the garden of the home he loved for over four decades.

After the president's death, Jackson's adopted children continued to live at *The Hermitage*. But, Andrew Jackson Jr. was no better at managing the property after his father's death than he had been in earlier years. The financial situation at *The Hermitage* continued to worsen. Andrew Jr. offered the property to the State of Tennessee for purchase in 1856. The state intended to hand the property over to the federal government for use as a military academy. Tennessee purchased the mansion and five hundred acres for $48,000, and the Jackson family moved to one of their plantations in Mississippi to live. Unfortunately, just two years later, the state's plans for the property fell through, so the Jackson family returned to *The Hermitage* to live there as tenants-at-will.

By the time Union soldiers occupied the house during the War between the States, it had become dilapidated. One soldier writes, "The place must have been a fine one in its palmy days, but now through neglect it's pretty well run to weeds." Jackson heirs

President Andrew Jackson's favorite room in the house was his library, which was next to his bedroom. During his last years, he spent nearly all of his time in these two rooms and in the garden. (Image courtesy of Andrew Jackson's Hermitage, Nashville, TN)

The Hermitage mansion viewed from the gardens shows the Greek Revival façade attached to an earlier brick structure that was more Federal in style. (Kitchens)

continued to live in the house until 1893, but the home was not improved or restored during those decades.[3]

The saviors of *The Hermitage* were concerned citizens who formed a group to restore the historic home. The Ladies' Hermitage Association was formed in 1889 in an effort to convince the State of Tennessee, who owned *The Hermitage*, to avoid giving the property to the Confederate Soldiers' Home Association for use as a home for indigent Confederate veterans. The Tennessee legislature chartered the Ladies' Hermitage Association in 1889 to "beautify, preserve and adorn the same through all coming years, in a manner most befitting the great man [Jackson]." However, the state still conveyed the bulk of the property to the Confederate Soldiers' Home, but carved out the house, gardens, cemetery, and twenty-five surrounding acres for the Ladies' Hermitage Association. Immediately upon receiving their charter, the Ladies' Association began renovating the house and grounds. To raise money for the purpose, they held plays, concerts, and barbecues. As early as 1897 the organization was already trying to reacquire some of Jackson's furnishings and personal effects. After a visit by President Theodore Roosevelt in 1907, the United States Congress finally appropriated funds to the Ladies' Association to make needed repairs to the structure.

In later years, the State of Tennessee conveyed much of the original *Hermitage* property to the association. Jackson's restored home, since 1961, has been designated as a National Historic Landmark. The Ladies' Hermitage Association continues to own and operate the historic home and greets over 250,000 visitors each year.[4]

Thanks to the hard work and loving care of the Kaslows, Amon Evans, and others, Rattle and Snap remains as one of Tennessee's most imposing antebellum mansions. (Kitchens)

RATTLE AND SNAP PLANTATION
Won on a Bet

♀ Maury County, Tennessee

Col. William Polk ranked as one of the most prominent men in colonial and post-Revolutionary North Carolina. Raised in Mecklenburg County, he later lived in Raleigh. Polk fought bravely during the American Revolution surviving with George Washington in the Valley Forge campaign and then spending most of the rest of the war opposing British general Cornwallis in the southern campaign throughout South Carolina and North Carolina. By 1781 he was commissioned as a lieutenant colonel. It was in that year that he fought with Gen. Nathanael Greene at the Battle of Eutaw Springs when Colonel Polk's horse was shot from under him and killed. His horse fell motionless to the ground trapping Polk underneath. Seeking to take advantage of the situation, a British soldier prepared to finish off Colonel Polk by raising a bayonet to deliver the mortal blow, but the fatal blow was dealt to the Red Coat when Polk's sergeant arrived in time to kill the enemy soldier.

In the years following the Revolutionary War, Polk was elected to the North Carolina General Assembly and was appointed as the surveyor general of North Carolina's Middle District, which is now the Middle Tennessee area. He was also appointed by George Washington to serve as the supervisor of Internal Revenue for the District of North Carolina. Polk held this position for seventeen years.

In his position as surveyor general, Polk was able to acquire vast acreage in what is now Middle Tennessee. However, one parcel of property he wanted was not yet available. It was owned or controlled by North Carolina's governor. Around 1820, Polk engaged the governor in a game of chance, apparently known as "rattle and snap," in which the acreage on which *Rattle and Snap* now stands was the price of the wager offered by the governor. The governor shook ("rattled") the dried beans or dice and then "snapped" them onto a flat surface. He lost the bet. Colonel Polk won 5,468 acres of fertile land on a bet. Perhaps to highlight his obvious good fortune or perhaps to remind his descendants of the possible consequences of wagers, Polk named his new property "Rattle and Snap." By the time of his death in 1834, Colonel Polk had acquired 100,000 acres of land in Tennessee, easily making him one of the largest land-holders in the state.

Colonel Polk gave pieces of the *Rattle and Snap* acreage to four of his sons by his second wife, Sarah Hawkins. Each of his sons built substantial mansions on large estates on either side of the road from Mount Pleasant to Columbia. Lucius Polk built *Hamilton Place* in 1832; Leonidas Polk built *Ashwood Hall* in 1833; Rufus Polk built *Westbrook* probably around 1840; and George Washington Polk built *Rattle and Snap* in 1842.

George Polk's father was an immensely wealthy man, but George had become successful in his own right as a banker and land speculator. He and his wife accepted the Maury County property the colonel had given them and began planning a house to be built on the site. Construction of the home known as *Rattle and Snap* started in 1842. George's brothers, Lucius and Leonidas, already had built imposing mansions nearby, but George's new residence would be one of the finest mansions erected anywhere in Tennessee during the antebellum period. The limestone used in its foundation was quarried nearby. A brick kiln was built to fire the tens of thousands of bricks required to build such a large home. Most of the wood used in its construction was cut on the property as well. Since some of Polk's slaves were skilled artisans, he was able to use his slave workforce to not only build the mansion, but also to craft some of its exquisite architectural decorative elements. However, the ten massive fluted columns and their intricate Corinthian capitals were manufactured in Cincinnati and shipped in sections by boat to Nashville, and then hauled by oxcarts to *Rattle and Snap*. Capping each twenty-six-foot-tall column are cast-iron capitals that had to be carefully assembled and secured into place on site.

Once Polk's 16,000-square-foot mansion was completed in 1845, it was one of the finest showplaces in all of Tennessee. Once set at the center of an oak forest, the brick mansion stands more than two stories over a limestone foundation. Only the façade is stuccoed in a tannish color, but all other exterior walls remain as exposed brick. The interior is as lavishly appointed as the exterior. Including the ell extending from the back of the mansion, *Rattle and Snap* includes over twenty large rooms, most of which are trimmed in intricate woodwork and decorative plaster medallions and cornices.

Polk's plantation house departs in several aspects from the more typical homes of the wealthy during this period. Rather than the typical front entry with doors surrounded by glass transom and sidelights, Polk's entryway has a central entrance with double doors. However, rather than sidelights, *Rattle and Snap*'s builder inserted smaller and wholly separate doors flanking each side of the main entry. Legend explains the unusual door arrangement as one intended to accommodate women's wide hoop-skirts through the central doorway, while the flanking doors provided ingress and egress for the gentlemen. Another unusual feature of Polk's house is the center hall, which does not extend from the front entrance to a rear entry, but is more of a central room from which Polk's other public rooms radiated. The center hall is lavishly decorated with classical architectural features, including Tower of the Winds columns dividing the room into a front hall and rear hall, and highly detailed plaster cornices and ceiling medallion.

To the left of the hall are massive double parlors, which are divided only by fluted columns matching those in the central hall. The double parlors provided the family an excessively large space from which to entertain their many family members and

Legend holds that the wide central doors were meant to accommodate women's wide hoop skirts, and the men were expected to enter through the small side doors. (Kitchens)

important guests. Another of the unique features of Polk's home is the double dining rooms. While other large homes of planters had a large formal dining room and a rather small family dining room elsewhere in the house, Polk's residence has two dining rooms adjacent to each other, which can be made into one huge dining hall by opening pocket doors that separate them. Fifteen-feet-tall ceilings on the first floor add to its grandeur. Upper-floor ceilings are fourteen feet high. The second floor contains at least seven bedrooms, most of which radiate from a central hall the same size as the hall below. The floors are connected by a broad elliptical staircase rising from the main floor's side hall and extending three floors into the attic.

During the antebellum period, *Rattle and Snap* prospered. Polk grew a variety of crops, including cotton, hay, and alfalfa, both for use by the Polk family and slaves living on the plantation and for income for the estate's operation. George's plantation, and those of his brothers living nearby, all grew hemp. The Polks were under contract by the United States Navy to produce hemp to make rope. They also used excess hemp to make clothing and other materials required on their plantations. George's plantation was worked by slaves who lived in frame cabins on other parts of the property. None of the slave cabins survive today, but some of the original cabins on George Polk's farm were moved to and remain at the Sam Davis plantation in Rutherford County, Tennessee.

During the 170 years since *Rattle and Snap* was built, it has repeatedly been in danger of destruction. In spring of 1862 a unit of Union soldiers under Maj. Gen. Don

Carlos Buell invaded *Rattle and Snap* on their way to Shiloh. The unit's captain ordered the mansion to be burned. However, while the captain waited in the foyer for the family to gather some belongings, he noticed that a painting of George Polk showed him wearing a Masonic ring. The order to burn the house was briefly stayed until the captain could report Polk's relationship to the Masons to Major General Buell. Once Buell discovered that Polk was a brother in the Masons, he issued orders to spare the house from the torch. Caroline Polk Horton, George Polk's youngest daughter, recounts how the family sought to hide their silver and valuables in anticipation of the Union army's visit to their home. The most secure location they could find was in the hollow center of a column on the front of the house. The Polk's youngest and smallest boy was lowered into a column from the attic and he placed baskets of silver and other precious items to rest in the columns. The baskets remained securely in place until the family finally removed them after the war ended.

The War between the States resulted in the same financial devastation for George Polk as it did for most other wealthy southerners. When he could no longer maintain *Rattle and Snap*, he sold the home and plantation in 1867 to Joseph J. Granberry, who renamed the home *Oakwood Hall* because of the many oak trees in the park around the house. Just a few years later, the home once again avoided destruction when a powerful windstorm ravaged the property by destroying most of the massive oaks around the house, but somehow spared the sturdy brick structure.

Rattle and Snap's double parlors once stored hay, but they have been returned to their original glory in recent years. (Kitchens)

Rattle and Snap's side hall opens onto this side portico with Tower of the Winds columns leading to the estate's formal gardens. (Kitchens)

Rattle and Snap's next owners brought the most dangerous risks to the mansion's existence. In 1919 the Granberry family sold the plantation to the Ridley and Dale families, who used the lands for farming and leased the mansion to tenants. Over the course of the next few decades, fewer tenants lived in the house and the house was slowly converted to use as a barn. Farm implements were stored there. The classical wooden columns in the central hall were removed and stored under the house so that the hall could be used to store hay and other crops. At one point, a wooden frame-work was erected in the central hall from which tobacco was hung to be cured. The once breathtaking double parlors were converted to use as a hay and feed warehouse. During these years, the house spiraled into disrepair. Hogs, cows, chickens, and other animals wandered through the mansion at will. Vandals found their way into the house, stealing or destroying most of the fine Italian-marble mantels Polk imported to adorn his parlors, dining rooms, and bedrooms.[1] For nearly two decades *Rattle and Snap* continued to deteriorate until it was purchased by Oliver Babcock Jr. and his wife, Jane, in 1953.

The Babcocks saved the house. Many believe that if the Babcocks had not come along when they did, *Rattle and Snap* would have been too far gone to be saved. They worked on the house for eighteen months before it was sufficiently restored to be habitable for their family. During the renovation they added five bathrooms, closets, and a modern kitchen to the house. They also wired it for electricity and plumbed it for

The entry hall at Rattle and Snap impresses the visitor as much today as it must have 150 years ago. (HABS)

running water and modern bathroom facilities. For the next two decades, the Babcock family resided in the rescued home.

After the Babcocks sold the house in 1972, it once again fell in disrepair, passing through the hands of several owners until finally it was purchased by Amon Carter Evans. The Evans family had owned the *Tennesseean* newspaper and after Amon inherited it, he sold the newspaper for $58,000,000. So when Amon Carter Evans purchased *Rattle and Snap* in 1979, he had plenty of money to properly restore the home. He vowed to fully restore Polk's great antebellum mansion to its 1845 grandeur. Indeed, he took his vow seriously. Evans hired some of the country's most renowned experts to perform the work. He hired Daniel Flaherity, who had helped renovate the US Capitol Building's molding and plasterwork, to work on the plaster at *Rattle and Snap*. He retained Malcolm Robeson, who had worked for England's Queen Elizabeth to faux paint woodwork, to re-create the antebellum faux marbleization and faux wood graining. Evans paid attention to every detail. He even retained one of the nation's experts

The wide central hall on Rattle and Snap's second floor serves as an upstairs parlor today displaying an impressive array of period antiques. (Kitchens)

in period draperies to re-create period-appropriate window dressings for his new home. Where previous owners had divided rooms by adding walls, Evans had those walls removed and restored to its original 1845 appearance, while still keeping some of the modern installations of plumbing and electricity. More than anyone else, Amon Evans truly saved the mansion and its historical character.[2]

Rattle and Snap is now owned and lovingly cared for by Dr. Michael and Bobbi Kaslow. Michael Kaslow descends from a family who lived in nearby Mount Pleasant, Tennessee, during the War between the States. Michael would travel with his mother from their home in California to Mount Pleasant as a child to visit relatives. In 2003 when the Kaslows learned that George Polk's mansion along with one hundred acres of surrounding property was for sale, he returned to Tennessee and purchased it. The Kaslows have continued the restoration of the dwelling and they have furnished it with high-quality period pieces. The Kaslows are very proud of this grand estate. They generously open their home for group tours on a periodic basis. Bobbi Kaslow has also furnished the carriage house to comfortably house those wishing to stay overnight. She also caters meals in the mansion to permit others to experience what it must have been like to live in such a masterpiece of architecture in antebellum days. Bobbi Kaslow expressed how she and her husband view their ownership of *Rattle and Snap*: "We don't think of ourselves as owner, but as a custodian. You have to share the house because of its significant history."[3]

CONCLUSION

From Peril to Promise: Why Preservation Matters

On the night of February 20, 1908, the antebellum mansion at Tanglewood Plantation, on the outskirts of Pendleton, South Carolina, caught fire and burned to the ground leaving only a stone foundation, two brick chimneys, and a row of four Ionic columns. Within a year the mansion was reconstructed incorporating the surviving elements. But two generations later the home burned again and the owners walked away and chose not to rebuild.

Not every antebellum dwelling that has been lost in the South has succumbed so dramatically. Most have simply been the victims of age and neglect. Time marches on and houses that were once filled with life are forgotten. Every southern state is home to hundreds, even thousands, of such structures that sit in advanced states of deterioration.

In researching and photographing the colonial and antebellum houses in this book that have been lovingly preserved or authentically restored, it is painfully obvious that those dwellings are the exception rather than the rule. There is a far larger number of houses that are in danger of complete loss if something is not done to save them. They can be seen while driving through the foothills, piedmont, and lowcountry of the Carolinas and across Virginia. They are plentiful in Georgia, Alabama, and Mississippi where cash crops once flourished on great plantations and smaller farms, and they can be found in abundance in the fertile lands of Tennessee, on horse farms in Kentucky, and down the River Road and in the bayous of Louisiana.

In Lawrence County, Alabama, Saunders Hall sits forlorn and neglected amid hundreds of acres of cotton fields. The once-grand plantation house, constructed around 1830 for Rev. Turner Saunders, features a tetrastyle portico upheld by four Tuscan columns, and single-story side wings that are uncommon to Alabama. Despite it architectural significance and its rich history the house is hastening to ruin with no champion to rescue it.

Standing on a knoll in Troup County, Georgia, the Forest Home Plantation house has not been lived in for decades and shows great signs of distress. The sturdy Greek

All that remains of the mansion on the former Tanglewood Plantation, near Pendleton, South Carolina, is a stone foundation, a row of columns, and two brick chimneys. The antebellum structure was destroyed by fire in 1908. (Bush)

Sunlight illuminates the decaying façade of Saunders Hall, one of Alabama's finest antebellum treasures. (Kitchens)

Revival–style dwelling still boasts a two-story veranda supported by fluted, Doric-style columns, and tripartite windows and doorways surrounded by highly carved wooden trim. There are currently no plans to save the structure and it is likely to continue its downward spiral.

Overlooking the headwaters of Cove Creek against a backdrop of mountains in McDowell County, North Carolina, the Joshua Hall Plantation house is only a shell. Most all of the windows and doors of the two-story, stucco-over-brick house are open to the elements. Many pieces of its fine interior trim have been stolen through the years and some of the floors on the lower level have rotted away. The house, erected in 1852, is still owned by Hall family descendants and lateral relations, but there are no plans to save it.

Years of abandonment and a botched restoration in the 1990s have left the antebellum Conner-Hodges House, located in rural Greenwood County, South Carolina, with numerous challenges for any future restorer. The two-story frame house dates to 1832. It has been severely damaged by vandals and needs extensive work to its chimneys and foundation. The property is managed by the Historic Cokesbury Commission, which desires full restoration of the property, but the organization is currently unable to commit funds to that endeavor and no new buyer has surfaced.

Located at the end of a long dirt drive within the town limits of Natchez, Mississippi, the great house known as *Arlington* sits as a ghostly apparition with sagging floors and staircases, rotted windows and doors, and a collapsed rear portico. The two-story

Forest Home Plantation, in Georgia, has become dilapidated with rotting columns, broken windows, and severely decayed porch floor. (Kitchens)

The plantation house of Joshua Hall, located in western North Carolina, is nearly hidden each spring and summer by a covering of vines that run rampant throughout the structure. (Lattimore)

brick house was designed and built for planter John Hampton White, who died during construction in 1819. His widow saw the home through to completion. While it once held a reputation as one of the grandest and most well-appointed homes in Natchez, for decades now it has been sitting abandoned and vandalized. There are currently no plans for restoration.

The homes mentioned above are the unsolicited representatives here of a burgeoning number of similar houses throughout the region. While no complete survey exists, it is believed that thousands of colonial and antebellum homes across the South sit

The most striking architectural feature of the dilapidated Conner-Hodges mansion, near Hodges, South Carolina, is a portico supported by rotting wooden columns. (Bush)

An evening view of Arlington mansion, in Natchez, Mississippi, displaying the structure's current state of decay. (Bourque)

in desperate need of repair or complete restoration. Many of those homes will be lost without intervention by interested persons or organizations dedicated to preserving them. News reports and headlines often mention the loss of historic homes, abandoned or occupied, to arson or other unfortunate occurrences. Sadly, many homes disappear entirely with little notice at all.

While a myriad of reasons exist as to why many older homes were abandoned in the first place, there are often an equal number of reasons why they have remained vacant and have continued to decay. Even when property owners have desired that their aging homes be preserved and restored, there are often so many challenges facing them that their hopes and dreams of a brighter future for their older dwelling are never realized. As all preservationists know, restoring older homes is a daunting task in good financial times. It is an ever more difficult proposition in a poor economy, which is often the case for rural areas where many remaining plantation homes are located. In the end, the greatest reality facing anyone interested in historic preservation is that not every older home or building can, or will, be saved.

As the essays in this book showcase, there is no one-size-fits-all path to preservation. Each preserved property was saved in a different way, by different people, and often for different reasons. And no one preservation plan is perfect. One fact is true: preserving historic properties takes time, dedication, money, skill, and labor. Nearly every successful historic restoration is accomplished through the active efforts of a few individuals who take the lead to champion the cause.

Although the historic preservation movement in the South was born in the nineteenth century with the restoration of George Washington's Mount Vernon in Virginia and Andrew Jackson's Tennessee plantation known as *The Hermitage*, it really came into its own a century later in the 1960s and 1970s, when Americans increasingly turned their attention to the nation's past. In the years before America's bicentennial in 1976, there was a rush to document and preserve as many historic sites as possible. Numerous historical societies were formed to focus on historic homes and other buildings, and a growing number of homeowners began choosing to purchase and restore older houses instead of opting to build new dwellings as had been the dominant trend in the years immediately following World War II.

During that era of relative prosperity when it seemed to many that preservation success stories would soon inspire the restoration of just about every ailing home and public building from the past, many important structures continued to be lost. In retrospect, it is now clear that only a small percentage of older homes can be saved.

Today in the twenty-first century, obstacles beyond economic challenges increasingly face properties that are in need of work. Changing attitudes about the past and the era in which some structures were built are making some people apprehensive about investing in a historic structure. Preserving antebellum homes in the South often means confronting the region's history of slavery and the use of enslaved African Americans in the construction of mansions and smaller homes for planters and successful farmers. Studying the past and forging a greater respect and understanding of the South's history, pleasant or unpleasant, can yield a greater appreciation for the structures from the past and a greater desire for the preservation of each aging structure that survives from an earlier time.

J. Myrick Howard, who since 1978 has been executive director of Preservation North Carolina, says that overcoming each of those obstacles is imperative to the continued success of the preservation movement in today's cultural climate. In his book, *Buying Time for Heritage: How to Save an Endangered Historic Property*, Howard relates that preservation projects can provide common ground for diverse groups of people. The collective participation of different peoples often enriches the outcome of the project and provides a deeper understanding of the historical importance of the building or dwelling being saved and of the history of the region.

"Many (architectural) preservationists conclude that preservation is a most powerful tool for building community," writes Howard. "Preservation brings a diverse crowd together under the same tent. African-Americans and conservative whites can come together in the preservation of a landmark that tells powerful stories about both cultures. Gays and straights can work side by side to preserve historic neighborhoods. Management and labor can advocate for the preservation of the places where their parents worked. Wealthy and poor can both benefit from living in historic environs."

The goal of *Southern Splendor: Saving Architectural Treasures of the Old South* is to celebrate restoration and preservation success stories accomplished by a diverse group of individuals, heritage organizations, foundations, and corporations, and to inspire similar projects in the future. It has also been the goal of each author to highlight and celebrate the collective contributions of both white and black southerners to the architectural history of the region in relation to its plantation heritage.

This volume is not, however, a "how-to" guide. While examples of preservation done well are presented, true step-by-step instructions of how to preserve historic homes is beyond the scope of this book. There have been several important books written on the topic of historic preservation, and those readers who are inspired to save a piece of the past should read such general guides as *Historic Preservation: An Introduction to Its History, Principles and Practice* by Norman Tyler and *Historic Preservation Technology: A Primer* by Robert A. Young.

Practical guides to everything from masonry to preservation law can give insight into all aspects of a project and help individuals and groups put preservation into practice. A few examples of helpful volumes include *Housekeeping for Historic Homes and House Museums* by Melissa Heaver (a National Trust publication); *A Richer Heritage: Historic Preservation in the Twenty-First Century* by Robert E. Stipe; and *A Layperson's Guide to Preservation Law: Federal, State, and Local Laws Governing Historic Resources* by Julia Miller (a National Trust publication).

Individuals interested in preserving a property should certainly gather all of the information they can from historic preservation organizations. The National Trust for Historic Preservation and the National Park Service's National Register of Historic Places are good places to start. Nearly every state has excellent organizations devoted to historic preservation, and many larger cities have similar resources.

The architectural treasures of the American South may not be as old as the antiquities found in Europe and on other continents with architecture stretching back thousands of years, but they are no less important in helping convey a stronger understanding of the past. For that reason, historic preservation in the South is paramount. As is revealed in this text, there is no thick dark line that separates properties worthy of preservation from those properties that are not. For those historic houses fortunate to survive in good repair, or to have been the focus of dedicated restoration projects in the past, the fact remains that they too often exist on a continuum of repair and decline, restoration and threat.

But, the space between those solidly maintained and those at great risk of fading into the past forever—the space between peril and preservation—is commodious and often complex. It is that space, however, and those who dare to traverse it that are the keys to saving the South's greatest architectural treasures. In the twenty-first century, those treasures have the potential to create jobs, promote tourism, revitalize local economies, and engender greater understanding of the South's important part of America's architectural and cultural heritage.

"Historic homes are among the best resources we have for teaching future generations about the past," says Walter W. Gallas, executive director of the Louisiana Landmark Society. "We cannot ignore their importance to our collective history and to the story of this country, whether they are great plantation mansions or simple farmhouses. There are architectural treasures all over this state (and the region) that are calling out for help."

Michael Bedenbaugh, executive director of the Palmetto Trust for Historic Preservation, is encouraged by the many homes and public structures that he sees that have been preserved or authentically restored in South Carolina and beyond. But, he is equally distressed by the number of structures that sit neglected or abandoned with little hope for improvement.

"We must keep working for the preservation of historic homes," states Bedenbaugh, who has witnessed several hundred restoration projects in his career. "I'm not too cavalier in my opinions not to recognize that a large number of older structures will be lost. But, the goal of people who understand and appreciate the importance of preservation and the impact that it has on our history, particularly here in the South, should always be to hold out hope until the last hour that a building or home can be rescued. If in the end they are lost, then at least we did our part to try and save them."

NOTES

INTRODUCTION

1. John B. Rehder, *Delta Sugar: Louisiana's Vanishing Plantation Landscape* (Baltimore: Johns Hopkins University Press, 1999), 53.

2. Estill Curtis Pennington, *Look Away: Reality and Sentiment in Southern Art* (Spartanburg, SC: Saraland Press, 1989).

3. Personal interview, May 14, 2009.

4. Personal interview, June 10, 2014.

LOUISIANA

Destrehan Plantation

1. The history of the Destrehan family and of their plantation is well documented. Dr. William D. Reeves exhaustively researched the history of the plantation for the River Road Historical Society, and Dr. Eugene Cizeck, a pillar of preservation in Louisiana, has worked on preserving and researching Destrehan for decades. The latter, joined by historians John Lawrence and Richard Sexton, authored *Destrehan: The Man, the House, the Legacy* in 2008. Original family papers can be found at the Historic New Orleans Collection, and the River Road Historical Society Archives contains a treasure trove of information about the estate.

2. Michael F. Knight, "The Rost Home Colony, St. Charles Parish, Louisiana," *Prologue Magazine* 33, no. 3 (Fall 2001).

Houma House

1. The history of Houmas House has been meticulously documented by Jim Blanchard in his enormous book *Louisiana's Sugar Palace*. It has also been well documented by the Historic American Buildings Survey and the National Register of Historic Places. Interesting archival materials related to the plantation's history can be found in the "Houmas Plantations and William Porcher Miles Materials Collection, 1760–1927," at the University of North Carolina Library.

Laura

1. The word *Creole* as it applies to Laura Plantation identifies the estate's inhabitants as the colonial descendants of white Europeans, who shared distinct culture, language, and customs quite different from the Anglo-derived culture of British colonial North America. The word Creole in this sense does not denote mixed race, as later it implied.

2. Joy Dickinson, "Creole Culture: Plantation Maintaining Traditions," *Advocate* (Baton Rouge), December 26, 1997.

3. Laura Locoul Gore, *Memories of the Old Plantation Home* (Vacherie, LA: Zoe Company, 2001).

4. Lilly Jackson, "Company's Coming—Renovators Ready a Once-Decaying 19th-Century Landmark for Tourists," *New Orleans Times-Picayune*, October 24, 1993.

5. Carol Anne Blitzer, "Rising from the Ashes: Laura Plantation Restored after Catastrophic Fire in 2004," *Advocate* (Baton Rouge), December 17, 2006.

6. Matthew Brown, "Owner Vows to Rebuild," *New Orleans Times-Picayune*, August 11, 2004.

7. Lolly Bowean, "A New Chapter—Despite a Fire at 200-Year-Old Laura Plantation Four Months Ago, the Stories of Slavery and Creole Culture Continue as Owners Restore the River Road Landmark," *New Orleans Times-Picayune*, November 30, 2004.

Nottoway

1. The history of Nottoway Plantation has been well researched and documented. The book *Nottoway Plantation: America's Largest Antebellum Mansion* by Robin Sommers Castaldi (White Castle, LA: Nottoway Plantation, 2013) is a very good source that details much of this history. Robert S. Brantley's *Henry Howard: Louisiana's Architect* (New Orleans: Historic New Orleans Collection, 2015) is a definitive ode to Nottoway's famed architect and gives a beautiful description of the architecture and construction of the plantation mansion.

Whitney Plantation

1. Whitney Plantation Historic District, National Register of Historic Places Nomination Document. http://www.crt.state.la.us/hp/nationalregister/nhl/document2.asp?name=48011001 .pdf&title=Whitney+PlanPlanta+Historic+District (accessed March 4, 2014).

2. Rehder, *Delta Sugar*, 263–65.

3. James Gill, "The Formosa Plant: The Rape of the Land Continues," *New Orleans Times-Picayune*, April 4, 1990.

4. Martha Carr, "Rusting along the River Road," *New Orleans Times-Picayune*, August 12, 1997.

5. Rehder, *Delta Sugar*, 279–80.

Saint Joseph Plantation

1. Alexa Hinton, "Restoring the Family's Crown Jewel," *Courier*, June 13, 2004.

2. Hinton, "Restoring the Family's Crown Jewel."

3. Hinton, "Restoring the Family's Crown Jewel."

MISSISSIPPI

Jefferson Davis's Beauvoir

1. The intricate history of Beauvoir can be pieced together using a mountain of materials found scattered among many various sources. There are several important collections that hold ample private letters, papers, and other documents relating to Jefferson Davis and specifically to Beauvoir. The Jefferson Davis Presidential Library collection at Beauvoir is, of course, the most extensive as it relates to the

estate itself. The Mississippi Department of Archives and History also houses an extensive collection. The Jefferson Davis Papers housed at William Stanley Hoole Special Collections Library, University of Alabama, Tuscaloosa, Alabama, also comprises a wealth of primary material. The Sarah Dorsey period is noticeably deficient of primary source material, a situation that stems from her own desire to destroy such papers. In an 1894 letter, Varina Davis notes, "Mrs. Dorsey instructed Mr. Davis to burn all her letters and papers immediately after her death unread, except such business letters as referred to her property, which he did." Of previous scholarly works, any study of Beauvoir should begin with Richard R. Flowers's *The Chronicles of Beauvoir* (Biloxi: Beauvoir Press, 2009), a definite work that was meticulously researched and compiled by Beauvoir's own curator. Ava Lisa Maxey's master's thesis, *The Gardens and Grounds of Beauvoir: A Landscape History*, also provides an excellent academic history of the estate. The story of Beauvoir's destruction during Hurricane Katrina and of its restoration thereafter was assembled using the contemporary news accounts of these events and the firsthand accounts and interviews of those who experienced the devastating events of the storm and were instrumental in the estate's restoration.

2. Flowers, *The Chronicles of Beauvoir*, 11; Harrison County Chancery Clerk Records.

3. For more information on Hurricane Plantation, see Marc R. Matrana's *Lost Plantations of the South* (Jackson: University Press of Mississippi, 2009), 150–51.

4. Ray M. Thompson, "Know Your Coast: How Beauvoir Got Its Name," *Biloxi (Miss.) Daily Herald*, February 13, 1957.

5. Austin Mortimer Dahlgren, Letter from Beauvoir, Mississippi, to marry Edgar Vannoy Dahlgren, April 22, 1877. Dahlgren Family Papers, The Tennessee Historical Society, Nashville, Tennessee. As quoted in Flowers, *The Chronicles of Beauvoir*, 34.

6. Lisa M. Krieger, "Beauvoir Will Be Restored," *Sun Herald*, September 14, 2005.

Waverly

1. The story of Waverly is well documented in *Waverly: Memories of a Mississippi Plantation* by Heath Childs (Columbus, MS: Higginbotham's Southern Printing, 2000). A plethora of information can also be found in the nearly 600-page report "Waverly Plantation: Ethnoarchaeology of a Tenant Farming Community" by William Hampton Adams, which can be found in its entirety online and in regional libraries and archives.

Hollywood Plantation

1. Margaret Louise Barry and Eustace H. Winn Sr., *The Burrus Family: Bolivar County, Mississippi* (Mississippi, 1984), 3.

2. Barry and Winn, *The Burrus Family*, 4.

3. Barry and Winn, *The Burrus Family*, 5.

4. Barry and Winn, *The Burrus Family*.

5. Barry and Winn, *The Burrus Family*, 6.

6. Barry and Winn, *The Burrus Family*, 19.

7. http://thebabydollhouse.com/baby-doll/.

ALABAMA

Belle Mont

1. Robert Gamble, *Alabama Catalog: A Guide to Early Architecture of the State* (Tuscaloosa: University of Alabama Press, 1986), 212; and http://www.preserveala.org/bellemont.aspx.

2. National Register for Historic Places Nomination Form for Belmont filed in February 1982.

3. Jenna Tidwell, "Belle of the South," unidentified newspaper, May 1, 2012, n.p.

4. "Spirit of a Freeman under Yankee Wrongs," *Montgomery Daily Advertiser*, vol. 15, June 12, 1863.

5. Letter from Isaac Winston Jr. to Maj. Gen. Don Carlos Buell, n.d. A copy of the transcribed version of this letter is held at the Belle Mont Mansion office.

Cherokee

1. Ralph Hammond, *Ante-bellum Mansions of Alabama* (New York: Architectural Book Publishing Co., 1951), 95–96; and National League of American Pen Women, *Historic Homes of Alabama and Their Traditions* (Birmingham: Birmingham Publishing Co., 1935), 90.
2. National League of American Pen Women, *Historic Homes of Alabama*, 90; http://www.jeminson mansion.com/.
3. National League of American Pen Women, *Historic Homes of Alabama*, 93.

First White House of the Confederacy

1. *The First White House of the Confederacy* (Montgomery: First White House Association, 1989), 2; National League of American Pen Women, *Historic Homes of Alabama and Their Traditions* (Birmingham: Birmingham Publ. Co., 1935), 51.
2. National League of American Pen Women, *Historic Homes of Alabama and Their Traditions*, 51.
3. National League of American Pen Women, *Historic Homes of Alabama and Their Traditions*, 52.
4. *The First White House of the Confederacy*, 27.
5. *The First White House of the Confederacy*, 5.

Gaineswood

1. http://en.wikipedia.org/wiki/Gaineswood.
2. Ralph Hammond, *Ante-bellum Mansions of Alabama* (New York: Architectural Book Publishing Co., 1951), 116; Jennifer Hale, *Historic Plantations of Alabama's Black Belt* (Charleston: History Press, 2009), 67.
3. http://en.wikipedia.org/wiki/Gaineswood.
4. Hammond, *Ante-bellum Mansions of Alabama*, 117.
5. Hammond, *Ante-bellum Mansions of Alabama*, 120.
6. Hammond, *Ante-bellum Mansions of Alabama*, 118.

Harris-Tate-Thompson House

1. Thomas McAdory Owen, *History of Alabama and Directory of Alabama Biography* (Spartanburg: Reprint Co., 1978), 1645; National Register Nomination File, Tate-Thompson house.
2. National Register Nomination File, Tate-Thompson house.
3. Mary Ann Neeley, *Old Alabama Town: An Illustrated Guide* (Tuscaloosa: University of Alabama Press, 2002), 99–100.

Sturdivant Hall

1. Jennifer Hale, *Historic Plantations of Alabama's Black Belt* (Charleston: History Press, 2009), 85.
2. Hale, *Historic Plantations of Alabama's Black Belt*, 88.
3. Ralph Hammond, *Ante-Bellum Mansions of Alabama* (New York: Architectural Book Publ. Co., 1951), 141.

GEORGIA

Bankshaven

1. Robert L. Raley, "Daniel Pratt, Architect and Builder in Georgia," *Magazine Antiques*, September 1972, 425.
2. Raley, "Daniel Pratt, Architect and Builder in Georgia," 425.
3. Raley, "Daniel Pratt, Architect and Builder in Georgia," 425.
4. Carolyn White Williams, *History of Jones County, Georgia: 1807–1907 Memorial Edition* (Fernandina Beach: Wolff Publishing, 2003), 202–4.
5. Williams, *History of Jones County, Georgia*, 203.

Chief Vann House

1. http://en/wikipedia.org/wiki/Chief_Vann_House_Historic_Site.
2. http://en/wikipedia.org/wiki/Chief_Vann_House_Historic_Site; http://www.aboutnorthgeorgia .com/ang/James_Vann; and http://www.georgiaencyclopedia.org/articles/history-archeology/chief-vann -house.
3. http://en/wikipedia.org/wiki/Chief_Vann_House_Historic_Site; and http://www.aboutnorthgeorgia .com/ang/James_Vann.
4. http://en/wikipedia.org/wiki/Chief_Vann_House_Historic_Site.
5. http://en/wikipedia.org/wiki/Chief_Vann_House_Historic_Site.
6. http://en/wikipedia.org/wiki/Chief_Vann_House_Historic_Site.
7. http://en/wikipedia.org/wiki/Chief_Vann_House_Historic_Site.

Thomas R. R. Cobb House

1. Charlotte Marshall, ed., *The Tangible Past in Athens, Georgia* (Dexter, MI: Thomson-Shore, 2014), 421.
2. Marshall, *The Tangible Past in Athens, Georgia*, 424, 427; http://en.wikipedia.org/wiki/Thoma_Reade _Rootes_Cobb.
3. Marshall, *The Tangible Past in Athens, Georgia*, 421.
4. Marshall, *The Tangible Past in Athens, Georgia*, 425.
5. Marshall, *The Tangible Past in Athens, Georgia*, 428.
6. Marshall, *The Tangible Past in Athens, Georgia*, 429–31.
7. Marshall, *The Tangible Past in Athens, Georgia*, 431–34.

Green-Meldrim House

1. http://www.visit-historic-savannah.com/green-meldrim-house/.
2. National Register of Historic Places Nomination form (May 1976).
3. Gen. William T. Sherman, *Memoirs of General William T. Sherman* (New York: D. Appleton, 1876), 494–95.
4. http://www.visit-historic-savannah.com/green-meldrim-house/.

Hay House

1. http://tomitronics.com/old _buildings.
2. http://tomitronics.com/old _buildings.
3. http://www.georgiatrust.org/historic_sites/hayhouse/history.php; Medora Field Perkerson, *White Columns in Georgia* (New York: Bonanza Books, 1952), 225; and Mills B. Lane, *Architecture of the Old South: Georgia* (New York: Abbeville Press, 1986), 236.

4. National Register of Historic Places Nomination Form for Johnston-Felton-Hay house, submitted November 1973.

5. National Register of Historic Places Nomination Form for Johnston-Felton-Hay house, submitted Nov. 1973; and www.georgiatrust.org/historic_sites/hayhouse.

6. National Register of Historic Places Nomination Form for Johnston-Felton-Hay house, submitted November 1973.

7. National Register of Historic Places Nomination Form for Johnston-Felton-Hay house, submitted November 1973.

8. www.georgiatrust.org/historic_sites/hayhouse.

Lockerly (Rose Hill)

1. http://www.lockerly.org.

2. Jesse Burke, "Dissecting a Plantation King: The Agricultural and Slave History of Daniel Tucker" (Senior thesis, Georgia College and State University, April 18, 2014).

3. Burke, "Dissecting a Plantation King."

4. John Linley, *Architecture of Middle Georgia: The Oconee Area* (Athens: University of Georgia Press, 1972), 80.

5. http://www.lockerly.org.

VIRGINIA

Arlington House

1. Mary Anna Randolph Custis Lee, Special Collections, University of Virginia.

2. Historic American Buildings Survey, Arlington House, 1940.

3. National Register of Historic Places, Nomination Form, 1966.

4. Michael Hardy, personal interview, 2012.

5. Hardy, personal interview.

6. Murray H. Nelligan, *Arlington House* (Burke, VA: Chatelain Press, 2005).

7. United States of America, National Park Service, *Arlington House: The Robert E. Lee Memorial* (Washington, DC: US Department of the Interior, 1985).

8. National Park Service, *Arlington House*.

9. Maj. L. M. Leisenring, "The Restoration of Arlington House: As Carried Out by the Office of the Quartermaster General," *Quartermaster Review* (Fort Lee, VA) March–April 1934.

10. Leisenring, "The Restoration of Arlington House."

11. National Register of Historic Places, Nomination Form, 1966.

12. National Park Service, *Arlington House*.

Berry Hill Plantation

1. National Register of Historic Places, Nomination Form, November 25, 1969.

2. Mills Lane, *Architecture of the Old South: Virginia* (Savannah: Beehive Press, 1997), 191.

3. Lane, *Architecture of the Old South*, 191.

4. Leland Luck, telephone interview, June 14, 2014.

5. Luck interview.

6. Luck interview.

Monticello

1. Marc Leepson, *Saving Monticello: The Levy Family's Epic Quest to Rescue the House That Jefferson Built* (New York: Free Press, 2001).

2. Leepson, *Saving Monticello*.

3. Thomas Jefferson, Letter to Baron Geisman, September 6, 1785. A copy of the transcribed version of this letter is held at the Belle Mont Mansion office.

4. Thomas Jefferson, Letter to George Gilmer, August 12, 1787. A copy of the transcribed version of this letter is held at the Belle Mont Mansion office.

5. Henry N. Ferguson, "The Man Who Saved Monticello," *American History Illustrated*, February 1980: 20–27.

6. Randle Bond Truett, *Monticello: Home of Thomas Jefferson* (New York: Hastings House, 1957).

7. Ferguson, "The Man Who Saved Monticello."

8. Ferguson, "The Man Who Saved Monticello."

9. Ferguson, "The Man Who Saved Monticello."

10. Ferguson, "The Man Who Saved Monticello."

11. Risa Ryland, personal interview, September 2013.

Mountain View Plantation

1. Derek Orr, personal interview, October 2015.

2. Mack H. Sturgill, *Abijah Thomas and His Octagonal House* (Marion, VA: Tucker Printing, 1990).

3. Sturgill, *Abijah Thomas*.

4. Historic American Buildings Survey, Library of Congress, 1946.

5. Historic American Buildings Survey, Library of Congress, 1946.

6. Sturgill, *Abijah Thomas*.

7. Sturgill, *Abijah Thomas*.

8. Orr interview.

9. Orr, personal interview.

10. Orr, personal interview.

White House of the Confederacy

1. Ruth Ann Coski, *The White House of the Confederacy: A Pictorial Tour* (Richmond: Museum of the Confederacy, 2012).

2. Coski, *The White House of the Confederacy*.

3. Coski, *The White House of the Confederacy*.

4. Letter from Varina Howell Davis to Mrs. John Story, Richmond, Virginia, 1903.

5. Coski, *The White House of the Confederacy*.

6. Frances Hasty, "New Chapter for the Confederate White House," *Fayetteville Observer*, April 3, 1988.

7. Hasty, "New Chapter for the Confederate White House."

8. Hasty, "New Chapter for the Confederate White House."

9. Michael Hardy, telephone interview, 2012.

NORTH CAROLINA

Creekside Plantation

1. Louisa Emmons, personal interview, April 10, 2014.

2. Emmons, personal interview.

3. Thomas T. Waterman, *The Early Architecture of North Carolina* (Chapel Hill: University of North Carolina Press, 1937).

4. Waterman, *The Early Architecture of North Carolina*.

5. Emmons, personal interview.

6. Emmons, personal interview.

7. Emmons, personal interview.

8. Emmons, personal interview.

9. Ted Alexander, personal interview, June 14, 2014.

10. Emmons, personal interview.

Fox Haven Plantation

1. Susan Millar Williams and Stephen G. Hoffius, *Upheaval in Charleston: Earthquake and Murder on the Eve of Jim Crow* (Athens: University of Georgia Press, 2011).

2. Delphine Jones, personal interview, August 11, 2015.

3. The History of Union County, South Carolina, Union County Historical Association, 1977.

4. Clarence Griffin, *Western North Carolina Sketches* (Asheville: Miller Printing Company, 1940).

5. Griffin, *Western North Carolina Sketches.*

6. Griffin, *Western North Carolina Sketches.*

7. Virginia Rucker, "Fox Haven Has Been Witness to Much of Rutherford's History," *Forest City (NC) Daily Courier*, April 11, 1984.

8. Rucker, "Fox Haven Has Been Witness to Much of Rutherford's History."

9. Jones, personal interview.

Green River Plantation

1. Ellen Cantrell, personal interview, 1993.

2. Cantrell, personal interview.

3. Thomas Tileston Waterman, *The Early Architecture of North Carolina* (Chapel Hill: University of North Carolina Press, 1941).

4. An exhibition of Jacob Marlin's work, including the portrait of Rachel Carson, was held at the North Carolina Museum of Art in 1961. An exhibition catalog was published.

5. Robin Spencer Lattimore, *Across Two Centuries: The Lost World of Green River Plantation* (Rutherfordton, NC: Hilltop Publications, 2003).

6. W. A. Sondley, *The History of Buncombe County, N.C.* (Asheville: Advocate Printing Company, 1930).

7. Amanda Cantrell, personal interview, 2015.

8. Ted Alexander, personal interview, June 14, 2015.

9. Connie Carson, personal interview, 1997.

Hope Plantation

1. William Bushong, *North Carolina's Executive Mansion: The First Hundred Years* (Raleigh: Executive Mansion Fine Arts Committee, 1991). Print.

2. Wayland Jenkins and Eric Hause, *The Miracle of Hope Plantation* (Windsor, NC: Historic Hope Foundation, 2002). Print.

3. Jenkins and Hause, *The Miracle of Hope Plantation.*

4. Jenkins and Hause, *The Miracle of Hope Plantation.*

5. Catherine Bishir, *North Carolina Architecture* (Chapel Hill: University of North Carolina Press, 1990). Print.

6. Jenkins and Hause, *The Miracle of Hope Plantation.*

7. Jenkins and Hause, *The Miracle of Hope Plantation.*

8. UNC-TV "North Carolina Weekend," 2011.

9. Gregory Tyler, personal interview, 2009.

10. UNC-TV interview, "Our State," 2011.

11. Tyler, personal interview.

Sidney Villa Plantation

1. Jacob E. Cooke, *Tench Coxe and the Early Republic* (Chapel Hill: University of North Carolina Press, 1962).

2. Cooke, *Tench Coxe and the Early Republic*.

3. Original documents in author's possession.

4. Original documents in author's possession.

5. Original documents in author's possession.

6. Original documents in author's possession.

7. Original documents in author's possession.

SOUTH CAROLINA

Drayton Hall

1. *Historic Preservation*, the magazine of the National Trust for Historic Preservation, vol. 43, no. 2 (1995).

2. *Historic Preservation* 43, no. 2 (1995).

3. Historic American Buildings Survey, Library of Congress, Drayton Hall, 1973.

4. *Historic Preservation* 43, no. 2 (1995).

5. Carl P. Borick, *A Gallant Defense: The Siege of Charleston, 1780* (Columbia: University of South Carolina Press, 2003).

6. *Historic Preservation* 43, no. 2 (1995).

7. *Historic Preservation* 43, no. 2 (1995).

8. SC-ETV, 2006.

Homestead House

1. Wade Fairey, telephone interview, May 10, 2014.

2. Fairey, telephone interview.

3. Fairey, telephone interview.

4. Michael C. Scoggins, *A Brief History of Historic Brattonsville* (York, SC: York County Culture and Heritage Commission, 2004).

5. Scoggins, *A Brief History of Historic Brattonsville*.

6. Scoggins, *A Brief History of Historic Brattonsville*.

7. Michael Scoggins, telephone interview, 2014.

8. Scoggins, telephone interview.

9. National Register of Historic Places nomination, February 14, 1971.

10. Fairey, telephone interview.

11. Fairey, telephone interview.

Millford Plantation

1. Richard Hampton Jenrette, *Adventures with Old Houses* (Charleston, SC: Wyrick & Company, 2000).

2. Jenrette, *Adventures with Old Houses*.

3. Jenrette, *Adventures with Old Houses*.

4. Jenrette, *Adventures with Old Houses*.

5. Jenrette, *Adventures with Old Houses*.

Kensington Plantation

1. Thomas T. Watermann, Historic American Buildings Survey, US Government, 1937.
2. National Register of Historic Places nomination, July 1971.
3. National Register of Historic Places nomination, July 1971.
4. Bob Redding, "Kensington: Antebellum Mansion Restored by Union Camp," *Sumter Daily Item*, May 31, 1985.
5. Redding, "Kensington."
6. National Register of Historic Places nomination, July 1971.
7. Redding, "Kensington."
8. Redding, "Kensington."
9. Redding, "Kensington."
10. Kim Wirth, telephone interview, June 25, 2014.
11. Michael Bedenbaugh, telephone interview, June 25, 2014.

Rose Hill Plantation

1. Union County Historical Foundation, *A History of Union County, South Carolina* (Union: A Press, 1977).
2. Ola Jean Kelly, personal interview, March 27, 2013.
3. Kelly, personal interview.
4. Kelly, personal interview.
5. Kelly, personal interview.
6. Union County Historical Foundation, *A History of Union County, South Carolina*.
7. Union County Historical Foundation, *A History of Union County, South Carolina*.
8. Union County Historical Foundation, *A History of Union County, South Carolina*.
9. Kelly, personal interview.
10. Elizabeth Moses, personal interview, 2015.
11. Trampas Alderman, personal interview, March 27, 2013.

Woodburn Plantation

1. Beth Ann Klosky, *The Pendleton Legacy: An Illustrated History of the District* (Columbia: Sandlapper Press, 1971).
2. Mary Esther Huger, *The Recollection of a Happy Childhood* (Pendleton, SC: Foundation for Historic Restoration in the Pendleton Area, 1976).
3. A copy of the diary is held by the Pendleton Historic Foundation.
4. Quote from the Pendleton Historic Foundation charter as read in Woodburn Plantation's nomination to the National Register of Historic Places, February 25, 1971.
5. Tim Drake, personal interview, June 20, 2014.
6. Jackie Reynolds, personal interview, June 20, 2014.

KENTUCKY

Ward Hall Plantation

1. *Ward Hall, Georgetown, Kentucky: External Envelope Restoration Plan: Phase 1, Revised Draft*, March 17, 2012; and Interview with David Stuart on October 2014.
2. *Ward Hall, Georgetown, Kentucky.*
3. http://www.findagrave.com/cgi-bin/fg.cgi?page=gr&GRid=97066606.
4. Pieter Estersohn, *Kentucky: Historic Houses and Horse Farms of Bluegrass Country* (New York: Monacelli Press, 2014), 88; http://www.findagrave.com/cgi-bin/fg.cgi?page=gr&GRid=97066606.

5. *Ward Hall, Georgetown, Kentucky.*

6. Interview with David Stuart of the Ward Hall Preservation Foundation, October 2014.

7. *Ward Hall, Georgetown, Kentucky.*

Waveland

1. Peter Estersohn, *Kentucky: Historic Houses and Horse Farms of Bluegrass Country* (New York: Monacelli Press, 2014), 118; and David C. McMurtry, *Waveland: Home of the Bryans* (Lexington, KY: Mil-Mac Publishers, 2010), 56–57.

2. McMurtry, *Waveland*, 57.

3. https://en.wikipedia.org/wiki/John_McMurtry_(architect).

4. McMurtry, *Waveland*, 124.

5. McMurtry, *Waveland*, 105.

6. McMurtry, *Waveland*, 79–80.

7. McMurtry, *Waveland*, 80.

8. McMurtry, *Waveland*, 182–84; Estersohn, *Kentucky*, 120.

9. Estersohn, *Kentucky*, 201–6.

White Hall

1. Lashe D. Mullins and Charles K. Mullins, *A History of White Hall: House of Clay* (Charleston: History Press, 2012), 19–20.

2. Mullins and Mullins, *A History of White Hall*, 20.

3. Mullins and Mullins, *A History of White Hall*.

4. Mullins and Mullins, *A History of White Hall*, 21–22.

5. Mullins and Mullins, *A History of White Hall*, 23.

6. Mullins and Mullins, *A History of White Hall*, 31.

7. Mullins and Mullins, *A History of White Hall*, 33.

8. Mullins and Mullins, *A History of White Hall*, 39–40.

9. https://en.wikipedia.org/wiki/Cassius_Marcellus_Clay_(politician).

10. https://en.wikipedia.org/wiki/Cassius_Marcellus_Clay_(politician); and Mullins and Mullins, *A History of White Hall*, 46.

11. Mullins and Mullins, *A History of White Hall*, 43.

12. Mullins and Mullins, *A History of White Hall*, 57.

13. Mullins and Mullins, *A History of White Hall*, 60.

14. Mullins and Mullins, *A History of White Hall*, 76–79.

15. Mullins and Mullins, *A History of White Hall*, 114–16.

TENNESSEE

Fairvue Plantation

1. http://tennesseeencyclopedia.net/entry.php?rec=507; Thomas B. Brumbaugh, Martha I. Strayhorn, and Gary Gore, eds., *Architecture of Middle Tennessee* (Nashville: Vanderbilt, 1974), 144.

2. Roberta Seawell Brandau, ed., *History of Homes and Gardens of Tennessee* (Nashville: Parthenon Press, 1936), 268.

3. Brandau, *History of Homes and Gardens of Tennessee*, 269; Brumbaugh, Strayhorn, and Gore, *Architecture of Middle Tennessee*, 144.

4. Wardin, *Belmont Mansion*, 4.

5. Brandau, *History of Homes and Gardens of Tennessee*, 271; Brumbaugh, Strayhorn, and Gore, *Architecture of Middle Tennessee*, 144.

Carnton Plantation

1. Cindy Sargent and Robert Hicks, eds., *Carnton Plantation* (Nashville: McQuiddy Classic Printing, 2010).

2. *Carnton: Plantation and Battlefield Guidebook* (Battle of Franklin Trust).

3. Sargent and Hicks, *Carnton Plantation*, 14.

4. *Carnton: Plantation and Battlefield Guidebook*, 20.

Clouston Hall

1. "Town and Country Tour of Homes," *Tennessean*, June 5–6, 2010.

2. Nancy Mueller, "1821 House Was Built for Parties," *Tennessean-Williamson A.M.*, July 31, 2009, 13W.

3. Mueller, "1821 House Was Built for Parties," 13W.

4. "Town and Country Tour of Homes."

5. Mueller, "1821 House Was Built for Parties," 13W.

6. "Town and Country Tour of Homes."

Belmont

1. See *Fairvue Plantation: Country House Extraordinaire*.

2. Thomas B. Brumbaugh, Martha I. Strayhorn, Gary G. Gore, eds., *Architecture of Middle Tennessee* (Nashville: Vanderbilt University, 1974), 156; Dr. Albert W. Warden Jr., *Belmont Mansion: The Home of Joseph and Adelicia Acklen* (Nashville: Belmont Mansion Association, 2005), 7.

3. Warden, *Belmont Mansion*, 7–8.

4. Warden, *Belmont Mansion*, 9–11.

5. Warden, *Belmont Mansion*, 11–12.

6. Warden, *Belmont Mansion*, 19.

7. Warden, *Belmont Mansion*, 22.

Hermitage Plantation

1. Ladies' Hermitage Association, *The Hermitage: Home of Andrew Jackson* (1997), 22–25.

2. Ladies' Hermitage Association, *The Hermitage*, 25–31.

3. Ladies' Hermitage Association, *The Hermitage*, 46–47.

4. http://tennesseeencyclopedia.net/entry.php?rec=758.

Rattle and Snap Plantation

1. http://www.midtneyewitnesses.com/still-standing/columbia/rattle-snap; Blanche Evans, "The Story of Rattle and Snap: How Too Much Money Saved the Most Beautiful Plantation Home in the South," September 4, 2007, http://realtytimes.com/todaysheadlines1; "Vacation Guide 2008: For the Shoals Area and Beyond," *East Lauderdale News* (Rogersville, Alabama), 7–9.

2. Interview with Dr. Michael and Bobbi Kaslow in October 2014.

3. Interview with Dr. Michael and Bobbi Kaslow.

SELECTED BIBLIOGRAPHY

Arrigo, Joseph. *Louisiana's Plantation Homes: The Grace and Grandeur*. Stillwater, MN: Voyageur Press, 1991.

Baldwin, William P., and N. Jane Iseley. *Lowcountry Plantations Today*. Greensboro, NC: Legacy Publications, 2002.

Baldwin, William P., and Agnes L. Baldwin. *Plantations of the Lowcountry: South Carolina 1697–1865* (revised edition). Greensboro, NC: Legacy Publications, 1987.

Brandau, Roberta Seawell, ed., *History of Homes and Gardens of Tennessee*. Nashville: Parthenon Press, 1936.

Castaldi, Robin Sommers. *Nottoway Plantation: The South's Largest Antebellum Mansion*. White Castle, LA: Nottoway Properties, 2013.

Cizek, Eugene D., John H. Lawrence, and Richard Sexton. *Destrehan: The Man, the House, the Legacy*. Destrehan, LA: River Road Historical Society, 2008.

Claiborne, Virginia Christine, Ella Williams Smith, and Caroline Pickrell Strudwick. *Homes and Gardens in Old Virginia*. Richmond: Garrett and Massie, 1953.

Collier, Malinda W., John M. Coski, Richard C. Cote, Tucker H. Hill, and Guy R. Swanson. *White House of the Confederacy: An Illustrated History*. Richmond: Cadmus, 1993.

Cooper, Chip, Harry Knopke, and Robert Gamble. *Silent in the Land*. Tuscaloosa: CKM Press, 1993.

Dalzell, Robert F., and Lee Baldwin Dalzell. *George Washington's Mount Vernon*. New York: Oxford University Press, 1998.

Daspit, Fred. *Louisiana Architecture, 1714–1820*. Lafayette: Center for Louisiana Studies, 1996.

——. *Louisiana Architecture, 1820–1840*. Lafayette: Center for Louisiana Studies, 2005.

——. *Louisiana Architecture, 1840–1860*. Lafayette: Center for Louisiana Studies, 2006.

Emmons, Louisa Alexander. *Tales from a Civil War Plantation: Creekside*. Lexington, KY: Heritage Press, 2013.

Estersohn, Pieter, and W. Gay Reading. *Kentucky: Historic Houses and Horse Farms of Bluegrass Country*. New York: Monacelli Press, 2014.

Franklin, Paul M., and Nancy Mikula. *South Carolina's Plantations and Historic Homes*. St. Paul, MN: Voyageur Press, 2006.

Gillette, Jane Brown. "American Classic: The Oldest Surviving Example of Georgian Palladian Architecture in the American South, Drayton Hall Stands in Splendid Defiance of the Passage of Time." *Historic Preservation* 43, no. 2 (1992).

Gore, Laura Locoul. *Memories of the Old Plantation Home and a Creole Family Album*. Vacherie, LA: Zoe Company, 2007.

Hammond, Ralph. *Antebellum Mansions of Alabama*. New York: Bonanza Books, 1961.

Horn, Stanley F. *The Hermitage: Home of Old Hickory*. Nashville: Ladies' Hermitage Association, 1950.

Howard, J. Myrick. *Buying Time for Heritage: How to Save an Endangered Historic Property*. Raleigh: Preservation North Carolina, 2007.

Jenrette, Richard Hampton. *Adventures with Old Houses*. Charleston: Wyrick & Company, 2000.

Johnston, Frances Benjamin, and Thomas Tileston Waterman. *The Early Architecture of North Carolina*. Chapel Hill: University of North Carolina Press, 1941.

Kennedy, Roger G. *Greek Revival America*. New York: Stewart, Tabori & Chang, 1989.

Kibler, James Everett. *Our Father's Fields: A Southern Story*. Columbia: University of South Carolina Press, 1998.

Kitchens, Michael W. *Ghosts of Grandeur: Georgia's Lost Antebellum Homes and Plantations*. Virginia Beach: Donning Company Publishers, 2012.

Lancaster, Clay. *Antebellum Architecture of Kentucky*. Lexington: University Press of Kentucky, 1991.

Lane, Mills. *Architecture of the Old South*. New York: Abbeville Press, 1993.

Lattimore, Robin Spencer. *Across Two Centuries: The Lost World of Green River Plantation*. Rutherfordton, NC: Hilltop Publications, 2003.

———. *Belles of the Backcountry: The History of Fox Haven and Cleghorn Plantations*. Rutherfordton, NC: Hilltop Publications, 2016.

———. *Rural Splendor: Plantation Houses of the Carolinas*. Rutherfordton, NC: Hilltop Publications, 2010.

———. *Southern Plantations: The South's Grandest Homes*. Oxford, England: Shire Books, 2012.

Leepson, Marc. *Saving Monticello: The Levy Family's Epic Quest to Rescue the House That Jefferson Built*. New York: Free Press, 2001.

Lewis, Richard Anthony. *Robert E. Tebbs—Photographer to Architects: Louisiana Plantations in 1926*. Baton Rouge: Louisiana State University Press, 2011.

Marsh, Kenneth F., and Blanche Marsh. *Plantation Heritage in Upcountry, South Carolina*. Asheville: Biltmore Press, 1962.

Matrana, Marc. R. *Lost Plantation: The Rise and Fall of Seven Oaks*. Jackson: University Press of Mississippi, 2005.

———. *Lost Plantations of the South*. Jackson: University Press of Mississippi, 2009.

McLeod, Stephen A., ed. *The Mount Vernon Ladies' Association: 150 Years of Restoring George Washington's Home*. Mount Vernon, VA: Mount Vernon Ladies' Association, 2009.

Miller, Mary Carol. *Great Houses of Mississippi*. Jackson: University Press of Mississippi, 2004.

National League of American Pen Women. *Historic Home of Alabama and Their Traditions*. Birmingham: Birmingham Publishing Co., 1935.

Nichols, Frederick Doveton. *The Early Architecture of Georgia*. Chapel Hill: University of North Carolina Press, 1957.

Ossman, Laurie. *Great Houses of the South*. New York: Rizzoli, 2010.

Overdyke, W. Darrell. *Louisiana Plantation Homes: Colonial and Antebellum*. New York: American Legacy Press, 1975.

Pennington, Estill Curtis. *Look Away: Reality and Sentiment in Southern Art*. Spartanburg, SC: Saraland Press, 1989.

Perkerson, Medora Field. *White Columns of Georgia*. New York: Bonanza Books, 1962.

Sexton, Richard. *Vestiges of Grandeur: The Plantations of Louisiana's River Road*. San Francisco: Chronicle Books, 1999.

Smith, J. Frazer. *White Pillars: The Architecture of the South*. New York: Bramhall House, 1961.

Smith, Reid. *Majestic Middle Tennessee*. Gretna, LA: Pelican Publishing, 1990.

Smith, Reid, and John Owens. *The Majesty of Natchez*. Gretna, LA: Pelican Publishing, 1986.

Stoney, Samuel Gaillard. *Plantations of the Carolina Lowcountry* (revised edition). Charleston: Carolina Art Association, 1969.

Vlach, John Michael. *Back of the Big House: The Architecture of Plantation Slavery*. Chapel Hill: University of North Carolina Press, 1993.

Wiencek, Henry. *Great American Homes: Plantations of the Old South*. Birmingham: Oxmoor House, 1988.

———. *Great American Homes: Mansions of the Virginia Gentry*. Birmingham: Oxmoor House, 1988.

Woofter, T. J., Jr. *Landlord and Tenant on the Cotton Plantation*. Washington, DC: US Government, Works Progress Administration, Division of Social Research, 1936.

INDEX

Page numbers in **bold** indicate an illustration.

V

Van Buren, Abram, 276
Van Buren, Martin, 276, 297
Vann, James, 137–39
Vann, Joseph, 139–42

W

Waguespack, Joseph, 55
Waguespack family, 30, 55, 57–58
Walsh, Frances, 344, 345
Walthall, W. T., 66
Walton, Thomas George, 212,
    214, **215**, 216
Ward, Junius, 297–98, 300
Ward, Matilda Viley, 297, 298
Ward, Sarah Johnson, 297
Ward, William, 297
Ward Hall Plantation, 297–303
Ward Hall Preservation
    Foundation, 300–302
Wardin, Albert W., Jr., 347
Washam, Grace, 288
Washington, George, 5, 175, 355
Waterman, Thomas T., 213–14
Watson-Brown Foundation,
    147, 148
Watts, Edward, 123, 126
Waveland, 305–10
Waverly Novels, The (Scott),
    77, 82
Waverly Plantation, 77–83
Welham Plantation, 46
West Indies architecture, 73
White, John Hampton, 365
White Hall, 311–17
White Hall State Historic Site,
    317
White House Association of
    Alabama, 107, 108
White House of the
    Confederacy, 203–8
Whitfield, Nathan Bryan,
    109–10, 113, 114
Whitney Plantation, 47–53
Wilkins, Eliza, 182
Wilkins, J. H., 241
Wilson, Rebekah, 230
Winn, Eustace H., Jr., 88
Winston, Catherine Baker, 93
Winston, Isaac, Jr., 93–94
Winston, Isaac, Sr., 93, 95
Winter, Joseph S., 103

Wirth, Kim, 280
Womack, Rusty, 338–39
Woodburn Plantation, 289–94

Y

Yancey, William Lowndes, 100
York County, South Carolina,
    259
York County Historical
    Commission, 263
Young, George, 80
Young, George Hampden, 77,
    79, 80, 82
Young, William, 80

Z

Zalia, Elénore, 12
Zalia, Louise, 12